My Cocaine Museum

my cocain

My Cocaine Museum

Michael Taussig

The University of Chicago Press
Chicago and London

museum

The University of Chicago Press, Chicago 60637

The University of Chicago Press, Ltd., London

13 12 11 10 09   3 4 5

ISBN: 0-226-79008-8 (cloth)

ISBN: 0-226-79009-6 (paper)

Library of Congress Cataloging-in-Publication Data

Taussig, Michael T.

  My cocaine museum / Michael Taussig.

     p. cm.

  ISBN 0-226-79008-8 (cloth : alk. paper) — ISBN

0-226-79009-6 (pbk. : alk. paper)

  1. Indians of South America—Colombia—Santa María

(Cauca)—Social conditions. 2. Indians of South America—

Colombia—Santa María (Cauca)—Economic conditions. 3.

Indians, Treatment of—Colombia—Santa María (Cauca). 4.

Slavery—Colombia—Santa María (Cauca)—History. 5. Gold

mines and mining—Colombia—Santa María (Cauca). 6.

Cocaine industry—Colombia—Santa María (Cauca). 7. Drug

traffic—Colombia—Santa María (Cauca). 8. Santa María

(Cauca, Colombia)—Social conditions. 9. Santa María (Cauca,

Colombia)—Economic conditions. I. Title.

F2269.1.S24T28 2004

986.1'53—dc22

                                   2003021831

The University of Chicago Press, Chicago 60637

The University of Chicago Press, Ltd., London

© 2004 by Michael Taussig

All rights reserved. Published 2004

Printed in the United States of America

13 12 11 10 09 08 07 06   2 3 4 5

ISBN: 0-226-79008-8 (cloth)

ISBN: 0-226-79009-6 (paper)

Library of Congress Cataloging-in-Publication Data

Taussig, Michael T.

My cocaine museum / Michael Taussig.

p. cm.

ISBN 0-226-79008-8 (cloth : alk. paper) — ISBN

0-226-79009-6 (pbk. : alk. paper)

1. Indians of South America—Colombia—Santa María
(Cauca)—Social conditions. 2. Indians of South America—
Colombia—Santa María (Cauca)—Economic conditions. 3.
Indians, Treatment of—Colombia—Santa María (Cauca). 4.
Slavery—Colombia—Santa María (Cauca)—History. 5. Gold
mines and mining—Colombia—Santa María (Cauca). 6.
Cocaine industry—Colombia—Santa María (Cauca). 7. Drug
traffic—Colombia—Santa María (Cauca). 8. Santa María
(Cauca, Colombia)—Social conditions. 9. Santa María (Cauca,
Colombia)—Economic conditions. I. Title.

F2269.1.S24T28 2004

986.1'53—dc22

2003021831

♾ The paper used in this publication meets the minimum re-
quirements of the American National Standard for Information
Sciences—Permanence of Paper for Printed Library Materials,
ANSI Z39.48-1992.

For Joyce Monges

Right from the start, the great collector is struck by the confusion,
by the scatter, in which the things of the world are found.

—Walter Benjamin

contents

You can find it when you face the sun, close your eyes, and watch the colored lines dance. Follow them, follow the heat, and you'll get there like I did, all the way to *My Cocaine Museum*. Not that there wasn't what you might call a proto-type, a most clear and definite and beautiful prototype, spooky in its own way too, the famous, the world-famous, the extraordinary Gold Museum itself. Not that it needs that sort of hype. No way. For this is no vulgar carnival sideshow. This has science behind it and a lot of soft lighting as well, not to mention big money and something even bigger than money: the image of money, which, as you know, was there in gold all along. And still is—as you see when you go downtown Bogotá, Colombia, and climb to the second floor of the Banco de la República off Carrera Séptima and there enter the glittering residues of the time before time when only the Indians were here, happy, so it seems, happy with their gold and happy with their coca too. Only later did it become cocaine.

Surrounded by slums on three sides, beggars and street performers in the park opposite, the museum provides a closed-off space, dark and solemn, in which pre-Colombian gold artifacts are displayed in spotlit cases. Said to possess 38,500 pieces of gold work, the museum, like gold itself, is an ornament adding dignity and art to the money-grubbing reality of the bank—not just any old bank, of course, but the Banco de la República, the bank of the nation-state, same as the Federal Reserve Bank in the U.S.A.

But what, then, is an ornament?

One block away on the Carrera Séptima stands the beautiful colonial church of San Francisco, which, like the museum, is stuffed full of gold shimmering in the dark. Country people and slum dwellers come and caress the foot of one of the saints, which as a consequence glows even more than the gold behind the altar. Hustlers working their way along the sidewalk outside are likely to be wearing gold chains in imitation of the guys who make it big in the drug trade. Like any book worth writing, *My Cocaine Museum* belongs to this sense of the ornament as something base like the foot of a saint or a hustler with a golden wrist, something that allows the thingness of things to glow in the dark.

To walk through the Gold Museum is to become vaguely conscious of how for millennia the mystery of gold has through myth and stories sustained the basis of money worldwide. But one story is missing. The museum is silent as to the fact that for more than three centuries of Spanish occupation what the colony stood for and depended upon was the labor of slaves from Africa in the gold mines. Indeed, this gold, along with the silver from Mexico and Peru, was what primed the pump of the capitalist takeoff in Europe, its *primitive accumulation*. Surely this concerns the bank, its birthright, after all?

It seems so monstrously unjust, this denial, so limited and mean a vision incapable of imagining what it was like diving for gold in the wild coastal rivers, moving boulders with your bare hands, standing barefoot in mud and rain day after day, so unable to even tip your hat to the brutal labor people still perform today alongside the spirits of their parents and grandparents and of all the generations that before them had dug out the country's wealth. It seemed such a rip-off of my work as an anthropologist too, using anthropology and archaeology to dignify the bank with the bittersweet spoils of genocide and looting.

The Gold Museum is also silent about the fact that if it was gold that determined the political economy of the colony, it is *cocaine*—or rather the U.S. prohibition of it—that shapes the country today. Not to talk about cocaine, not to display it, is to continue with the same denial of reality that the museum practices in relation to slavery. Like gold, cocaine is imbued with violence and greed, glitter that reeks of transgression. What's more, cocaine has roots deep in prehistory too.

Like gold, coca was of great interest to the Indians long before the arrival of Europeans. Indeed, among the most significant objects in the Gold Museum are its golden *poporos*, curvaceous containers shaped like a Coke bottle and used by Indians to contain the lime made from burnt and crushed seashells that, added to toasted coca leaves, facilitates the release of cocaine into the gut and bloodstream. You insert a stick into the spout of the *poporo* and then withdraw it so as to put gobs of lime in your mouth while chewing coca leaves. I say "your mouth" but I must mean "their mouths," plural, as with the men seated all night around a fire, like the Indians of the Sierra Nevada de Santa Marta, as I was informed by María del Rosario Ferro just yesterday. Gathered together like this, they are discussing a communal problem—whether to allow her to stay with them, and why the heck is she there, anyway?[1] When they take the end of the stick out of their mouth and reinsert it back into the *poporo,* they spend several minutes rotating the stick around the lips of the spout, making a soft suffusion of sound that spreads like wind stirring in the forests of time. Actually, they do not so much rotate the end of the stick around the lip of the spout of the *poporo* as they seem to be writing in curves and dashes punctuated by little stabbings. There are maybe as many as a hundred men doing this simultaneously, each with his own *poporo* and his own woven cotton shoulder bag containing toasted coca leaves. It is dark.

---

1. María del Rosario Ferro is a young anthropologist who, in the 1990s, spent five years living with the Indians of the Sierra Nevada de Santa Marta on the coast of northern Colombia. She spent two years living with Arahuacos and another three years with Kogis. It is she who in 2003 introduced me to the Kogi priest Mamo Luca and to the Wiwa religious leader Ramón Gil, and told me many of the things I relate here about coca and gold.

It is loud, this softer-than-soft sound, she tells me, the sound thus magnified, maybe like the sound of the Caribbean Sea from which the shells come as far as this high mountain.

As I understand this phenomenon, the speed and rhythm of the jerky rotating movement around the spout of the *poporo,* and hence of the soft suffusing of scratching sounds, correspond to the movement of speech and thought, the Arahuaco word for thinking being the same as breathing in the spirit (*kunsamunu*). But of course these are not the squeaky-clean *golden poporos* we see resplendent in the Gold Museum in Bogotá that stand naked and exposed, bereft of any sign of human use, let alone of any sign of this exceedingly strange crust of coca-saturated saliva around the mouth of the *poporo.* Rightly, the museum is fixated on the object, which puts an end to speaking, let alone the relation between breathing and thinking. Here, gold freezes breath no less than thought as we gaze absentmindedly at the auratic glow, completely uninformed as to the wonders of what these *poporos* might mean. Too bad.

But then would dried spittle last long in the rarefied atmosphere of a museum? A museum abhors clutter. There can be little sympathy for Walter Benjamin's enthusiasm when unpacking his library, that "from the start, the great collector is struck by the confusion, by the scatter, in which the things of the world are found."[2] For what this scatter implies for him is its fantastic otherworldly character, as when he says: "Every passion borders on the chaotic, but the collector's passion borders on the chaos of memories. More than that: the chance, the fate, that suffuses before my eyes are conspicuously present in the accustomed confusion of these books."[3] To impose order on such chaos is to render tribute to chance, such that the final arrangement adds up to what he calls a "magic encyclopedia," which in itself serves to interpret fate. This corresponds nicely with the Indians in the Sierra Nevada, writing their thoughts onto the crust of dried spit around the mouth of their *poporos.* Something like this also underlies William Burroughs's attitude to the disorder we call order, as when he notes that the chapters he is writing, of what will become *Naked Lunch,* "form a mosaic with the cryptic significance of juxtaposition, like objects abandoned in a

2. Walter Benjamin, "The Collector," in *The Arcades Project,* ed. Rolf Tiedemann, trans. Howard Eiland and Kevin McLaughlin (Cambridge: Harvard University Press, 1999), p. 211.

3. Walter Benjamin, "Unpacking My Library: A Talk about Book Collecting" (1931), in *Illuminations: Essays and Reflections,* ed. Hannah Arendt, trans. Harry Zohn (New York: Schocken, 1968), p. 60.

hotel drawer, a form of still life."[4] And the aim of that? To make people aware of what they already know but didn't know they knew.[5]

For all its nastiness, spit is vulnerable to both time and good taste. Spit is hardly the sort of thing—if thing it be—that would serve the needs of a bank's claim to culture. Spit is the very opposite of gold in Western economics, such that it lends itself to the evacuation of equations many of us live by, those equations connecting beauty with goodness and goodness with making sense by finding or imposing forms on the welter of experience that is the universe. Spit is anarchic as regards form. What other philosophy might therefore be at stake here, "just around the corner"? A philosophy not of form but of substance and force—such as gold, such as cocaine—*transgressive substances,* I call them, aswarm with all manner of peril that may not provide much by way of stable form to the world but certainly much by way of exuberance and perturbation. Indeed, spit did find its Western philosopher in 1929 in Georges Bataille, who, for one of his cranky dictionary entries in his magazine, *Documents* (that lasted only two years but still manages to amaze), wrote this:

> A dictionary begins when it no longer gives the meaning of words, but their tasks. Thus *formless* is not only an adjective having a given meaning, but a term that serves to bring things down in the world, generally requiring that each thing has its form. What it designates has no rights in any sense and gets itself squashed everywhere, like a spider or an earthworm. In fact for academic men to be happy, the universe would have to take shape. All of philosophy has no other goal: it is a matter of giving a frock coat to what is, a mathematical frock coat. On the other hand, affirming that the universe resembles nothing and is only *formless* amounts to saying that the universe is something like a spider or spit.[6]

---

4. William S. Burroughs, letter to Allen Ginsberg from Tanger, October 21, 1955, in *The Letters of William S. Burroughs: 1945 to 1959,* ed. Olivier Harris (London: Picador, 1993), p. 289.

5. Robert A. Sobieszek, *Ports of Entry: William S. Burroughs and the Arts* (Los Angeles: Los Angeles County Museum of Art and Thames and Hudson, 1996), p. 118.

6. Georges Bataille, "Informe," *Documents* 7 (December 1929): 384; translated by Alan Stoekl as "Formless," in Georges Bataille, *Visions of Excess: Selected Writings, 1927–1939* (Minneapolis: University of Minnesota Press, 1985), p. 31. A fabulous exploration of Bataille's spider-and-spit theme is *Formless: A User's Guide,* by Yves-Alain Bois and Rosalind Krauss (New York: Zone Books, 1997).

Not so much *My Cocaine Museum* as *My Spit Museum*?

As for the Indians of the sierra, this dried crust of spit around the mouth of the *popro* grows over time and is shaped carefully to form a cylinder, says Gerardo Reichel-Dolmatoff in his celebrated study of the Kogi, among whom he lived between 1946 and 1950. It is absolutely forbidden for Kogi women to chew coca, and Reichel-Dolmatoff sees the *popro* as in fact a sexual rival of the women. When a young man is initiated, he is given his first *popro* filled with lime. He thus "marries" his "woman" in this ceremony and perforates the *popro* at this time in imitation of a ritual defloration. "All the necessities of life," concludes Reichel-Dolmatoff, "are concentrated in this small instrument that for the Kogi comes to mean food, woman, and memory. No wonder the Kogi man and his *popro* are inseparable."[7]

Petted and patted over time by incessant scribbling with the tip of the stick, the crust of dried coca-and-lime-thickened saliva is as likely to be a flat disc as a cylinder, an object of beauty far exceeding any gold work in the museum. It is perfectly symmetrical. Faint greenish lines like a spider's web wander around its sides; while viewed from above, the disc contains faint rings like that of a cut tree trunk. In his nine months camped out in the mountains of Boyacá, the crust, or *kalamutsa* (in Kogi speech), thus created by Mamo Luca, a Kogi priest I met in 2003, was roughly three-quarters of an inch thick and two and half inches in diameter. When asked, he referred to his obsessive petting and patting as "writing thoughts," the crust itself being his "document." More like a magic encyclopedia, I thought, it being the Mamo's task to continuously exert his thoughts while chewing coca to figuring out for the sake of his community what costs Mother Earth has incurred due to the wrongdoings of human beings. "Pretty much what I aspire to do with *My Cocaine Museum*," I said to myself.

The ruddy brown body of his *popro* was only six inches high, fitting snugly in his left hand, which it never once seemed to leave, night or day. Indeed, the *popro* is more like a living extension of the body, or should I say of the mind,

---

7. Gerardo Reichel-Dolmatoff, *Los Kogi: Una tribu de la Sierra Nevada de Santa Marta, Colombia* (1950), 2 vols., 2nd ed. (Bogotá: Procultura, 1985), vol. 1, pp. 88–90.

than it is a mechanical artifact. The crust of the *poporo* of Ramón Gil, in the foothills of the Sierra Nevada near Santa Marta, was even more impressive, being about six inches wide, like a pie, and two and half inches thick.

Invited for a consultation in 2003 to the Gold Museum in Bogotá, and then asked as to the possibility of his carrying out a "cleansing" of the museum's 38,500 gold artifacts, Ramón Gil said he would need the menstrual blood of the museum's female staff, plus the semen of the men, including that of the board of directors of the Banco de la República. Needless to say, his demand was not met and the gold work remains in its polluted state. According to Mamo Luca—who dares not enter the museum on account of that pollution—gold is valuable because it is the menstrual blood of Mother Earth in which is concentrated all her power and that can only be extracted through appropriate ritual ensuring that all is in harmony at the site of extraction—e.g., "that the river is good, the animals are good, the plants and the woods are good." Essential to such purifying ritual, paying Mother Earth for the defilement of gold extraction, is thinking—yes! thinking—and such thought is achieved through imbibing coca and "writing thoughts" onto the previous thoughts embodied in the yellow crust of dried spittle around the mouth of the *poporo*. And according to Mamo Luca, before the birth of the sun, people used gold instead of crushed seashells in their *poporos*.

The centerpiece of the museum's display is a *poporo* with four golden balls around its orifice. In a darkened room, placed against black felt without the slightest hint of irony or self-consciousness, this spotlit *poporo* has the following text beneath it:

> This poporo from Quimbaya, which began the collection of the Gold Museum in 1939, identifies Colombians with their nationality and history.

Another *poporo,* thinner than most, is shaped like an erect penis. Others take the form of a jaguar, full-bellied fruit, or a person that is half-alligator. There is one *poporo* shaped as a golden woman, naked, with birds hanging from her wrists, and we are informed that burnt human bones were the source of the lime it contained. Gold and cocaine are firmly connected since ancient times, before even the birth of the sun, by art, sex, magic, and mythology, no less than by chemistry.

The Gold Museum is already *My Cocaine Museum*. But it is only when we know of these connections that we can, as Antonin Artaud put it, "awaken the gods that sleep in museums,"[8] not to mention the ghosts of African slaves, who with their bare hands dug out the gold that kept the colony and Spain itself afloat for more than three hundred years. However, unlike the Indians, destroyed by Europe and centuries later "awakened" by the aesthetic and stupendous monetary values accorded pre-Colombian gold work, these other ghosts are truly invisible and their polluting power—their miasma—all the more disturbing.

And that is why I have undertaken to create this, *My Cocaine Museum.*

Unlike the Gold Museum located plumb in the center of the nation's capital, my museum lies at the furthermost extremity of the nation where the Pacific Ocean seeps into four hundred miles of mangrove swamps and trackless forest, where the air barely moves and the rain never stops. This is where slaves from Africa were brought to mine gold in the headwaters of the rivers flowing fast down the Andes, which run north to south but a few miles from the sea. This is where I have visited a few weeks at a time every summer in the 1990s through to 2002, and before that in 1971 and in 1976, intending to write a book about the gold-mining village of Santa María located at the headwaters of the Río Timbiquí.

During those years, as gold dwindled to little more than memories, cocaine appeared on the horizon. It had spread west over the Andes from the Amazon basin, where U.S. government–enforced spraying with defoliants drove coca cultivation into these forests of the Pacific Coast. By 1999 cocaine traffickers were coming to Guapi, the largest river port in the region and merely one river south of the Timbiquí, buying cocaine tons at a time several rivers south. Living it up in

---

8. Antonin Artaud, *Le Theatre et son double* (Paris: Gallimard, 1964), p. 52. I thank Ed Scheer for this connection.

the Hotel del Río Guapi, these traffickers would take off in fast launches in the morning and return at nightfall to carouse with the local police. The excitement was palpable, and along the middle reaches of the Saija, but one river north of the Timbiquí, the largest guerrilla army in Latin America—the FARC—had coca fields as well.[9]

In other areas of Colombia, cocaine draws not only the guerrilla but behind them come the paramilitaries with the thinly concealed support of the state's military apparatus. Dependent on cocaine trafficking, the paramilitaries torture and kill peasants they claim are collaborating with the guerrilla. Other than in the north near Panamá in the Chocó region, the Pacific Coast knew none of this spectacular paramilitary violence till the massacre of peasants in April 2001 in coca-growing areas at the headwaters of the Río Naya, several rivers north of the Timbiquí. To the south of the Timbiquí in that same year, paramilitaries had assassinated human rights workers in the port of Tumaco, on the border with Ecuador, and were edging in on coca fields in the Patía drainage. In October they took up temporary residence in the lower Timbiquí too, causing waves of anxiety if not a general hysteria. Since then, fears have abated but the nightmare of imminent paramilitary bloodshed can never, ever be discounted. It is in this sense that *My Cocaine Museum* stands with its door ajar on the impending apocalypse.

Is the danger proportionate to the value of these gorgeous "flowers of evil," gold and cocaine? With gold we see perhaps the irony more than the danger, the irony of poverty-stricken miners at the end of the world up to their waists in water and mud, searching, at times for years, for the stuff of dreams and legends, before throwing in the towel. Likewise with cocaine, the drama is intense, so intense that what this drama opens your eyes and heart to is a weird but invigorating place where words and elemental forces of nature form hybrid entities, neither natural nor human, more like the foot of a saint or the golden wrist of a hustler that glows in the dark. It is here, philosophically speaking, where *My*

---

9. FARC, an acronym for the Revolutionary Armed Forces of Colombia, has some fifteen thousand combatants and dates from the mid-1960s, when peasants belonging to the Liberal Party, who had been persecuted for over a decade by the national government and the Conservative Party, set up "red republics" under Communist Party influence or leadership so as to protect themselves.

Cocaine Museum begins, where transgressive substances make you want to reach out for a new language of nature, lost to memories of prehistorical time that the present state of emergency recalls.

It goes like this: gold and cocaine are *fetishes,* which is to say substances that seem to be a good deal more than mineral or vegetable matter. They come across more like people than things, spiritual entities that are neither, and this is what gives them their strange beauty. As fetishes, gold and cocaine play subtle tricks upon human understanding. For it is precisely as mineral or as vegetable matter that they appear to speak for themselves and carry the weight of human history in the guise of natural history. And this is how I want *My Cocaine Museum* to speak as well—as a fetish.

This is the language I want, a substantial language, aroused through prolonged engagement with gold and cocaine, reeking in its stammering intensity of delirium and failure. Why failure? Because unwinding the fetish is not yet given on the horizon of human possibility. Would that we could strip these fetishes of their mythology and thus expose the true and real substances themselves, naked and alone in their primal state of natural being. Yet even if we could, we would thereby destroy that which animates us, those subtle tricks played on human understanding by substances that appear to speak for themselves. The language I want is just that language that runs along the seam where matter and myth connect and disconnect continuously. Thus, *My Cocaine Museum* does not—I repeat, does not— try to tease apart nature from culture, real stuff from the made-up stuff, but instead accepts the life-and-death play of nature with second nature as an irreducible reality so as to let that curious play express itself all the more eloquently.

As a museum dedicated to natural history, *My Cocaine Museum* follows the flow of the river from the headwater village of Santa María deep in the forest, past the provincial capital of Santa Bárbara lying downstream just above salt water, across the still waters of the river mouth to the swamps that form the puffy edges of the coast itself. Some ten miles out at sea as its terminal exhibit, *My Cocaine Museum* disappears into itself on an ex-prison island that is now a national park, a museum island of natural history that early on in the Spanish conquest of the New World was given the name of Gorgona after she whose face turned those who looked at her to stone. The Gorgon haunts *My Cocaine Museum.* No doubt about it. She comes before the gods, before nature was separated out from culture. She comes before time, they said, living at the end of the known world near the night where time is space. She petrifies. She is the patron saint of museums. Yet my site moves. There is more to the Gorgon than at first appears.

But I am not that interested in museums. I find them dead and even hostile places, created for a bored bourgeoisie bereft of life and experience. What I am interested in is the life of gold and the life of cocaine where one is dying and the other taking off, although cocaine has more than its fair share of death too. What interests me and I hope you, too, about the end of the earth where the rain never stops and the trees reach the sky is an ambition as old as the hills, namely, to combine a history of things with a history of people forced by slavery to find their way through these things. What sort of things? Heat and rain, forests and rivers, stones and swamps, color and islands—those sort of things—and especially the miasma emanating from the swamp. And why? So that along with the ghosts of slavery haunting the museum, nature itself is released along with the rush of the time-compacted magic of gold and cocaine.

My Cocaine Museum

gold

Looking ahead through the rain with the roar of the river on our left, we made out the clatter of machinery and a rusty funnel, the height of a two-story building, into which the hillside on the other side of the river was disappearing as so much rubble to be filched for gold. This was the newly arrived Russian mining company. A tractor trailer crawled like a yellow centipede on its countless tires. Orange water vomited from a pipeline, spilling over the turmoil of boulders that had once been a purposeful river. Awkwardly balancing on sliding heaps of stones, a mestizo man with a black rubber cape stood guard with a shotgun. Some village children and barely clad women who had been panning for gold at the edges of this mountain of rubble walked calmly in front of the trailer, balancing their wooden pans upside down on their heads as umbrellas. Not that they seemed to care much about the rain. It seemed like a cute, even comic, act, amid this grotesque drama, those black silhouettes against the warm sheets of rain, the gray sky, and the leaden air. We'd returned to the beginning and end of time when the planet was formed from molten chaos and was now, thanks to modern machinery, disappearing back into it. "What is your mission? What is your mission?" people asked as we struggled through the mud to the village that had once housed slaves from Africa brought to mine gold by hand.

In the beginning, time compressed itself into space as continental drift. Sliding over one another and the earth's molten core, tectonic plates heaved, the mountains shook, islands rose from the seabed, and the rivers went underground. To local miners, such as Ricardo Grueso, a descendant of the African slaves brought here to mine gold in the eighteenth century, this tumultuous past is the story of gold, its alchemical coming-into-being. Gold is the exudate of a corrupt natural order subject to divine wrath. In Ricardo's view—and it is hardly his alone—it was the Flood as described in the Old Testament that ravaged the earth and by means of this violent kneading of the earth's elements forced the rivers underground and filled them with gold.[1] Miners, mostly men, wend their subterranean way searching for the old rivers coursing deep in the earth. They know when they are close on account of the fossils they find, such as shells from the sea and huge tree trunks, leaves as well, tossed in turmoil under the earth by the Decisive Diluvial Undoing. In fact, they call fossils *diluvios.* As you get close to the underground river, the rock may harden as if nature is determined to keep you out. The miners call this abnormally hard rock *huevos de peña,* "eggs of bedrock." It is dark black with strange whorls that look like small shells have been pressed in expressing a prehistoric language. Miners using pickaxes can extend a mine a meter a day. When they hit *huevos de peña,* it's more like a meter in six months. But the fossilized leaves that cover the gold, Ricardo said, they are so petrified they turn to powder at your touch and the gold you find there is no less powdery, so fine they call it *liquid.*

The women bend almost double from the waist and like magic get the *batea* to make this swirling movement so it spins out gravel. Shaped like a saucer

1. In his gem of a book on gold mining in Colombia, first published in English in 1834, the Swedish mining engineer Pedro Nisser notes the following as regards the peculiar geological formations where gold can be found: "The miners of this country attribute this formation to the *revolución del diluvio* [in Spanish in the original], meaning the impact of the biblical Flood." Pedro Nisser, *La Minería en la Nueva Granada* (1834), trans. María Victória Mejía Duque (Bogotá: Banco de la República, 1900), p. 47.

about two and a half feet in diameter, a *batea* is carved whole out of one piece of wood, by men who make canoes and paddles as well, with nothing more than a machete and a tiny plane. A *batea* might be used as a baby's crib or as a container for clothes taken down to the river to wash, but its main use is to find gold. As they rotate the *batea*, the women dip the edge into the river so a little water spills in with every swirl as gravel is ejected. After a few minutes of spinning the *batea* like this, spinning and dipping, there remains a black sand fine as soot in which they look for specks of gold. It is an astonishingly beautiful movement. I try but the gravelly water sloshes around and I lose it all. When the women stoop, the body bends into the running water through the medium of this spinning wooden disc. The trick is to get the rotating action working in harmony with the up-and-down action just at the level of the water in the stream so that as the non-gold-bearing material is ejected by centrifugal force, a little water is allowed to spill in by a centripetal force. What sort of machine could do that? The women drift along the streams when and where they wish. Nobody can stop them now. The river is theirs.

It was not always like this. Years ago at the beginning of the twentieth century, the New Timbiquí Gold Mines Ltd., head office 10 rue Taitbon, Paris, prohibited panning for gold because it gave people a measure of independence and the company needed every able body for miles around. It was like a police state up the river then. The sort of thing you read about in books. Sweaty white men trapped in the equatorial forest fathering black children in a barbaric country. Company store. Company currency. Company jail. It was Justiniano Ocoró who led the fight in the late 1920s when the company was but a feeble shadow of its former self and the fight centered on this right to pan gold on your own account along the rivers.

I say "on your own account" but I must mean "on women's account." *Mazamorreo* it is called in the legal documents presented by Ocoró in the state capital, but the woman use another name—*playando*—meaning "to beach" or "beaching," passing from one beach to another, washing sand and gravel for specks of gold. Now women go every day, solitary or in groups of two or three, with clothes to wash and kids in tow. One woman in her sixties, Eustaquia Ocoró, with a yellow hard hat and in bare feet, sometimes takes a guitar along with her. Even tiny kids work the *batea*, almost as big as themselves.

On average, but of course there is no average, a woman finds gold equivalent to a dollar a day. How much actual gold is that? One grain is what they say they get on average. The word is *grano* and it is a weight as balanced by one corn seed placed on a small metal pan, part of a homemade balance made of wood and string suspended from the forefinger of the shopkeeper who buys gold as well as selling basic foodstuff, matches, soap, and so forth. A unit of weight known as the *grano* was used in the scale of weights and measures in the slave mines here—in 1819, for instance, one *castellano* equaled eight *tomines,* which equaled ninety-six *granos,* with the *grano,* so I read in the dictionary, as equivalent to forty-eight milligrams. But the *grano* was also a measure of the *fineness* of gold (quite different to *weight*) as indicated by the carat, there being in the history of the word *carat* its meaning "four grains," for instance. Which is all very confusing, especially when you take into account that the young blond chap from the interior who buys gold in Guapi has never even heard of the *grano.* "*Grano? Grano?* You mean *gramo!*" But then what else would you expect but confusion and complexity with a commodity as special as gold, the mother of all commodities, including money itself, the commodity that carries in its innermost being, so to speak, the languages of the Bible and African slavery, to name but two items in its polyglot heritage? And if you think measuring one's daily income by a corn seed is pathetic, what about a matchstick? For the amounts found now are so small that this is also a unit of measurement up here in Santa María, even though you will not find this unit of weight or fineness in any dictionary I know of. Four matchsticks = one *grano.*

I am surprised at how often I get the same answer from the women as to how much gold they find in a day. A *grano* a day, they say. It seems so routine. Perhaps they just say this to make the conversation simpler with a nice round figure, knowing full well that each day is different and you can go days without finding anything. Perhaps this is what the person buying the gold tells them. Perhaps they work to that figure and then call it quits for the day. Or perhaps what they get varies day to day, but nobody wants the others to know if they score big. Later I learn how sensitive people here are to envy and inequality, to sorcery and poisons as payback. I hear stories of the devil as the owner of gold but never of subsistence crops such as plantain or corn. Gold mining is a transgression. Of what I am not sure. It is also necessary for survival, and that is getting harder and harder to achieve. Indeed, it now looks like the devil has no more gold to give, and the village faces slow death just as happens in fables about those who strike a deal with the fabled prince of darkness. But then there's cocaine, the devil in modern guise.

Right from the beginning, the Christian and Jewish God loved gold too. Perhaps not in quite the same way as the devil, but it certainly seems like He couldn't get enough of it. When He first appeared to mankind, He stated his side of the contract: "Thou shalt not make unto thee any graven image," said God, "or any likeness *of any thing* . . . but build me an altar and sacrifice upon it." Moses killed oxen and sprinkled the altar with their blood. Whereupon from the clouds on Mount Sinai, God commanded the people of Israel to bring him gifts to build a temple that was to be covered inside and out with gold. The holy of holies was the "mercy seat," either side of which were two golden cherubim with their wings open. "And there," said God, "I shall meet with and command thee." In the beginning was the word. And the word was gold.

But here's the strange thing: gold is also the epitome of evil, a veritable code word for all we want but in our innermost hearts know we must not have. Remember the Golden Calf they all danced around as naked in fact as they were in spirit? And with reference to yellow in his famous book on color, Goethe noted in 1810 that gold in its perfectly unmixed state gives us what he called a new and high idea of yellowness. It is an agreeable and gladdening color, which in its utmost power is serene and noble. Yet yellow, he goes on to say, is extremely liable to contamination, and he singles out sulfur as an example for having something unpleasant about it—this same sulfur, or "pale sulfur," that van Gogh said he used to create an atmosphere of the devil's furnace in his painting *Night Café*. "By a slight and scarcely perceptible change," writes Goethe, "the beautiful impression of fire and gold is transformed into one not undeserving the epithet foul; and the colour of honour and joy reversed to that ignominy and aversion. To this impression the yellow hats of bankrupts and the yellow circles of Jews may have owed their origin."[2] Like cocaine, perhaps even more so, gold has its seamy underside seething with danger, prohibition, secrecy, and hidden histories. Gold is legendary for driving men crazy as in B. Traven's *Treasure of the Sierra Madre*, made into a film by John Huston, starring Humphrey Bogart. Gold drives men crazy because the desire it stimulates is boundless, reeking of danger that needs to be hemmed in by a firewall of fairy tales and superstition. Gold is famous for destroying entire nations and empires. Is it not the received wisdom

---

2. Johann Wolfgang von Goethe, *Theory of Colours* (1840), trans. Charles Lock Eastlake (Cambridge: MIT, 1970), pp. 306–8.

concerning the far-flung Spanish empire that gold brought it to its knees, that gold and silver from the New World undermined the wealth of Spain, making it a hopeless backwater of defeated armies, a reactionary church, and stagnant intellectual life? If money is the source of all evil, gold is this in spades.

Indeed, it has been argued—notably by Sigmund Freud—that gold is shit, especially with reference to the gold offered by the devil that turns out in many stories, Colombian as well as European, to be monumentally self-destructive. The world delights in opposites. Anthropologist and ex–bank teller Saba Waheed informed me that the commonest substances found on bank notes in the United States are shit and cocaine. The world delights in opposites. Yet this marriage of money to fecal matter and cocaine threatens opposition itself. The two sides of the coin implode, and we are left with exorbitant residue that shoots beyond form. Such is gold. Such is cocaine. Matter out of place, happy in just Being, variants of miasma from the swamps; formless, yet contagious. Why *formless?* The fossilized leaves that cover the gold in its archaic riverbeds, Ricardo said, they are so petrified they turn to powder at your touch.

My first sight of the Russian miners was of shirtless men staggering into the dusk along the uneven cobblestones of the one street that is Santa María, clutching at bottles of rum that in those gigantic hands seemed more like toys. It was unnerving, for you rarely see shirtless men in other parts of Colombia, let alone white ones on the Pacific Coast, and their lurching desperation made them stand out like clowns on a stage. And these chain-smoking men, more often drunk than not, were desperate. They would laugh and weep in quick succession, their Colombian translator told me, and often fight. For apart from the rigors of the climate and the remoteness of the location, they had not been paid, so it was said, either in pesos or in rubles, much less in the precious dollars they had been promised. They were invaders, yet also prisoners stuck up an isolated river in the Colombian jungle, one hundred of them, according to a submission to the circuit court in Guapi, and seventy-four Colombian employees as well.[3] They could barely muster a word in Spanish. "Santa María! *No problema!* Santa María! *No problema!*" That was about it. Except for the word *contrato* (meaning contract). The locals treated them with scant respect. The Russians slunk in and out of the

---

3. Later changed to 106 Russians.

village back to their camp by the airstrip. When I asked what most impressed them about Colombia, one responded with wide-open eyes, "The goods in Buenaventura!" The main port on the Pacific Coast, Buenaventura bakes in a muddy estuary of cheap shoes, cheap scotch, and cheap lives. The Russians pass around my son's red flashlight. It passes from hand to hand in its smooth perfection. I am the first white man handing out beads, cloth, and guns to these semi-naked barbarians living off hope and fearing strange gods (names supplied on request). I shall write a book about their cruel customs and become famous. They buy a bottle of rum and fill seven glasses. We stand up and drink. They are not miners, I say to myself. They are earth movers. We brace ourselves.

People here tell me you can go for days panning gold without finding any. Yet this is the only source of cash for most people. Years ago it was different. But now the village lives more on memories of gold than gold itself. Perhaps this is the nature of gold. Before it must have been a fairy-tale place with all that gold concentrated there at the end of the world in the primeval forest where the rain never stops and the river leaps its way down the mountain on its way to the sea; all that gold that the Indians made into exotic art for their bodies, for their dead, and for the lime containers needed for the ingestion of coca; all that gold the African slaves dug out and washed for their owners, the Arboledas and the Mosqueras, living on the other side of the cordillera in the whitewashed capital of Popayán, nestled in the mountains of the interior far from these gray skies and pounding rain; all that gold the ex-slaves tunneled out for the French engineers of the New Timbiquí Gold Mines early in the twentieth century. All that. Gone. It seems. And the ultimate throw of the dice by these hapless gamblers? To stay put and keep looking. Not that they had much choice. Not when your cash income is down to a dollar a day.

Gambling and mining have this in common: each in its own way enters into a game with nature—the first with probabilities, the second with the history of the world, which, in relation to mining, is also called geology, meaning the wisdom or, latterly, the science of the good earth on which we tread so lightly. The history of the earth, in this region at least, is a restless ever-changing one with earthquakes and catastrophes such as the Flood, no less than with the sedimentation of heavy metals down to bedrock accompanied by the erosion of surfaces by water, as with the rain that beats down like a hammer here in these equatorial forests. For people with experience garnered over many lifetimes of collective trial and error, playing with nature means mimetic play—imitating nature in order to fuse with the force imitated so as to manipulate it. The simpler the technology, the more subtle this mimetic play will be: women born in the forest with their *bateas* swirling in the stream, as compared to men flown in from the ex–Soviet Union with bulldozers leveling a mountain. When a woman stands arched over in the shallows rocking the *batea* full of gravel, she is in effect a replica of the millennial work of the river itself, washing its way down the mountain to the bedrock, where gold, as the heaviest metal, comes to rest.

The element of chance associated with mimetic play has a curious relation to fantasy, which sets off such play from what we usually mean by work, like when you hear music coming from a deep pond in the river where gold naturally collects as in a giant sluice box. It was Gustavo Díaz Guzbén, a resident of Santa María, who first told me about this music, later confirmed by women who dive for gold. Because he called it music, I imagined it to be melodic, perhaps like the music of the marimba that hangs in the church during Easter. But what he meant by music was a noise like a machine or like a wild wind he heard swimming underwater with a stone tied to his back at San Vicente. He surfaced and asked if an airplane had passed by. He later figured out the music was the caretaker, the *cuidandero,* of the gold, with whom you have to strike some sort of deal so as to get at his hoard. What sort of deal? That's the problem. Other times the caretaker appears in the darkness of a subterranean mine as a hen followed by its chicks. First thing you notice is the "*pio, pio . . .*" of its clucking. Or it comes as a toad. Or as a dog . . . Strange things, said Lilia Zuñiga, who also lives in Santa María, ugly things, *cosas marranas.* Moving shadows. Accidents. You put down a crowbar, come back, and it has moved.

It seems there are plenty of men who make a deal with the caretaker and are quite prepared to provide him with the souls he demands, which means they use magic or poisons slipped into the food or drink of the victim, until that day when they, too, have to pay with their own lives, like Leopoldo. He was considered a rich man on account of his mine about half a mile downriver with its rocky mouth agape, dark and sweaty, right on the river's edge. It must have been the last of the truly productive mines. You can still see the iron rails for the gondola coming out of it, like a ghost train. I don't think people were all that surprised when Leopoldo died a few years back, choked on his set of false teeth, the man steering the canoe told me, almost with a smile, I thought, as we shot by downstream. The river had been raging and Leopoldo tried to cross it in a canoe and tipped over with his boots on and was dragged down.

As an afterthought to such fatalism, Lilia once remarked that when all of a sudden people make a lot of money, they go crazy. I don't think she meant this to displace what Gustavo or Eustaquia—or herself, for that matter—had told me. Not at all. It was more like a commonsense observation and a layer, if you like to put it that way, a layer you put on top of all those strange and sinister ideas about gold. To me what's important about her remark is how it makes you realize what being a miner is like, spending your whole life in grinding poverty and then one day, maybe, finding a lode and with that the world explodes.

But women never get involved with the devil. On that she was adamant, even though she once pointed out to me the woman who had made the Russians leave. *Volteando los rastros,* they call it. It's a way of making people leave the village even if they don't want to by placing a spell over their footprint. Women have their secrets, as men do, but not for gold and not with the devil; secrets to defend yourself, secrets so you can work without getting tired, secrets to cure snakebite, secrets to staunch the flow of blood, secrets to attract lovers, secrets to climb a chontaduro palm . . . These secrets are prayers, or what in English we call spells. When students of culture explain superstition, they tend to emphasize its role in reducing anxiety in situations where persons, no matter how rational, lack control, but it has been pointed out that magic is just as likely to provoke anxiety as reduce it. Other times it is said that magic in the form of sorcery exists as the effect of envy and has as its aim the reduction of inequality between persons. Still other scholars say magic and sorcery serve to maintain harmony between person and nature. But none of this explains the metamorphoses of the devil, his animal forms, the music from the pond, or the little detail of Leopoldo's boots, let alone his choking on his false teeth. Nor does it begin to explain the magic of gold itself, why it is inherently evil yet so attractive.

At one point Eustaquia said that when God made the world, he gave its gold to the devil as his part. Does this mean that sooner or later all gold miners end up in league with the devil and are fated for self-destruction? Of course not.

That's simply too melodramatic. But the idea is there—who can deny its truth?—along with others, some more pragmatic, some more lighthearted. Her seventy-year-old husband, Andrés, knee-deep in mud in the mine they have been digging with their bare hands for over a year without finding gold, overheard our conversation and told the story of a man who had a compact with the devil but wanted to bail out. "Only if you can guess my age," said the devil. "What can I do?" cried the man to his wife, who after thinking awhile replied, "Just wait. I'll fix it." She lay down on the path where the devil walked and spread her legs wide. "When the devil saw that apparatus," Andres said, "he was so startled she was able to ask him his age. 'Thirty-three,' he replied. And so it was that the man got out of his compact." Rabelais tells a similar story of that apparatus scaring off the devil, which Freud cites in his two-page essay on the Gorgon, Medusa, whose face turned men to stone, it being Freud's contention that this is more than a face, like those Greek figures of Baubo, face and woman's genitals, combined. Ten miles out to sea, the ex-prison island of Gorgona knows none of this. A mere island, after all, tip of an underwater mountain range thrown up by volcanic eruptions, beaten down by never-ending rain showers and memories; memories of staging the Spanish conquest of South America, memories of eighteenth-century British pirates and, in our time, the ghostly forms of prisoners incarcerated there for life.

The dramatic emergence of the cocaine economy in a few localities in the southernmost towns of the coast has had the strange effect of resuscitating gold jewelry, which pours forth as a beautiful soft yellow substance like butter with a hint of the orange of the setting sun. Most often it is worked into broad bands of filigree up to an inch wide. Hector—handsome and strong, aged twenty-eight, with a university degree in literature, reader of Proust, and now back on the coast as a mechanic in the one and only town with any life—worked six months in a cocaine laboratory in the jungle along the sprawling Patía River south of Guapi. He wears a gold necklace weighing four and half ounces from the apex of which hangs a large 36, which I assumed was his age. No! he said. That was the number of ounces of gold the miner had discovered in one hit diving under the bed of the headwaters of the Río Guapi. He had this necklace made from that gold; spent all the rest on liquor, women, and weapons; and had to give the 36 to Hector to pay off debts.

Upstream, however, there are no such necklaces to be seen, and little of that vibrant, daredevil youth economy bursting to the surface, fists full of gold destined for liquor, women, and weapons. But there are many people, especially women, who have visions. These they call *revelaciones* and distinguish them from dreams. The night after she found half an ounce of gold in a stream at San Jerónimo last year, Eustaquia, for instance, had a *revelación*. She saw a black bull come toward her. As it approached, it changed into a young black man. Very handsome, she said later. He stretched out his hand to greet her. It was white with eight fingers.

"I've heard you sing in church," he said, "sweet and clear."

"You should come to church," she countered, and with that he disappeared. When she went back to the stream where she had found the gold, it was covered by a landslide.

I ask a friend upriver in Santa María what happens to the gold he mines and sells. He says it goes to the Banco de la República in Bogotá, which sells it to other countries. "What happens to it then?" "I really don't know. They put it in museums . . ." His speech fades. Lilia shrugs. It's for jewelry, she thinks. And for money. People sell it for money. It goes to the Banco de la República and they get money for it . . . In a burst of self-righteousness, I ask myself how come the world-famous Gold Museum of the Banco de la República in Bogotá has nothing about African slavery or about the lives of these gold miners whose ancestors were bought as slaves to mine the gold that was for centuries the basis of the colony—*just as cocaine is today*? So what would a Cocaine Museum look like? It is so tempting, so almost within grasp, this project whose time has come . . .

Within grasp?

Project?

Where better, then, to start than with the twelve-inch-long bright red wrench, lovingly displayed on our TV screens in New York City last week, as described to me by my teenage son, an inveterate watcher of TV? Is not this oversize wrench the most wonderful icon for *My Cocaine Museum*? I mean, where better to start than with the mundane world of *tools*, antithesis of all that is exorbitant and wild about cocaine, and yet have this *particular* tool, which, being so fake and being so grand, so far exceeds the world of usefulness that it actually hooks up with the razzle-dazzle of the drug world? How these two worlds of utility and luxury cooperate, to form deceptive amalgams that only people privy to the secret can prize apart, is a good part of our story and therefore of our museum too.

For according to U.S. federal prosecutors, gold dealers on Forty-seventh Street in Manhattan are paid by cocaine smugglers to have their jewelers melt gold into screws, belt buckles, wrenches, and other hardware, which are exported to Colombia, from where the cocaine came in the first place. U.S. attorney in Manhattan James B. Comey points to "the vicious cycle of drugs to money to gold back to money."[1]

Could we not have predicted this, given what we already know about the tight connections in prehistory between gold and cocaine? The exotic and erotic gold *poporos* in the Gold Museum have long unified the world of gold with the world of coca. Used to contain lime from crushed seashells and burnt bones so as to speed up the breakdown of the coca leaf into cocaine, the *poporo* unifies the practical world with the star-bursting world of cocaine and cannot be too far removed from the beauty of the oversize red wrench, at once so practical and impractical. "On 47th Street, everything is on trust," says a jeweler, making it all the easier, it appears, for an undercover agent from the El Dorado Task Force who came saying he wanted to smuggle gold into Colombia and needed to change its shape. The jeweler replied to UC (which is how the undercover agent is now referred to) that he would provide gold in any shape UC wanted.

Any shape UC wanted.

How perfect is gold, the great shape-changer, the liquid metal, the formless

---

1. Benjamin Weiser with Daisy Hernandez, "Drug Money Laundered into Gold, U.S. Says," *New York Times*, June 6, 2003, sec. A, p. 1.

form. How perfect for our Cocaine Museum to have such hefty metaphysical kinship with a substance that, like the language of the poet, can be twisted and tuned to the music of the spheres. I can think of only one other substance that rivals gold and cocaine in this regard and that is cement, once known as liquid stone, which now covers America.

Where better to start, then, than in the canyons of Gotham, with Wall Street brokers buying their drugs from a Dominican man in a nice suit in the men's room sniffing cocaine. At the same time across the East River at Kennedy Airport, there is a Chesapeake Bay retriever, also sniffing, urged on by its U.S. Customs–uniformed mistress, "Go, boy! Go find it! Good boy!" as small-statured Colombians draw back in horror at the baggage carousel when their clear plastic-wrapped oversize suitcases come lumbering into sight and smell—plastic-wrapped in Colombia by special businesses that come to your home the day before the flight to seal your baggage against a little slippage.

A real American decides enuf is enuf. The dog has gotten out of control, he decides, and he tells its handler to back off as the dog jumps up and down slobbering on his chest. "You have your constitutional rights," says the handler. "Here everyone is guilty until smelt innocent," and she urges the dog to leap higher. You need a large dog for this sort of work. The small ones may be smarter but get trampled on. Whoa! Watch out! Dogs and their happy masters and mistresses come running helter-skelter down the aisle as if out in the park for a romp. They must be thinking of the dogs leaping for red meat under the wings of the planes out on the tarmac far away at Bogotá. Lucky Third World dogs. When the animal is at play, the prehistoric is most likely to be snagged.

Sometimes they find a frightened Colombian they suspect of having swallowed cocaine-filled condoms before the flight. They force-purge the suspect. I mean, how many days do you think the DEA's gonna wait on some constipated mule? In the toilet bowl swim tightly knotted condoms like pairs of frightened eyes, blown up Salvador Dalí–like streaming out of the bowl, across the floor, and along the ceiling, showing the whites of terror as other condoms explode in the soggy blackness within the stomachs of couriers.

Far from the surefooted world of dogs, yet no less dependent on instinct because they cannot distinguish coca from many other plants, are the satellite images used to prove the success of the War Against Drugs, spraying defoliants onto peasants' food crops as well as onto coca, forcing the coca deeper into the forest and now over the mountains and into the Pacific Coast. The U.S. ambassador to Colombia has been quoted as saying, "It's quite possible we've underestimated the coca in Colombia. Everywhere we look there is more coca than we expected."[2] Remember the "body counts" in Nam?

The noose is tightening, says the priest. Along with the cocaine come the guerrilla, and behind the guerrilla come the paramilitaries in a war without mercy for control of the coca fields and therefore of what little is left of the staggeringly incompetent Colombian state. You edge into a dark room with sounds of a creature in distress illuminated by a red glow casting shadows of vultures on the wall of the slaughterhouse early morning as amidst the smell of warm manure, the lowing of cattle, and thuds of the ax, poor country people line up closer together shivering to drink the hot blood for their health as the president of the United States of America signs the Waiver of Human Rights in the Rose Garden that releases one billion dollars' worth of helicopters fluttering out of the darkness like the bats the Indians made of gold, the caption to which tells us that being between categories—neither mice nor birds—bats signified malignity in the form of sorcery, and compares the helicopters with the horses of the conquistadores breathing fire and lightning on terrified Indians.

But the Indians were always good with poisons and mind-bending drugs such that high-tech solutions turn out to be not all that effective in the jungle, so don't despair: there's every chance the war and the massive economy it sustains will keep roaring along for many years yet. Speaking of Indians, here's a familiar figure to greet you, that huge photo you see in the airport as you walk to immigration of a stoic Indian lady seated on the ground in the marketplace with limestone and coca leaves for sale and in front of her, of all things, William Burroughs's refrigerator from Lawrence, Kansas, with a sign on its door, *Just Say No*, as an Indian teenager saunters past with a Nike sign on his chest saying *Just Do It* and a smiling Nancy Reagan floats overhead like the Cheshire cat gazing thoughtfully at an automobile with the trunk open and two corpses stuffed inside it with their hands tied behind their backs and neat bullet holes, one each through the right temple and one each through the crown of the head. *El tiro de gracias.* Professional job, exclaim the mourners crowding around the open coffin and holding the neatly dressed children high for a better view. "I know when I die," I say

2. Juan Forrero, *New York Times,* July 30, 2001, sec. A, p. 4.

VELORIO
HENRY
CHANTRE

PUERTO
TEJADA
10 OCT.
1998

JUST SAYNO   JUST SAY NO   JUST SAY NO   JUST SAY

to Raúl, "I want it to be here in this pueblo with these people around me." He looks at me oddly. I have scared him.

One of the bodies is Henry Chantre, who while doing his military service in the Colombian army used to pick up and transport drugs into Cali for his officers—so they say—and when discharged got into trafficking himself, a shiny SUV, a blond wife, handsome little children, and one day a deal went sour and he was found stuffed in the trunk of an abandoned car by the bridge across the Río Cauca. A long way from Manhattan's East River. In one sense. Strange, these rivers, so elemental, first thing the conqueror does is find a river snaking its way into the heart of darkness and all of that, for trade, really, canoes, rafts, that sort of thing, rail and road an afterthought decades or centuries later, water spanning the globe, the bridge spanning the river connecting Cali to this little town south, where Henry Chantre lies staring at you, the town milling round, the bridge being where most of the bodies end up getting dumped, heaven knows why; what weird law of nature is this, the river, the bridge, why always the same spot, macabre compulsion to dump bodies in the burnt-out cars and gutters there in the no-man's-land by the bridge between categories, like the bats, neither bird nor mouse, sanctified soil teeming with chaos and contradiction here by the river where black men dive to excavate sand for the drug-driven construction industry in Cali. Father Bartolomé de las Casas, sixteenth-century savior of Indians in the New World, wrote passionately about the cruelty in making Indians dive for pearls off the island of Margarita in the Caribbean. Nowadays, long after African slavery has been abolished, the slavery that replaced the slavery of Indians, it's considered routine to dive for sand, not pearls, the strong ponies so obedient braced against the current, carrying wooden buckets.

We need figures, human figures, as strong as these squat ponies braced against the current, and in the early morning mist by the river comes in single file the guerrilla, who, except for their cheap rubber boots and machetes, look the same as the Colombian army, which looks exactly the same as the U.S. Army and all armies from here to eternity, most especially the paramilitaries, who do the real fighting, slitting the throats of peasants and schoolteachers alleged to collaborate with the guerrilla, hanging others on meat hooks in the slaughterhouse for days before executing them, not to mention what they do to live bodies with the peasants' own chain saws, leaving the evidence hanging by the side of the road for all to see, and worst of all, me telling you about it. Hence the restraint in the display case in our Cocaine Museum with nothing more than a black ski mask, an orange Stihl chain saw, and a laptop computer, its screen glowing in the shadows. When they arrive at an isolated village, the paras are known to pull out a computer and read from it a list of names of people they are going to execute, names supplied by the Colombian army, which, of course, has no earthly connection with the paramilitaries. Just digital. "It was a terrible thing," said a young peasant in July 2000, in the hills above Tuluá, "to see how death was there in that apparatus."

The paras are frank even if they like to be photographed wearing black ski masks despite their being hot and prickly. As of July 2000, some 70 percent of the paras' income, so they as well as the experts say, comes from the coca and marijuana cultivated in areas under their control in the north of the county, drugs that will make their way stateside. Yet up till that date, at least, the paras get off scot-free. Their coca was rarely subject to eradication, and the government's armed forces had never, ever confronted the paramilitaries. Instead the thrust of the U.S.-enforced war was to attack the south where the guerrilla are strongest and leave the north free. The War Against Drugs is actually funded by cocaine and is not against drugs at all. It is a War for Drugs.

Our guide motions to the ripples spreading over the river where corpses are daily dumped, and men dive for sand for the remnants of what was once a thriving industry, building the city of Cali, rising rainbow-hued through layers of equatorial sunbeams thickened by exhaust fumes. Transformed by drug money invested in high-rise construction and automobiles, the city now wallows in decay, with many of its apartment towers and restaurants empty. Nothing like cocaine to speed up the business cycle.

In the next room of our Cocaine Museum are the remains of peasant plots like bomb craters filled with water lilies in the good flat land from which the earth has been scooped out eight or more feet deep so as to make bricks and roof tiles for when the building boom in the city was in full swing. This rich black soil was once the ashes of the volcanoes that floated down onto the lake that was this valley in prehistoric times. Peasants sold it, their birthright, taking advantage of the high prices for raw dirt and because agribusiness created ecological mayhem with their traditional crops. Then the boom stopped and now there is no work at all. There is no farm anymore. Just a water hole with lilies that the kids love to swim in.

And to tell the truth, for a lot of people even if there was "work" in the city, nobody would want it. Dragging your arse around from one humiliating and massively underpaid job to another—less money, really, than the women get panning gold on the Timbiquí (can you believe it!). That's all over now, the idea of work work. Only a desperate mother or a small child would still believe there was something to be gained by selling fried fish or iced soya drinks by the roadside, accumulating the pennies. But for the young men *now* there's more to *life*, and who really believes he'll make it past twenty-five years of age? If they don't kill each other, then there's the *limpieza*, when the invisible killers come in their pickups and on their motorbikes. At fourteen these kids get their first gun. Motorbikes. Automatic weapons. Nikes. Maybe some grenades as well. That's the dream. Except that for some reason it's harder and harder to get ahold of, and drug dreams stagnate in the swamps in the lowest part of the city like Aguablanca, where all drains drain and the reeds grow tall through the bellies of stinking rats and toads. *Aguablanca*. White Water. The gangs multiply and the door is shoved in by the tough guys with their crowbar to steal the TV as well as the sneakers off the feet of the sleeping child; the *bazuco* makes you feel so good, your skin ripples, and you feel like floating while the police who otherwise never show and the local death squads hunt down and kill addicts, transvestites, and gays—the *desechables*, or "throwaways"—whose bodies are found twisted front to back as when thrown off the back of pickups in the sugarcane fields owned by but twenty-two families, fields that roll like the ocean from one side of the valley to the other as the tide sucks you in with authentic Indian flute music and the moonlit howls of cocaine-sniffing dogs welcome you to the Gold Museum of the Banco de la República.

Something like that.

My Cocaine Museum.

A *revelación*.

cocaine mu

One day cocaine will return to being the prehistoric soul mate of gold, what fairy
tales can never have enough of because gold has the unique function of being
both symbol and reality of value. When Massachusetts sealer and outrider Captain Amasa Delano, whose published diary provided Herman Melville with his
story "Benito Cereno," visited the mint in Lima, Peru, in 1805, he found himself
in a fortress-like building occupying an entire block.[1] The gold ore was wetted
and kneaded by blacks treading on it with their feet on a paved brick surface after
which they put mercury on it so as to separate out the gold. Then the metal was
heated, becoming red as blood. To get the liquid metal to run from its crucible,

---

1. Charles Olson cites Delano in *Call Me Ishmael* (Baltimore: John Hopkins, 1997) p. 117: "[Melville] was a
sea frontiersman like the whalers Fanning, Delano and other outriders."

the spout was touched with a stick with a piece of cloth around it. When this stick made contact, there was a flash and the metal began to run in a stream not much thicker than a pipe stem. The bars of gold formed were subsequently squeezed flat by rollers until the thickness of a dollar or doubloon, by which time the bars had become sheets four feet long. A powerful press cut coins out from these thin sheets like a cookie cutter, and the pieces were turned to receive a milled edge. Then came the weighing. Rarely were the coins too heavy. If they were, they were let through. But if too light, a man selected a tiny pin of precious metal from a box and with a special instrument made a hole in the coin into which he pushed the pin so as to make the correct weight. The machine that inserted the pin had leverage up to one hundred tons. They were working on thousands of coins when Delano visited and could pin fifteen a minute, or one every four seconds. The bullion was brought to the mint just like farmers brought corn to a mill. As soon as it was coined, it was taken away by its owners.[2]

I can neither recall nor imagine a better way of making money both mysterious and everyday than through this meaty description of its fabrication. Here in their minting, gold and silver coins become enchanted, material things, aglow with a power emanating from deep within. All sense of money as a symbol, of money as the embodiment of societal value, disappears as we become suffused by the practical details of its production, including those strange value-added pins. Karl Marx famously described money—in its function as capital—as like a *fetish,* by which he meant to imply that money could easily seem to multiply all on its own, as when your money in a savings account accrues interest. What happens, he said, is that human labor provides the element that makes for such multiplication. By paying workers less than what they produce, money expands. *Voilà!* I'll go along with that, but nevertheless I continue to think it strange that the *fetish* character of money is so enduring in our thoughts no less than in our language. Money as capital is irreducibly a fetish, bigger than any explanation, and that, I submit, is what it both takes from and adds to gold. Gold is the ur-stuff, what we might call the "original capital," the "quintessence" of capital, and it comes chockablock full of dreams, fairy tales, biblical resonance, and mountains

---

2. Amasa Delano, *Narrative of Voyages and Travels in the Northern and Southern Hemispheres* (1817) (New York: Praeger, 1970), pp. 498–508.

of excess creating further excesses. Hence what is intriguing to me in Amasa Delano's depiction of making gold coins is that he—or, rather, the process of fabrication—actually displaces that aspect of gold as money by concentrating our attention on the practicalities of how money is made. The comparison with corn is superb in this regard. But let us look at these "practicalities" a little longer. Aren't they at the same time a poetry, vivid and shocking? Don't they make nature no less than the economy look strange?

This sums up for me what is crucially important about the work of the gold miners in Santa María. The gold becomes like corn, we might say. Indeed, is it not generally weighed off against a grain of corn? But not so fast! The fetish quality that Marx discerned may dissipate, but another form of wonder takes it place, as in Delano's description. And this is the wonder of the practical workaday world combined with the wonder of the material world, which here in this land of ceaseless rains and suffocating heat has contrived to create golden rivers. Moreover, as the long-standing belief in this region instructs us, the gold secreted in underground riverbeds is in its own way enchanted, product of the mechanical, material forces unleashed by the Flood, which is when the world turned upside down. And what about the connections between gold mining and the Prince of Darkness? Hence as we move from Karl Marx's fetish to the "plain facts" of the material world, we seem to do little more than displace one enchantment by another, which is, I think, a very good thing because the materiality of the material world and of the workaday world is far too easily taken for granted, especially in societies with advanced technology. What is required now as the world lurches toward ecological and political self-destruction is continuous surprise as to the material facts of Being, something I think Walter Benjamin put nicely in his 1929 essay on surrealism, where he counseled—against the easy mysticisms and New Age enthusiasms of his era—the need for a "dialectical optic" that discerns the mystery in the everyday, no less than the everydayness of the mystery.[3] In that case, surely money qualifies as the most surreal of all our objects, yet it takes stories like Amasa Delano's and those I have recounted from Santa María to bring this forth.

---

3. Walter Benjamin, "Surrealism: The Last Snapshot of the European Intelligentsia" (1929), in *Reflections: Essays, Aphorisms, Autobiographical Writings*, ed. Peter Demetz, trans. Edmund Jephcott (New York: Schocken, 1986), p. 190. The actual wording is "a dialectical optic that perceives the everyday as impenetrable, the impenetrable as everyday."

Above all, gold is a tease; immaculate substance pleading for a form. Take the Spanish conquest of the Incas. On finding the intricately worked gold figures made by the Incas, the Spaniards melted them down into ingots. Hernándo Pizarro oversaw the big meltdown in Cajamarca in 1533. He had Indian smiths working on nine forges, and on many days they melted over six hundred pounds weight of gold. At the end of four months, they had melted eleven tons of golden vases, golden figures, golden jewelry, and golden furnishing ornaments. He then escorted the train of 225 llamas carrying the gold and silver to Lima. A load of baser gold arrived a few days later on the backs of sixty llamas.[4] Imagine this on a movie screen; those dun-colored mountain slopes of the central Andes that stretch forever, cut across by a line of stately llamas not even knowing what they carried, other than its weight. In the Temple of the Sun in the Incan capital of Cuzco, the Spanish found a garden whose plants were made of gold and silver. This, too, they melted down.

Inevitably money—like color—makes one think of stories of transmutation of form into substance and of substance into flows. The story of the Inca's garden tells us more about money than many an economic treatise. Pizarro melts the garden down into ingots nice and square that fit into boxes in ships' holds to go to Spain as bullion, the ur-form of money. The Indians want gold as the ultimate mimetic metal, flowing and ductile, with which they can *imitate* most anything. But the money boys want gold as that with which they can *acquire* most anything. Squared up as ingots or rounded as coins, their gold has done a good deal more than serve as a medium of exchange. It has made everything in the world exchangeable in what we now see as the big meltdown.

In opposition to Newton, sustained by his notion of God as the Great Geometer, whose mathematical ways of looking at things is certainly congenial to smelting the whole world and not only gold into money, I want to turn to Goethe's 400-page treatise on the theory of colors, a book filled with wonder and ingenious experiments that Newton's theories could not easily encompass.[5] Indeed, Goethe's experiments have been hailed as evidence for a newfangled "chaos theory." But it is more

---

4. John Hemming, *The Conquest of the Incas* (New York: Harcourt Brace Jovanovich, 1970), p. 73.
5. Goethe, *Theory of Colours*, pp. 195 ff.

instructive to regard his fascination as one that sidesteps theory with the notion that everything factual is already theory, beginning with the blueness of the sky.

Why thinking about color causes reality to tilt remains a mystery. Color is the genie escaped from the bottle. Philosophers argue endlessly about it, and it is color that propels Ludwig Wittgenstein, for example, to invest himself ever further into the riddles of language.[6] Color makes a mockery of language, it seems, and that is one reason why it is so sought after by William Burroughs in his war against image and language so as to accelerate his program of cultural erasure no less than accelerate back and forth through history—as with the hourglasses he describes, each with its own colored sand: red, green, black, blue, and white. Each sand represents "color time" and "color words."[7] Color is grist to his mill of amputated lyricism as in these lines (and there are plenty more):

The silence fell heavy and blue in mountain villages—Pulsing mineral silence as word dust falls from demagnetized patterns.[8]

It is color that turns language into word dust, patterns lose their ability to hold us in thrall, and silence falls—silence that is heavy, silence that is blue, the blue of waking dreams that come with *yagé*, the hallucinogenic vine Burroughs came across in his travels in the southwest of Colombia (and which, on the Pacific Coast, is called *pildé*). Which takes us back to Goethe's blue sky, where everything factual is already theory.

Goethe's experiments with color make us aware of how the best experimental method is very like a language game too, leaving us with . . . well, just the experiments, just the colors, the fascination, and the wonder. We see nature, then, all of it, in new ways. We see seeing, all of it, then, in new ways too.

Wiping away breath on glass and then breathing on it once again allows us, he writes, to see very vivid colors gliding through each other. As the moisture

6. Ludwig Wittgenstein, *Remarks on Colour,* ed. G. E. M. Anscombe (Berkeley: University of California Press, 1978).

7. William S. Burroughs, *The Soft Machine,* in *The Soft Machine, Nova Express, The Wild Boys: Three Novels by William S. Burroughs* (New York: Grove Press, 1980), p. 92.

8. William S. Burroughs, *Nova Express,* in *The Soft Machine, Nova Express, The Wild Boys: Three Novels by William S. Burroughs* (New York: Grove Press, 1980), p. 33.

evaporates, the colors change their place and at last vanish altogether. A similar iridescence appears in soap bubbles and in the froth of chocolate. When first created, bubbles are colorless. Then colored stripes like those in marble paper begin to appear. This is even easier to see in the bubbles of chocolate froth than in soap bubbles because chocolate bubbles are smaller and the heat provides an impulse toward movement and hence a succession of appearances. As the bubble gets close to bursting, you will see the colors are attracted to the highest point of the bubble in which a small circle appears that is yellow in its center while the other colored lines move constantly around this. Slowly this circle enlarges then sinks down and while its yellow center remains, the bubble becomes red and soon blue. Sometimes green is produced by the union of colors at the border. When metals are heated, colors rapidly succeed one another. At a certain temperature the metal will be overspread with yellow. As the temperature increases, the yellow becomes more intense and passes to red—the red of gold in the Lima smelting house—yet this is difficult to maintain because it hastens to a beautiful bright blue and then a light blue.

Goethe (whom I have been quoting and paraphrasing) says at this point that "these colors pass like breath over the plate of steel." Goethe's color world is one of movement and sudden change coming from who knows where and into what. It is like abstract expressionist painting or Mexican fireworks bursting into a black sky framed by jagged peaks. Walter Benjamin followed this way of thinking in his opposition of color to line. Color to him was a suffusion unlocking fantasy. It took you into a riotous world, nowhere more so than with the illustrations in children's books and the child's love of soap bubbles, not to mention, I might add, their love of chocolate. The point, however, is not to oppose color to line so much as engage their mischievous interaction. "Prince is a word with a star tied to it," a seven-year-old boy told Benjamin, the point being that color, image, and word manifest a mysterious unity more present or more obvious in primers than in adults' books. But let us turn this around, so to speak, and see the whole of nature and the whole of the human apparatus for sensing as similarly bound to color, image, and word. Let us appropriate from the world of children's books—"prince is a word with a star tied to it"—what we could designate, following Benjamin himself, a "hieroglyphic mode" of perception. It was not form so much as color that drew children to books, into which as with magic they disappeared. "The gazing child," he suggests, "enters into those pages, becoming suffused, like a cloud, with the riotous colors of the world of pictures. Sitting before his painted book . . . he overcomes the illusory barrier of the book's surface and passes through colored textures and brightly painted partitions to enter a stage on which fairy tales spring to life."[9]

The reader, whether of books or nature, passes into that which is being read.

Even as an adult, Goethe must have held on to childish characteristics. This would account for the ingenuity of his color experiments that convert physics into something closer to poetry as a language of nature in which effervescent swarming surfaces glide through each other . . . in an incandescent succession of appearances, temperatures, breath, and speeds. Transmutation is the name of the game, and it is no surprise that Goethe's color theory owes a great deal to alchemy, an art and science that emerged from the techniques of dyeing cloth rich colors in ancient Egypt, applied to the task of transmuting metals into gold. We could say, along with the poets and metallurgists of the ancient worlds, China and India included, and along with the Indians of South America, that there is some truth to the children's tale that at the foot of the rainbow sits a pot of gold. What's more, Goethe's theory that color emerges from intricate contrasts of light and shade is a theory that meshes with the color world of the Pacific Coast, whose gray skies and intense glare, thanks to the low-lying clouds and heat, displace solid colors with flickering luminosities. If you hold a sheet of black paper to the sun, Goethe said, "it will be seen to glisten in its minutest points with the most vivid colors." Making color come out of blackness seems miraculous to me. It is like seeing gold flecks emerge in the black pay dirt at the bottom of the spinning *batea* in a woman's strong hands dipping into the stream.

9. Walter Benjamin, "A Glimpse into the World of Children's Books," in *Selected Writings,* vol. 1, *1913–1926,* ed. Marcus Bullock and Michael W. Jennings, trans. Rodney Livingston et al. (Cambridge: Harvard University Press, 1996), p. 435.

On account of their physical prowess and their capacity to live in hot and unhealthy climates, Africans are supremely useful in the Tropics. It cannot have been without forethought that Providence made them part of the Antilles, Venezuela, the coasts of Peru, and of the states of Cauca, Panamá, Bolívar and Magdalena.

—Sergio Arboleda, son of the owner of the slave mine at Santa María at the headwaters of the Río Timbiquí in the province of Cauca[1]

heat

Like gold or cocaine, heat is a force like color that sets aside the understanding in place of something less conscious and more overflowing, radiance instead of line, immanence instead of that famous bird's-eye view. As our planet heats up and the Tropics spread, is it not possible that not only a new human body but a new type of bodily consciousness will be created in both temperate and tropical regions, a consciousness that reattaches the body to the cosmos? Two centuries ago, Charles Fourier certainly thought so, with his scheme to reorganize human society along anti-capitalist, socialist principles that encompassed sex, smell, and color, no less than money, work, and property, and he did so in

1. Sergio Arboleda, "La Colonia: Su constitucion social," in *Corona funebre en honor del Sr. Dr. Sergio Arboleda* (Ibagué: Impr. del Depto., 1890), p. 124. My translation.

order to save what he saw as our dying planet. A reinvigorated Earth, according to his estimation, would equilibrate heat so there would be less of it in the Torrid Zone and more of it at the Poles, heterosexuality would dissolve into pansexuality, the Tropics would acquire a climate like the south of France, and the Arctic would melt into seas of lemonade. Fourier is unsettling. But then so is global warming.

But let me first admit to a more narrowly aesthetic if only slightly less cosmic complaint connected to heat: that having made many visits in my adult life to what are called the Tropics, I am perplexed as to the absence of heat in movies and stories set in that Torrid Zone. And where much is made of heat, is it not the case that its torpor is turned inside out; that instead of sinking us deeper in sloth and discomfort, instead of allowing heat to melt even language itself, such heat becomes a trick and nothing more than a device to propel a plot? I have yet to see a movie that is serious about heat instead of treating it as a theater prop. The more sultry the weather, the more sinister the expectation: *Body Heat* no less than *The Wages of Fear* (my first foreign movie). But sultriness-in-itself? The languor that dissolves Being into a sticky wet puddle? If only Fourier had made films!

In my job it is essential that I read anthropological classics based on fieldwork in hot places—the Australian desert, the Trobriand Islands, Mozambique, Central Africa, West Africa, Sudan, the Amazon, the Yucatán, Sri Lanka, Indonesia . . . Yet I can think of only one account that devotes any attention to the feel of the heat and humidity in the Tropics—and this merely in its first two paragraphs—Bradd Shore's esteemed *Sala'ilua: A Samoan Mystery,* published in 1982. "The heat grows steadily in Samoa throughout the late morning and early afternoon" are his opening words. "It is hot and steamy even in the 'cool months' [note his quotation marks]. . . . On ordinary days, not much happens in Sala'ilua during these blazing hours. Conversation among the women and older girls sitting or reclining in the open *fale* becomes more muted. . . . The drone of soft music from the radio only adds to the general torpor. The weaving of mats slows in the heat and many simply sleep the afternoon out, occasionally lifting a hand to swat an annoying fly, or halfheartedly flick a fan to raise a transient breeze."[2] As a

2. Bradd Shore, *Sala'ilua: A Samoan Mystery* (New York: Columbia University Press, 1982), p. 5.

conscientious ethnographer, he feels guilty at his lack of energy and having to fight off a powerful urge to stare blankly at the sea. Yet as the subtitle of his book indicates ("A Samoan Mystery"), no less than the title of this first chapter ("A Death in the Family"), heat here is the same as in the movies: prelude to drama as antithesis to languor. A man called Tuato will soon be shot dead in the chest and found lying in a widening pool of blood.

True, the "father of anthropology" Bronislaw Malinowski wrote passionately of heat, but then that was restricted to his diary, infamous for its personal detail. "Strong fear of the tropics; abhorrence of heat and sultriness," he writes in the *winter* month of May 1914, in Brisbane, Australia, prior to his departure for New Guinea, and he goes on to note that he feels "a kind of panic fear of encountering heat as terrible as last June and July. I gave myself an injection of arsenic." To deal with the panic, he stocks up on a generous supply of cocaine, morphine, and emetics.[3] Indeed, you can read his diary as a weather chart with his body a thermometer recording heat and lassitude, heat and numbness, heat and arsenic. In the wonderful photographs assembled by Michael Young of Malinowski in the Trobriands in his customary fieldwork gear, we see him in dazzling whites, like a cricketer, buffered against the sun.[4] His smocklike elegant white shirt is buttoned to the neck, and he wears white riding breeches with off-white, knee-length, leather leggings. More often than not, his noble dome of a forehead is surmounted by a beautifully balanced pith helmet. Cleary this is a man prepared for heat. Indeed, he is strikingly similar to pictures we see all too often today of workmen and state security officers clearing out toxic dumps or investigating anthrax. The contrast with the almost naked natives, dark of skin, is staggering. But none of this heat or ways of living with it appears in the published ethnography, *Argonauts of the Western Pacific,* or *Coral Gardens and Their Magic,* where, instead, reality is *depicted.* It is distanced and visual whether in photographs or as expressed in words. Reality is defined as an out-of-body experience, namely, what we can see through a camera lens or from the bow of a moving canoe. Indeed, it goes even further than this; reality is itself a picture: "Further ahead, through the misty spray, the line of the horizon thickens here and there, as if faint pencil

3. Bronislaw Malinowski, *A Diary in the Strict Sense of the Term* (1967), 2nd ed. (London: Althone, 1989), p. 4.
4. Michael W. Young, *Malinowski's Kiriwina: Fieldwork Photography, 1915–1918* (Chicago: University of Chicago Press, 1998).

marks had been drawn upon it."[5] Heat has slipped off the sociological chart to become personal neurosis and private nightmare. But then there's cocaine along with morphine and emetics, another form of hot.

Sitting out the scorching summer in 1932 on the then-remote Mediterranean island of Ibiza, Walter Benjamin, sad, lonely, and very poor, wrote a four-page letter to a dear friend in Berlin. It is now published as an essay called "In the Sun," and as you read it, you get a sensation similar to what Goethe describes as the behavior of color sweeping across the surface of heated steel. Benjamin no longer sees but feels. And he no longer sees but is seen. The cosmos involutes. He is the all-seeing eye that is more than an eye. He writes about himself in the third person: "This sun was burning into his back. Resin and thyme impregnated the air in which he felt he was struggling for breath." A bumblebee brushes his ear, but no sooner does he feel this, then the bee has disappeared into a vortex of silence. It is suddenly brought home to him that as with the bee, so the summers before had disappeared into a vortex. "With astonishment he would recall that entire nations—Jews, Indians, Moors—had built their schools beneath a sun that seemed to make all thinking impossible for him."[6] The summer heat of the island is magnified through the prism of experience enlivened by smoking hashish and opium and writing up his dreams.[7] No wonder it was here in the summer that he sketched out his extraordinary essay "On the Mimetic Faculty," exploring the notion that in imitating something we actually become that thing, an intuition he applied to language as well—an essay that has to be opened up alongside his earlier Berlin notes on how, when taking hashish, one was provided with "the collusive knowledge about non-being," in which words became colored sequins.[8] We tend to think of observations like these as the result of "expanded consciousness." Rarely do we conclude that maybe they indicate just how re-

5. Bronislaw Malinowski, *Argonauts of the Western Pacific: An Account of Native Enterprise and Adventure in the Archipelagoes of Melanesian New Guinea* (1922) (Prospect Heights, Ill.: Waveland Press, 1984), p. 49.

6. Walter Benjamin, "In the Sun" (1932), in *Selected Writings*, vol. 2, *1927–1934*, ed. Michael W. Jennings, Howard Eiland, and Gary Smith, trans. Rodney Livingston et al. (Cambridge: Harvard University Press, 1999), pp. 662–65.

7. Vicente Valero, *Experiencia y pobreza: Walter Benjamin en Ibiza, 1932–1933* (Barcelona: Ediciones Península, 2001).

8. Walter Benjamin, "Main Features of My Second Impression of Hashish" and "Hashish, Beginning of March 1930," in *Selected Writings*, vol. 2, pp. 86, 328.

duced "normal" consciousness is, a consciousness we keep normal by having ready-made categories such as "drugs" and "dreams" so as to isolate the untoward. But then there is heat—drug and dream combined—getting hotter with each passing day.

In his book *Dispatches,* an insider's view of a year spent in front-line combat in Vietnam, which he covered for *Esquire* magazine in 1967, Michael Herr makes few references to the heat and humidity, which in fact must have been monstrous. Indeed, the very opening to the book uses the tropical heat as the force that warps perception of time and space in the form of an old French map of Southeast Asia hanging above his bed: "The paper had buckled in its frame after years in the wet Saigon heat, laying a kind of veil over the countries it depicted." In his deranged and exhausted view, Herr wonders if this map buckled by heat, depicting the ancient political geography of extinct kingdoms, could bring alive the dead, for that would be a truer map of Vietnam than the current maps, which revealed very little because "reading them was like trying to read the faces of the Vietnamese, and that was like trying to read the wind." Shapes and forms, as in maps, give way to moods and forces such as the wind and the heat. "We also knew that for years now there had been no country here but the war."[9]

Once he mentions pillows damp with sweat, the ceiling fans, and the air heavy, as though a terrible heat was coming on; or that time when in August the heat in I Corps "forgave nothing"; how Mutter's ridge had a terrible heat; how the photographer Sean Flynn back from six weeks with Special Forces in III Corps sat not saying a word about what had gone on up there, spaced out on the floor by the air conditioner trying to watch the sweat running down from his hairline; how the fatigues of photographer Dana Stone (who later disappeared, along with Sean Flynn) were completely darkened with sweat; and at one point, "Fuckin' heat . . . I . . . oh, man, I just . . . can't . . . fuckin' . . . *make it!*"[10]

But these references to heat are sparse. The truer sense of heat lies in the force buckling ancient maps so as to make them more true than new maps,

---

9. Michael Herr, *Dispatches* (1968) (New York: Vintage, 1991), p. 3.

10. Herr, *Dispatches,* p. 205.

the force that provides Herr with the new language he brought back from Vietnam. "There were all kinds of people who knew the background, the facts, the most minute details," he says, "but only a correspondent could give you the exact mood."

> Night sweats, harsh functionings of consciousness, drifting in and
> out of your head, pinned to a canvas cot somewhere, looking up at a
> strange ceiling or out through a tent flap at the glimmering sky of a
> combat zone. Or dozing and waking under mosquito netting in a
> mess of slick sweat, gagging for air that wasn't 90 percent moisture,
> one clean breath to dry-sluice your anxiety and the backwater smell
> of your own body. But all you got was and all there was were misty
> clots of air that corroded your appetite and burned your eyes and
> made your cigarettes taste like swollen insects rolled up and smoked
> alive, crackling and wet. . . . Sometimes you couldn't live with the
> terms any longer and headed for air-conditioners in Danang and
> Saigon. And sometimes the only reason you didn't panic was that
> you didn't have the energy.[11]

Unlike *Sala'ilua: A Samoan Mystery,* heat here is not the languor that sets the stage for a dramatic plot. Instead, it is the figure for an atmosphere in which natural history and political history become united in what is still referred to as the "Cold War." Heat for Herr is virtually unmentionable because the senses are overstimulated and numbed not only by drugs—they come later—but by the brutality of the war combined with the lies of the commanders and the politicians, such that it becomes impossible to tell it like it is. Not for nothing were the front-line combatants on the U.S. side called "grunts." So where does it go, this heat? Is it what melts the impressions he receives, running one into the other—that drifting of consciousness, of which he speaks, that dozing and waking? Is it that mess of slick sweat that is the story the book tells, that is no story at all but a hazy morass of disbelief that no story could encompass? Like drugs, the story comes later, for it is only when Herr is called upon to write a Hollywood film

---

11. Herr, *Dispatches,* pp. 226, 54.

script adapting Joseph Conrad's *Heart of Darkness* to Vietnam, that heat is used to fuel narrative effect, no less desperately sought by Hollywood than its need for cocaine. Running in sweat, Martin Sheen's face in the film *Apocalypse Now* tells that story, no less than the stains in the armpits of the uniforms of the soldiers who bundle him into the shower at the beginning of his mission as the ventilator fan swirls slowly overhead.

Sweat runs down the cleavage of the singer by the side of the Panama Canal. Her hips sway. The camera focuses on her thighs. These few tears of sweat are the only sign of heat and humidity you will see in the two-hour feature film *The Tailor of Panama,* and they serve not to project you into the steamy world of heat but into the steamy world of sex—our true tropics—in the British embassy, no less. As for the genre of the magazine essay, what Sylvia Plath called "the slicks," I have just finished reading in the *New Yorker* an article on the fate of the Panama Canal by John Lee Anderson, author of a megabiography of Che Guevara. But *not one word* about the incredible heat or humidity! Stuffed full of entertaining facts about political skulduggery, plus an account of his heroic crossing of the wild Isthmus of Darien with Cuna Indians, the writer is strangely removed from this basic bodily experience of heat and humidity, as if such experience is inimical to the act of writing itself. Instead what we get are the "concrete details" beloved of *New Yorker* magazine writing, testimony to the need to create the illusion of the real: the gold-colored blazer of a Spanish businessman looking for investment opportunities in the Canal zone, or the gold Rolex watch and gold pens peeking out of the pocket of a disgraced dictator with nowhere to live but the Republic of Panamá.[12] So much gold, we might say, and so little heat.

Gold and silver, of course, is what Panamá meant to Europeans for centuries, just as it does today in the form of secret bank accounts, flags of convenience, and hideaways for dictators on the run. But that gold and silver was joined at the hip to a suffocating climate. Thomas Gage found the heat so dreadful in Panamá City when he was there in 1637 that he spent about as much time commenting upon it in his published memoir as he did upon the fabulous streams of silver trans-shipped across the isthmus for the galleons waiting at Porto Bello on

---

12. John Lee Anderson, "233,000 Acres, Ocean Views," *New Yorker,* November 29, 1999, pp. 50–61.

the Caribbean coast. During the two weeks it took to load the wedges of silver at the latter port, he said some five hundred men died of fevers and flux associated with the heat and unhealthy climate.[13] "An open grave" was how he described it. Not Porto Bello but Porto Malo.

In a well-documented history of the buccaneer Henry Morgan, based on state papers in the colonial archive in Seville, Spain, it is stated that Porto Bello was generally considered the worst posting in the Spanish empire. "It really was a terrible place," continues the author, Peter Earle, "humid, smelly and suffocatingly hot, cut off from the cool breeze of the evening by the mountains and hills surrounding it. Strangers to the town invariably complained of the heat, the constant rain, the hordes of flies and mosquitoes, and the stench of filthy black mud that was laid bare at every low water." While locals might become used to it, many suffered from recurrent malaria and other diseases, "and nearly everyone sooner or later became sunk in a terrible lassitude."[14] And note that Porto Bello was chosen in 1584 because Nombre de Dios, the previous port, a few miles to the east, was considered too unhealthy.[15]

Small wonder, then, that farther east along the coast from Panamá, José Arcadio Buendía dreamt of a future city of mirrors to be built where he was sleeping that night. In his dream the city bore a strange name: Macondo. In fact, it was not a city that came to be built there but a tiny village lost in the swamp, and as he realized later, it wasn't mirrors he was dreaming about but ice. "Macondo would no longer be a burning place, where the hinges and door knockers twisted with the heat," Gabriel García Márquez writes in *One Hundred Years of Solitude*, a book that begins with these words: "Many years later, as he faced the firing squad, Colonel Aureliano Buendía was to remember that distant afternoon when his father took him to discover ice."[16] The colonel's father was none other than that ice dreamer, José Arcadio Buendía, and the ice that he took his son to

13. Thomas Gage, *Thomas Gage's Travels in the New World* (1648), ed. J. Eric Thompson (Lincoln: University of Oklahoma Press, 1985), pp. 327–31.

14. Peter Earle, *The Sack of Panamá* (Bury St. Edmunds, Suffolk: Norman & Hobhouse, 1981), pp. 54–55.

15. C. H. Haring, *The Buccaneers in the West Indies in the XVII Century* (1910) (Hamden, Conn.: Archon Books, 1966), pp. 17–18.

16. Gabriel García Márquez, *One Hundred Years of Solitude* (1967), trans. Gregory Rabassa (New York: Harper, 1991), p. 25.

see had been brought by gypsies, magical beings bearing magical gifts to this baking Caribbean village.

What are we to make of this extravagant mixture of gypsies and the last moment of life opening out to memories of first seeing ice as the place where this story begins? "Magical realism," they say. For which ice in a hot, backward, Third World, tropical country might seem emblematic. Yet is it not the stark fact of heat as everyday, all day, and the next day and the next that is the realism against which gypsies and magic here gain their fullness? And is it not the fact that heat is unrepresentable that makes us cling to ice, watery, translucent, lovely, and painful-to-touch ice? Through its heavenly antidote, ice, heat metamorphoses finally into rain. Toward the end of *One Hundred Years of Solitude*—and that's what it takes, *one hundred years*—it eventually rains. And it rains without stopping for four years, eleven months, and two days.

Watery, translucent, ever-so-presentable ice, how it glitters like diamonds in the one account I know of that does justice to heat-in-itself: Louis-Ferdinand Céline's *Journey to the End of the Night*, one of the texts Julia Kristeva singles out to illustrate her notion of abjection, meaning that all-too-common but thoroughly unrepresentable state of diffuse anxiety, depression, and self-loathing that seems to dissolve your very being.[17] Escaping his perdition as a soldier in World War I, Céline finds himself in a French freighter bound for Africa with a bunch of colonial administrators. Off Portugal, the heat comes down like a hammer:

> One morning we woke up to find ourselves overcome by a breathless sort of stove atmosphere, disquieting and frightful. The drinking water, the sea, the air, the sheets, our own sweat, everything was warm, sticky. From then onwards it was impossible, by day or by night, to feel anything cool in one's hand, under one's bottom, down one's throat, but the ice in the whiskey served at the ship's bar. An ugly despair settled on the passengers on board the *Admiral Bragueton;* they were condemned never to leave the bar, dripping, clinging to the

---

17. Julia Kristeva, *Powers of Horror: An Essay on Abjection,* trans. Leon S. Roudiez (New York: Columbia University Press, 1982).

ventilators, grasping little bits of ice, threatening each other after bridge and incoherently apologizing.

Reality dissolves.

In this maddeningly unchanging temperature the whole human freight of the ship clotted together in one vast tipsiness. People walked wanly about the deck, like jelly-fish at the bottom of a pool of stagnant water. It was then that one saw the whole of the white man's revolting nature displayed in freedom from all constraint, under provocation and untrammeled, his real self as you saw it in war. This tropic stove brought out human instincts in the same way as the heat of August induces toads and vipers to come out and flatten themselves against the fissured walls of prison buildings.[18]

Céline gets it right, and he gets it right because of colonialism. His World War I freighter bound for Africa is a microcosm of all that is morally wretched and absurd in the colonial experience, and it is this experience that fuses with a swarming sense of heat to produce a strangely familiar bodily unconscious—that of vipers and toads coming out of their cracks in August, flattening themselves against the fissured walls of prisons. We have all been there. But it takes Michael Herr's Vietnam War or Céline's freighter to make it clang in our brains. As global warming will—and for much the same colonial or postcolonial reasons.

---

18. Louis-Ferdinand Céline, *Journey to the End of the Night* (1934), trans. John H. P. Marks (New York: New Directions, 1960), pp. 109–10.

my cocai

Dampier's arrows

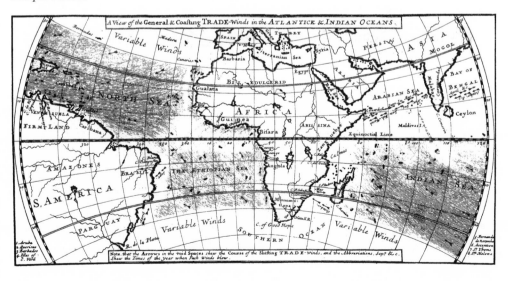

It is an embarrassing truism to point out how important knowledge of the weather and especially wind must have been to the making of the modern world. It is embarrassing because it should be so obvious and yet at the same time is so strange, further testimony to the way history has numbed us, such that if nature returns, it does so as uncanny. If you look at the maps of the world drawn toward the end of the 1600s by the British pirate William Dampier, who cruised the waters between the island of Gorgona and the Río Timbiquí, you see the vast oceans with tiny black arrows coursing across them like so many swallows darting in parallel lines.

These arrows show the "general and coasting trade winds" of the world without knowledge of which there could not have been, it seems safe to say, a modern world, and certainly not a colonial world drawing Africa, Asia, and the

Americas into the one orbit with Europe. In the last decades of the seventeenth century, the best maritime atlases contained no sailing directions for ports outside of Europe or instructions for making ocean passages, and "this," writes a British naval commander in 1931, "was the gap which Dampier determined to fill." Amazingly, "most of the information he obtained at first hand was so accurate and comprehensive that it has been handed on from generation to generation with little alteration." Dampier's "directions for using the Atlantic trade winds," he continues, "are still the best that can be given, and will be found with little alteration, in the Admiralty handbook upon ocean passages."[1] You feel Dampier would have had useful advice on global warming and El Niño. Today's manuals have titles like:

Admiralty Sailing Directions

while Dampier's book, abbreviated to *The Discourse of Winds,*[2] is more properly:

What a difference between these two titles! I look at Dampier's—at its length, its varied typography, its self-reference, its poetry and wide screen—and am reminded of Paul Valéry saying that once men imitated the patient process of nature, but now modern man no longer works at what cannot be abbreviated. The *Admiralty Sailing Directions* confidently manifests the modern state's assumed dominance of nature as in the use of Star Wars, smart bombs, and nuclear power–driven vessels in place of sail. But what such dominance grew out of was something else, a writing that in *The Discourse of Winds* speaks patiently, even lovingly, to the wind, and hence learns its languages—all the better to use it against itself, just as missionaries learn the natives' language so as to convert them, the

Cap. Dampier
HIS
DISCOURSE
OF THE
Trade-Winds, Breezes;
Storms, Seasons of the
Year, Tides and Currents of the TORRID
ZONE throughout the
World.

Ii 3

---

1. A. Colquhoun Bell, "An Explanatory Note on *The Discourse of Winds,*" in *Voyages and Discoveries,* by William Dampier, with introduction and notes by Clennell Wilkinson (London: Argonaut Press, 1931), p. 223.

2. William Dampier, *A New Voyage Round the World* (London: James Knapton, 1699), p. 220. It is Wilkinson who abbreviates this title to *The Discourse of Winds.*

same way we have all been taught to use our prehistoric instinctual selves to get a grip on our prehistoric instinctual selves. But then there's the stuff that curls over the edges to come back and haunt us, these tides and currents of the Torrid Zone. Which is why we love pirates, like Dampier, whose shifting shape we may still discern like wind in our ever-more impoverished weather talk.

For the cliché concerning the cliché of weather talk is that we talk about the weather as a way of avoiding talking about anything else, anything that would commit us to a point of view that might threaten the social bond for which weather talk is such a balm. When you stop to think about it, this is weird. Something important to your very sense of being, something beyond anybody's control, truly the wild beyond, namely, the weather, becomes hijacked as socializing grease for which grunts and groans might serve just as well. Hence Mark Twain's observation, "Everybody's talking about the weather but nobody's doing anything about it."[3] Weather talk is like wind rustling through our bodies as acknowledgment of sociality. Weather talk is soft and sweet, acknowledging our alienation from nature no less than from one another, relic of the superstition that to talk otherwise might rile it.

In this regard, I am struck by how people seem happy enough to cite heat as a number of degrees, a sure sign of what T. W. Adorno referred us to as *reification,* a mouthful, to be sure, by which he meant the habitual response in modern culture to abstract and then quantify even lived experience as if it were money. If you do this long enough, he maintained, the abstraction comes alive and seems self-empowered, like a person or a god. The upshot of this is that just as we find comfort in objectifying everything uniquely visceral in weather, such as heat, and express it in numbers of degrees Fahrenheit, so with that very same action we inadvertently grant it spectral status. Just as "money speaks," so do degrees of heat. Our TVs do even better in this regard ever since they discovered a striking mimesis of person with nature in the changing patterns of color on the weather channel, which we view in the air-conditioned balm of our living rooms. The prehistoric pixels glimmer and dilate as the viewer becomes opened up by cosmic views

3. Cited in Andrew Ross, *Strange Weather: Culture, Science, and Technology in the Age of Limits* (London: Verso, 1991), p. 267.

of the planet Earth as spied from the heavenly heights of satellite cameras. High-pressure systems head north from neighboring countries, and oceans are displayed under snowstorms as hurricanes with strange names like Floyd threaten continents in their moody journeys. This gives you insight into the return of prehistory; why they persist in calling it not a *weather* but a *meteorological* report, meteors being those things that flash across the sky leaving trails of fire, portents of disturbance in the body politic.

This is merely to say that the body itself talks a different talk than consciousness does in advanced capitalist society, nowhere more so than as regards heat and humidity. The weather thermostat of temperature and sweat controls built into our bodies operates outside of consciousness, which is just as well because we would be dead if it screwed up, and consciousness is notoriously error-prone, as Nietzsche, for one, never tired of telling us. Weather consciousness is thus unconscious, but not in Freud's sense of a psychic so much as a bodily unconscious, which is also the unconscious of the world, something like a branch of astrology connecting the tiny human body to the cosmos at large, the writhing storms over the Sahara no less than the twisters roaring through Kansas, the explosions on the sun, and the steady, dissolute gray drizzle that makes for misery and romance in London and Amsterdam. But, then, why is it that while we love to talk about the weather, what we say is so empty yet strangely satisfying? Could it be that what we mouth are the shreds and patches of previously vigorous magical correspondences? That fervent modernist Ludwig Wittgenstein says in this regard on first reading *The Golden Bough:* "And when I read Frazer I keep wanting to say: All these processes, these changes of meaning—we have them still in our word-language. . . . A whole mythology is deposited in our language."[4]

Hearken then to *mana,* the basis of magic, according to those early-twentieth-century anthropologists Marcel Mauss and Henri Hubert, who took *mana,* a Polynesian word, to mean a force and a substance that magicians tapped into so as to accomplish their fine work, *mana* being something "invisible, mar-

4. Cited by Rush Rhees, "Wittgenstein on Language and Ritual," in *Wittgenstein and His Times,* ed. Brian McGuinness (Chicago: University of Chicago Press, 1982), p. 69.

velous, and spiritual . . . which cannot be experienced since it truly absorbs all experience."[5] This is most curious and certainly seems to match the enigmatic nothingness of weather talk today, that great something that is simultaneously such a great nothing. Could weather supply the model for magic?

A few years later Mauss and Hubert's mentor, Emile Durkheim, found this curious impersonal force alive and well, pretty much wherever he looked in the extant ethnography of so-called primitive tribes. Among the Sioux of the U.S. plains, for instance, according to the anthropologist James O. Dorsey, it was known as *wakan*, embracing all mystery, all secret power, and all divinity. All the beings that the Dakota revere, "the earth, the four winds, the sun, the moon and the stars, are manifestations of this mysterious life and power." It is striking that although this mysterious power "enters into all," as Durkheim says, it is weather, wind, and stars that are most frequently conjured into expressing its presence: "Sometimes it is represented in the form of a wind, as a breath having its seat in the four cardinal points and moving everything: sometimes it is a voice heard in the crashing of the thunder; the sun, moon, and stars are *wakan*. It is not a definite and definable power, the power of doing this or that; it is Power in an absolute sense with no epithet or determination of any sort."[6]

Here's what I think: that *mana* expresses a sense of bodily consciousness writ large into cosmic consciousness; that such bodily consciousness is actually more like an unconscious, what might be called the "wisdom of the body" or the body's self-regulating autonomic nervous system; that so-called primitive societies created a magnificent theater of ritual and magic out of the network connecting this unconscious "wisdom of the body" with the cosmos at large. Hence while weather talk today retains some inklings of *mana*, the mystical and magical meanings have been eviscerated, the theater has been gutted, and the magic turned into pap because the cosmic frame of reference binding us to the natural world now barely exists. For us, weather no longer belongs to *wakan*, to divine mysteries, or to "pure force." Instead it has become a "floating signifier," the empty chatter with neighbors in the elevator. No more the voice speaking through

---

5. Marcel Mauss, *A General Theory of Magic*, trans. Robert Brain (New York: Norton, 1972), p. 111.
6. Emile Durkheim, *The Elementary Forms of Religious Life* (1915) (Glencoe, Ill.: Free Press, 1965), p. 221.

the crashing thunder. What remains of weather as cosmic frame and force is so-cial grease, mangled residue of what Durkheim alerted us to with *mana* as the basis of religion, society's worship of itself. But there is something more going on here such that weather talk today is not merely an absence or an impoverished form of prior practice and fantasy. Weather for us today is God after the death of God. "Do we not feel the breath of empty space?" asks Nietzsche.[7]

As usual, Walter Benjamin was here long before me. What else would you expect of a thinker who thrived on minutiae in which the supernatural is secular-ized but nevertheless maintains its auratic charge as profane illumination? What he said of the Russian storyteller Nikolai Leskov could be said of himself in this regard: "The lower Leskov descends on the scale of created things the more obvi-ously does his way of viewing things approach the mystical."[8] And in his notes on boredom and the weather in relation to dream worlds of modern capitalism, Benjamin writes:

> Nothing is more characteristic than that precisely this most intimate
> and mysterious affair, the working of the weather on humans, should
> have become the theme of their emptiest chatter. Nothing bores the
> ordinary man more than the cosmos. Hence for him the deepest
> connection between weather and boredom. How fine the ironic
> overcoming of this attitude in the story of the splenetic Englishman
> who wakes up one morning and shoots himself because it is raining.[9]

It is Benjamin's contention that weather is one of the highest and most ge-nial manifestations of cosmic forces. I ask myself what it would take for us to re-alize this; that every time you feel a breeze or watch a cloud pass, remember you are bearing witness to the workings of the cosmos bending a blade of grass or rustling wastepaper in the city street. Today we seem as far from that as ever. We are, as it were, in suspension, permanently thresholded, because fuller awareness

7. Friedrich Nietzsche, *The Gay Science: With a Prelude in Rhymes and an Appendix of Songs* (1887), trans. Walter Kaufmann (New York: Vintage, 1974), sec. 125, p. 181.

8. Walter Benjamin, "The Storyteller: Reflections on the Work of Nikolai Leskov" (1936), in *Illumina-tions: Essays and Reflections,* ed. Hannah Arendt, trans. Harry Zohn (New York: Schocken, 1968), p. 106.

9. Walter Benjamin, *The Arcades Project* (1982), ed. Rolf Tiedemann, trans. Howard Eiland and Kevin McLaughlin (Cambridge: Harvard University Press, 1999), pp. 101–2.

of the cosmos is blunted by the condition of modern life where even death is removed. Not for us the rain dance of the Zuni. Not for us thunder as the voice of God or the shamans descendant from the sun whose task it is to control the tempest. Only the glimpse remains and it remains as refuse to be picked over and played with in the *mana*-like speech of boredom-suffused weather talk, privileged medium of sociability like the clouds themselves, soft murmurings fleecy-lined in the elevator.

"The annual rainfall of the Pacific lowlands of Colombia is not only the highest in the Americas," writes the geographer Robert C. West, but "probably exceeds that of any other equatorial area in the world." Rarely is there a day without rain. For those who like their rain in numbers, the average annual rainfall exceeds 150 inches, many areas receive more than 250 inches, and some get battered by over 415—i.e., 34½ feet of water per year, almost three feet a month! Note that "a definite dry season is absent."[1] Which is why the two streets that exist in Santa María at the headwaters of the Río Timbiquí are cobbled and hard to walk on because of the uneven surface. I've never seen such streets elsewhere in Colombia and got

---

1. Robert C. West, *The Pacific Lowlands of Colombia: A Negroid Area of the American Tropics* (Baton Rouge: Louisiana State University Press, 1960), pp. 25, 8.

a shock to see this one, complete with marvelous stone-lined drainage channels. All this speaks to ingenuity, care—and massive amounts of rain. In other parts of rural Colombia beyond the Pacific Coast, the street would be either a muddy swamp or a concrete runway. Robert West was of the opinion that such cobbled streets were made by slaves from Africa in the eighteenth century when there were many mining villages along the middle and upper reaches of these coastal rivers.[2] Yet people in Santa María tell me it was the French mining company that cobbled this street in the opening decades of the twentieth century. Perhaps the company got the idea from what the slaves had built. Now people regard the cobblestones as too large, and a common punishment meted out by the *inspector de policía* is to order a person to replace a certain number of cobblestones with smaller ones. Often torrential, the rain makes you raise your voice on account of the noise made clattering on the iron roof. Your clothes are soon damp and smelly. Fungus appears on my leather wallet within two days. As soon as you get inside out of the rain, it's uncomfortably hot again. The distinction between air and water evaporates; sweat and rain are one. We have changed from air-breathing creatures into something else. Like amphibians we peer through a foggy humidity to draw apart curtains of water.

Soaked in sixteenth-century chronicles depicting the conquest of Peru by Francisco Pizarro, the famous nineteenth-century historian William Prescott imagined himself into the landscape of the Pacific Coast of Colombia as only a blind man could. "The land spread out into a vast swamp," he writes, "where the heavy rains had settled in pools of stagnant water, and the muddy soil afforded no foothold to the traveller [and Pizarro] was baffled by a succession of heavy tempests, accompanied with such tremendous peals of thunder and floods of rains as are found only in the terrible storms of the tropics." Elsewhere he describes the rain as descending "not so much in drops as in unbroken sheets of water."[3]

On sighting the island of Gorgona, which lies ten miles off the coast of Colombia, close to the mouth of the Río Timbiquí, the English privateer Woodes Rogers, several months out of Bristol, wrote in his diary:

---

2. West, *The Pacific Lowlands of Colombia*, p. 114.

3. William H. Prescott, *History of the Conquest of Peru, with a Preliminary View of the Civilization of the Incas*, 2 vols. (Boston: Phillips, Sampson, 1858), vol. 1, pp. 212–13, 222.

June 10th, 1709. We saw the Island at 6 in the evening, bearing SW Distance about 8 leagues. In the night we have much Rain with Lightning and Squalls of Wind, by which the Havre de Grace lost her main top-mast. This morning died Jonathan Smyth, a Smith by trade and Armourer's Mate on our Ship. . . . [S]everal of our Good Sailors dead, we are so weak that should we meet an Enemy in this Condition, we could make but a mean Defence. Everything looks dull and discouraging, but's in vain to look back or repine in these parts. [June 12th:] Hard rainy Weather, with little or no Wind. [June 16th:] Nothing remarkable pass'd from the 11th, but that we had frequent Thunder, Lightning and Rain, which retarded our careening the Duchess. [July 23rd:] At 6 last Night our cable broke, and we lost our Anchor: The Ground here is a black Mud, which in all hot Countries rots Cables in a very little time. We have often Thunder, Rain and Lightning in the Night, tho' clear dry days. This is accounted by the *Spaniards* the worst part of the coast for wet dirty weather. We have had enough of it, but God be thank'd are now pretty well, there not being above 30 Persons in all our ships unhealthy.[4]

On the island of Gorgona in 1684, the pirate William Dampier noted in his journal that "all this country is subject to great Rains. . . . I believe this is one reason why the Spaniards have made such small Discoveries in this and other Rivers on this Coast."[5] The pirate scribe Basil Ringrose, one of a pack of merry boys who broke through into the South Sea across the Isthmus of Panamá in 1680, recalled their Spanish prisoners telling them how difficult sailing was there on account of the fickleness of the wind south to latitude of three degrees, and, indeed, cruising southward close to Gorgona, he found this to be so. On June 13, 1680, for example, "there was very little wind, and most commonly none, for space of twenty-four hours." The current ran very strong toward the mainland and that same day they experienced much rain.

4. Woodes Rogers, *A Cruising Voyage Round the World* (1712) (New York: Longmans, Green, 1928), pp. 158–68.

5. William Dampier, *A New Voyage Around the World* (1729) (New York: Dover, 1968), pp. 119–20.

Yet, notwithstanding all this calmness of weather, the next day in the morning very early, by a sudden gale of wind which arose we made shift to split our main top-sail. We had all the night before and that day continued and incessant showers of rain, and made a S.W. by S. way; seeing all along as we went a multitude of dolphins, bonitos, and several other sorts of fish floating upon the seas, whereof in the afternoon we caught many, the weather being now changed from stormy to calm again—inasmuch as we could fish as we sailed along, or rather as we lay tumbling in the calm.[6]

Inland from Gorgona up the Río Timbiquí during Easter 1976, I get up in the middle of the night. The smell of feces and urine waft across the rocks by the river. Breadfruit trees and chontaduro palms with jagged leaves cut out the black sky at the back of Daniela's deserted house, where we are staying on the second floor with big holes in the floor over the sleeping Omar. If he sleeps. The houses are of wood, two stories high, with elaborately carved balconies. Someone, probably Juan Pablo, was playing a marimba, a xylophone made of bamboo and hardwood slats of chonta. It would be played till the wee hours of the morning, and I would wake not knowing if the tinkling sound was the rain or the marimba, the music of man and the music of nature conjoined and substitutable. That was the first and last marimba I heard on the coast. So although I'm told that there's one in every church in every pueblo, don't get the idea that this icon of coastness is played often. Far from it. It's rain. But what, then, of heat? Rain is noisy and spectacular, tangible and worth writing home about, filling up soggy diary pages as words swamp out into watery worlds binding heaven and earth. Rain makes music on tin roofs and emulates the marimba, while heat uses silence like nerve gas.

It's not a question of people of African descent having adapted to the rain or in simpler language just gotten used to the watery environment. It goes way beyond that. At times it seems like love. Certainly homeopathy. In the town of Guapi, it had not rained for three days. Then it pelted down, drumming on the

---

6. Basil Ringrose, in A. O. Exquemelin, *The Buccaneers of America* (1684–85), ed. William Swan Stallybrass (Williamstown, Mass.: Corner House, 1976), p. 340.

roof, and everyone shot outside. The young men played mini-football, slicing through curtains of rain and skidding through puddles like ducks, while girls and boys jumped into the swiftly moving river. "In the rain?" "Yes! *¡Es más sabroso!*" It was as if we lived in a drought-stricken desert suddenly relieved by rain, whereas in fact it rains like the dickens just about every day. A broken gutter spouts a torrent down onto the pavement. A girl and a boy dance in it to the music coming from the restaurant. She puts her hands on the wall and wags her bottom under the waterspout. Later the boy lies in a trance on the pavement in the same spot, rolling from side to side under the torrent for several minutes. A pack of kids zigzag like a school of fish along the street playing football and then dive into the rusting carcass of the wheel-less truck parked outside the mayor's office, beating on it for all they're worth and leaving the doors open as a parting gesture. Marsella scoots outside to get on her bike. No raincoat. No umbrella. And before peddling off in the pelting rain, she stoops over to scoop a bucket of water from a baby's plastic bathtub by the front gate and pour it over her head. Her mother comes in from two hours hunched over in an open launch thumping on the ocean's waves in a massive downpour. First thing she does is bathe in the rainwater brimming over a tank in the backyard.

At Santa Bárbara rain came down in torrents starting around five in the morning. I see kids playing basketball at 6:30 in the deluge. A girl aged about ten in a white singlet, black skirt, and rubber sandals stretches out belly-down on the cement of the basketball court for at least two minutes enjoying the rain. Now she gets up. Tries to shoot a basket but can only get the ball up a few feet and so goes to puddle in the ankle-deep water of the drainage channel at the edge of the court after which she jumps in with both feet so as to make a splash, which she loves and repeats again and again. A young guy in a bright yellow shirt comes and sits by her in the pouring rain with his feet in the water running along the drain. Now she has her sandals off as she walks up and down the drain with giant steps feeling the water running against her. She stoops to splash water over her face.

Upriver at Santa María the same water alchemy. A man works all day diving into the river excavating the bottom in search of gold. He is a fish. Immersed in moving water two to three meters down in the gloom. When he emerges, he immediately washes himself vigorously in the same water. Wendy Sulay, aged eight, comes home from the mine where she's been working along with maybe ten other kids after school, and dripping wet in the rain, we go straight to the river where we do the "*largo*," the long one, which means wade out to where the current is strongest and be swept one person behind the other in a dizzying arc, bobbing like dolphins over the boulders to return almost where we started, thanks to the bend in the river. Surfing! Then there's the *tambor,* when in a circle of kids, you stand a bit more than knee-high and stamp down hard. An orange bubble swells up, and you clap the palm of your hand down pretty fast but gentle onto it as it gets close to the surface, and a great boom sounds. Magic!

And in the riverside town of Guapi surrounded by water especially from the gray skies above, in all this water, I see two young men struggling with a two-wheeled wooden cart neatly laden with big blue bottles of WATER FOR SALE, brought all the way from the great port of Buenaventura way north and from God knows where before that!

my coca

Lilia

boredom

I should, however, begin with lethargy as well as with games—with the tumbling in the calm. Nothing could be less glamorous, or so resistant to representation. As the days pass like wet paste one into the other, your admiration for the spiritual and physical strength of the people here grows in leaps and bounds. Boredom hangs like a pall over the village smothered under its blanket of heat and humidity. In a well-intentioned effort to combat racist stereotyping, anthropologists are often moved to evoke equally stereotyped tropes of the cultural "dynamism" and cultural "richness" of the coast, yet I find it hard to know what is meant here. Certainly such statements reflect oddly on the rigor of everyday experience imposed by the climate and the physical brutality of the work necessary to stay alive. For what is elided by such tropes is the existential soul strength that monotony demands. Here ethnography fares poorly because this formative experience, namely, this sticky vacuum of heat and boredom, seems pretty well unconveyable and, worse still, all manner of narrative, paradox, and so-called data are then desperately shaped by the observer so as to jolt the emptiness with meaning.

Have I projected my boredom on to the village? This is the anthropologist's dilemma. Even nightmare. I ask Lilia if she feels bored. "I want to leave *running*! I want to fly!" she says with unnerving passion. "It's suffocating," she says. "Sometimes after I've finished my household chores, I go and sit downstairs and look up and down the empty street. Up and down. Nothing." She pauses and her eyes narrow. "Then out of the blue I begin to feel scared. Fear grips me . . ." Worst of all is when she thinks of this same fate befalling her children. Her husband feels the same. Most every night now around one o'clock in the morning, they switch on the radio program *Noche, Buenos Días*. Last night it was full of people mad at the government for the massive unemployment—the worst in Latin America and the worst ever recorded for Colombia. The people calling in on the radio were angry as hell, saying the figures the government emits on unemployment are false and underestimate the problem. What is more, the government is totally corrupt. This is the issue people always return to. One person on the radio said while it is true that the FARC guerrilla do bad things, at least they kill corrupt officials! I think of what it must be like to go to sleep in this dark rainy village with no electricity and wake yourself up at one o'clock to tune in to this other universe, this vast nation, the real Colombia that can only express itself on a national scale on the dark side of the moon, *Noche, Buenos Días*. But the old people, they are not bored, she says, except when there is little to eat.

Here is a puzzle. How is it we pepper our talk with "is" and "be" and "being," yet have not worked out a notion of what Being is? Greek philosophy before Plato saw this as the central problem, which means the problem from which all others flow. In religions the concept of God becomes a stand-in for the nature of Being. Martin Heidegger gave this problem an ingenious spin when he dared to ask, How is it with the Nothing? Which I guess is what Lilia asks too when she looks up and down the emptiness of the one and only street that is Santa María and feels anxiety grab her in her insufferable boredom. "I want to fly" is what she wants.

Heidegger thought you could get a handle on Being by sneaking up on it backward, so to speak, by approaching it through the Nothing. And what is it that opens up on to the Nothing in his opinion? In the first instance it is boredom, and here is what he says: "Profound boredom, drifting here and there in the abysses of our existence like a muffling fog, removes all things and human beings and oneself along with them in remarkable indifference. This boredom reveals beings as a whole."[1] But just when it seems like the Nothing has been gotten at, and hence beings as a whole, Heidegger loses nerve and abandons this maneuver in favor of *anxiety*—exactly like what happens to Lilia up a remote river on one of the world's more remote coasts as she oscillates between boredom and anxiety.

As a poet-philosopher, Heidegger has to make a trap with something that can orchestrate the tension between Being and Nothingness, it being absolutely fundamental in his eyes that the Being of beings presences itself only to disappear when actual, concrete beings come to occupy center stage and the mysterious Being of beings dissipates. Being exists, we might say, through its being "questioned" by specific, concrete beings as when Gustavo diving for gold hears music coming out of the pond or the FARC kill corrupt officials of the Being of beings we call the State, which in Spanish is called El Estado, past participle of *to be*.

The State is a presencing that Heidegger doesn't bother with much and just as tough a nut to crack as the Being of beings associated with fire, air, earth, and water. Lilia and her husband thus extend Heidegger. Through the rippling night air of radio waves coming through the forest—a quite different forest to those German ones Heidegger keeps talking about—they take him for a walk along winding paths to where he feels out of place, yet this is the place, the only place, where his metaphysical riddles could be solved. Certainly the anxiety is there, the anxiety to which Heidegger attributes powers no less than those the ancient alchemists attributed to the philosopher's stone. This anxiety has a certain quality of calmness, yet it is indeterminate and marked by generalized unease. "We cannot say what it is before which one feels ill at ease," he writes. In this state, things recede, and in this very receding, he suggests, things turn toward us: "More pre-

---

1. Martin Heidegger, "What Is Metaphysics?" (1929), in *Basic Writings*, ed. David Farrell Krell (San Francisco: Harper, 1993), p. 99.

cisely, anxiety leaves us hanging because it induces the slipping away of beings as a whole."[2] Thus we humans slip away from ourselves.

I want to make several equations that will please no one: that this terrible boredom that transforms into anxiety is very much the ethnographer's boredom too; and that this slipping away from oneself is not only what makes writing possible but is writing itself. Like boredom, this slipping away can be a terrible drag or else something we come to terms with as writers, enamored with slipping away from one's self and thereby able to open up the gap between writing and what the writing is about.

"What if it were true that writing is a lie?" asks Jean Genet. "What if it merely enabled us to conceal what was, and any account is, only eyewash? Without actually saying the opposite of what was, writing presents only its visible, acceptable, and so to speak, silent face, because it is incapable of showing the other one."[3]

What is remarkable to me about this passage and many others like it in his last book, *Prisoner of Love,* is that this book is not a work of fiction but basically an ethnography, begun in 1983 as a memoir of his stay with the PLO in their camps on the East Bank of the Jordan for two years, 1970 to 1972, and for a few months in 1984. Be it noted that this famous writer had not written a book for almost thirty years before this return to the written word, and he states that "before I started to write it I'd sworn to myself to tell the truth in this book."[4]

Yet what he ends up with is a book as much about writing as about the PLO!

"How can one simultaneously express all the contradictory emanations issuing from witnesses?" he asks despairingly. What's more, he feels his scenes are flat. They can ooze love; they can ooze friendship. But can they ooze contradiction? And his despair is bottomless when he considers page following page written in what he calls his own voice. Like all the other voices, he goes on to say, "my own is faked, and while the reader may guess as much, he can never know what tricks it employs." Recognized master of his craft, Genet alerts us to the cliché yet no less magnificent mystery of "voice," which no writer can do without. Telling us that the "only fairly true cause of my writing this book were the nuts I picked

---

2. Heidegger, "What Is Metaphysics?," pp. 100–1.

3. Jean Genet, *Prisoner of Love* (1986), trans. Barbara Bray (Hanover: Wesleyan University Press, 1989), p. 27.

4. Genet, *Prisoner of Love,* p. 27.

from the hedges at Ajloun," Genet continues: "But this sentence tries to hide the book, as each sentence tries to hide the one before, leaving on the page nothing but error: something of what often happened but what I could never subtly describe—though it's subtly enough I cease to understand it."[5] While recognizable as faked, he says, it is nevertheless effective, yet in saying as much, is he not faking even more, playing the ultimate trick, merely pretending to expose the trick of "voice" while leaving us hanging on the uncertainty of the contradiction by which its fakery makes for truth?

And if so, if I am correct in tracing the steady onward movement of his prose as a movement erasing itself as it proceeds, staring down the empty street gripped in anxiety that presences Being as it recedes in beings, I can only take heart in heat—that I, too, have chosen to make the act of writing and exposure of such no less important than what I am writing about. Indeed, it is precisely to privilege the facts such as heat in the Torrid Zone that writing self-consciously self-destructs midway between its skillful trickery and even more skillful revelation of such. Nietzsche says somewhere that for there to be a fact there has first to be a meaning. But what if the meaning is torpor?

Athletic young Russians silhouetted against the light of what I call the "Blue Bar," a family home with a dark blue painted front where prostitutes used to congregate before the Russians ran out of money and the prostitutes returned to Buenaventura. A genial bunch of galumphs, these Russians. The food here is simply awful, they say. Rice. Rice. And more rice. No fish. No meat. Ah! But in Russia it was so much better! They remind me of the crew of the Death Ship in the novel of that name by mystery man B. Traven, whom, so it is said, was a German anarchist who fled the Munich uprising of 1918 to live the rest of his long life in Mexico, where he wrote powerful stories about the Mexican Revolution.[6] In fact, one huge blond in red clothes worked twelve years on Soviet ships. Another put in nine years as a backhoe operator. The other two are welders. They think I and my two kids (aged twenty and ten) are spies, says their interpreter, a Colombian woman from Manizales who spent seven years in the USSR and dreams of being an actress. Sitting in the swelling downpour with two Russians last night

5. Genet, *Prisoner of Love*, p. 27.

6. B. Traven, *The Death Ship: The Story of an American Sailor* (1926), trans. Erich Sutton (New York: Collier Books, 1962), pp. 185–86.

drinking warm beer with rain dripping through the corrugated iron roof. The neck of the bottle smells like urine. These are the words we have in common: *Nyet,* Ukraine, contract, money, *arroz, banano,* Marx, Lenin. At night a long line of them with flashlights makes its way drunkenly up the hill to their camp where the airstrip is. The rain never stops. The church is up on the hill too, and next to it the empty house for the priest who comes at most twice a year. A Russian died abruptly from hepatitis and cerebral malaria, the nurse tells me. Later I learn she has a supernatural power to see when a person is going to die. Quite a few women have this power. Some men too. It comes from the spirits of the dead, the *ánimas,* which visit in one's *revelaciones,* which are like dreams. The *ánimas* have their *secreto,* explains Gustavo. Which is to say is the end of explanation.

Why do the Russians remind me of Traven's *Death Ship*? Written soon after the end of the First World War from the point of view of a laconic American sailor from "Sconsin" with fond memories of dairy cows, but now, having lost his papers, a miserable stoker on a tramp steamer, Traven describes the tough life on board such vessels. With the exception of the officers, all the sailors on his Death Ship are technically stateless, lacking the papers necessary for a passport or a sailor's card. Each sailor has a violent history of war, forced migrations, and shifting national boundaries, making the question of official papers ever more pressing. Indeed, the actual physical violence of that war, subject of so many memoirs as a watershed experience in the history of the world, seems rather minor compared with the violence of bureaucratic indifference and rules, especially in relation to the nation-state and the regulation of employment. Each sailor speaks a different language. The ship they work is a rusty coal-burning tub tracing a palpable destiny with death. Its owners in corporate headquarters in London, New York, or Aspen, Colorado, have many such unseaworthy ships condemned to founder as they are too costly to maintain properly. Almost a century before "globalization" becomes a cliché or the diaspora a watchword, the Death Ship becomes their embodiment in its endless voyage from port to port on the seven seas and represents in a compact microcosm what neo-liberalism adds up to; not the absence of state regulations, but yet another form of their manipulation. Remember, at sea there is no state, yet the reason the sailors work the Death Ship is because they have no passport and hence no national or legal identity. The vaunted absence of state regulation makes the sailors all the more susceptible to it. The age of the notorious press gang is way behind us. The so-called "Russians" up the Río Timbiquí were like this too—skilled mechanics and backhoe operators without yet a day's pay for their efforts. They came from all over the ex–Soviet Union and God knows where else beside, recruited by Mafia-like gangster outfits for the latest version of a pirate escapade to a lonely village stuck way the hell up a roaring river at the malarial end of the earth drenched in sweat with guys like Omar for company.

As regards the label Russians: Traven writes,

> That everybody was called according to his nationality was one of the great ironies of which there existed so many aboard the *Yorikke* [the name of the Death Ship]. Their native lands and the authorities of their native countries had denied them all citizenship, and therefore passports, for some reason or other. But on the *Yorikke* their nationality was the only thing they possessed to distinguish them from anybody else. Whether, however, the nationality they agreed to have was their true nationality was never proved.[7]

Everyone speaks a different language on the Death Ship. Yet the crew could tell each other any story they wanted in less than three hundred and fifty words, more or less. For their stories were "born in the heart and raised in the soul and fattened on one's own bitter or sweet experiences." And once told, there was nothing left unexplained or misunderstood. How, then, does Genet's troubled self-interrogation as a writer who feels the truth slip away as soon as he sets pen to paper compare to this self-confidence as to the worth of stories? By any measure a skilled writer, Genet eloquently expresses his lack of eloquence when it comes to the task of describing his two years in PLO camps, offices, and homes on the East Bank of the river Jordan. It might seem that fiction is a lot easier, but that is not true either. What these writers are grappling with is how nonfiction and fiction refuse to stay neatly separated. When we look further into Traven's

---

7. Traven, *Death Ship*, pp. 185–86.

sailors' stories "born," as he says, "in the heart" and "fattened on . . . experiences," it turns out that the stories are told not so much by people as by things,
in fact, by one big thing, the Death Ship itself. "The crew may leave the ship,"
notes Traven.

> Their stories never leave. A story penetrates the whole ship and
> every part of it, the iron, the steel, the wood, all the holds, the coal-
> bunkers, the engine-hall, the stoke-hold, even the bilge. Out of these
> parts, full of hundreds of thousands of stories, tales, and yarns, the
> ship tells the stories over again with all the details and minor twists.
> She tells the stories to her best comrades—that is, to the members of
> the crew. She tells the stories better and more exactly than they could
> ever be told in print.[8]

Like Genet, then, Traven admits to going beyond reality as the way of
doing it justice. In fact, he takes the ultimate and logical step, which is to claim
that language is by no means limited to humans and human society. When he
claims that the ship is the real storyteller, we might understand this to mean
that the ship is like a human being. But it could also mean that the language of
stories is the language of things, with a twist. And this twist is that the language
of things is privy to the people who live day by day with those things, have been
cruelly forced by circumstances of world history to work those things, and
nevertheless eventually grow to regard these things with empathy, loyalty, and
some fondness, even while hating them. Such intimacy is beyond good and evil,
and that is how it is also along the rivers, panning gold or seeking out archaic
rivers underground.

The best stories, then, are told by things, dying things, as it turns out, like
that Death Ship. We have come a long way from those who would stress the
affinity between person and thing that allows for a common language between
them. To the contrary, it is the alienation from nature that gives nature its
tongue, and prehistory thus returns in the struggle over the terms of the contract
that humankind sets up with the natural world. Homelessness is what returns us

---

8. Traven, *Death Ship*, p. 104.

to language as home. This is the premise of each and every story the Death Ship relates no less than Genet's memoir of the PLO. While Genet's nuts lie strewn across the page, as things, Traven's Death Ship plows the ocean talking to itself until death demonstrates that heaven is the one and only ship that will take on its homeless sailors without official papers.

One thing is a picture, drawn from the imagination. It was another thing to speed around a bend in the river and have the universe rip apart with the sound of a compressor and see a navy blue spaceman, his black face shrouded in glass, his head covered with the helmet of a wet suit. Down he goes down in the green water. Bubbles come to the surface. He is twelve feet down, they say. The raft is tied to trees on the bank because the current is strong. A hefty man with a slender pole pokes in a blue metal box from which gushes mud pumped up from the river bottom by the diver below, feeling his way in the dark. The man on the surface uses his pole to dislodge stones so the outflow can run freely down the sluice into which the gold-bearing pay dirt is meant to settle. You can't hear yourself think on account of the noise. It upsets your balance. Another man comes with a yellow gasoline container, pulls out the stick that serves as a plug, sucks on a tube, and empties out the gasoline into the motor supplying air to the man in the dark below. I wonder how much of the gas fumes go into the air he is breathing down there. What happens if the motor stops for lack of fuel? My mind keeps coming back to this man like a ghost digging down there, digging himself into the river bottom like into a grave, sucking on its gold.

It was in the town of Guapi in 1998 that I first heard of *buzos* and *draguetas*. I was sitting with a group of men gathered around Ricardo Grueso as he applied the finishing touches to the wooden bus he was making. It was a real bus, not a toy, and I hasten to make this clear because *buzos* and *draguetas* also sound more like marvelous toys than real things. *Buzo* means diver and a *dragueta* is a mini-dredge. I went home and painted a *dragueta* from my imagination, then showed it to Ricardo and his friends, who said it was perfect, only I'd forgotten to put in the sluice in which the gold-bearing gravel is washed so as to separate out the gold. Trust me, I was too interested in the drama and had forgotten the gold. As for the *dragueta*, I couldn't believe what they had told me. Even more to the point, I couldn't understand the basic concept. That's why I had to paint it, follow it out through its various moves and colors; a man diving into the river, swallowed by the darkness of the rushing waters, digging himself into and then under the riverbed. Come on! No way!

The basic idea of the mechanized *buzo* system of gold mining is that a person puts on a mask and wet suit and goes down to the river bottom, supplied by an air tube connected to a raft with an air compressor. This person, the *buzo,* then burrows into the river bottom with a sort of vacuum-cleaner tube, also connected to the air compressor, sucking up the mud. Slowly, fighting the current and unable to see anything on account of the murk, he scoops himself into a tunnel under the bottom of the river, searching for the bedrock where the gold will be. It is spectacularly dangerous, because of cave-ins, but also spectacularly rewarding. Everyone I spoke to, first thing they said was, "You can't see anything down there. It doesn't matter if it's night or day."

In 1993 there were lots of these mini-dredges clustered together fighting for space at Coteje, about two-thirds of the way upriver from Santa Bárbara to Santa María. A lot of gold was found and a lot of death too. Ricardo says there were eight people killed in about as many months, seven due to cave-ins, the other from whiskey and gunshots. Jesús Alberto told me he was in a store downriver at the time and a stranger walked in who seemed to recognize him. The stranger ordered a case of Chivas Regal, took out one bottle, and gave him the rest! Excess as a way of life. Fortunes made and lost overnight. Emigrants living in Cali scampered back, claiming this or that part of the river belonged to them and would demand a tax! If you didn't pay, they threatened to cut the air line. The *buzo* would usually get 10 percent of production. Some *buzos* made one million pesos, *minimo,* in two hours! Seven hundred and fifty dollars! Hard to believe. Ricardo is carried away by the enormity of it all, everyone nodding in agreement.

I'd become so entranced by these space-age figures emerging from the green water in their moth-eaten wet suits that I'd completely overlooked those other sorts of divers who simply take a huge breath and go down with a wooden bowl in their hands and a big stone strapped to their back. Nearly all are women. "Of course, in Santa María there are women divers!" Lilia told me. "And the blood pours from their nostrils they go so deep. They go as deep as any man diver with an air supply from a *dragueta.* Some have drowned."

The young man opposite where I live in Santa María works as a *buzo* with a wet suit and air compressor. His wife lives with him, and his girlfriend lives in the house next to me. Sometimes at night he likes to drink moonshine liquor called

biché and play music with friends, Ecuadorian music with sad flutes or else *vallenatos* from the Caribbean coast of Colombia plying your soul with sighing accordions. The stereo has big speakers and requires a gasoline-driven generator, which makes a hell of a racket. One night they were outside drinking *biché* getting drunk, the music louder and louder, the generator groaning to keep up. Behind the houses, the little Río Sesé ripples over the stones under the palms and breadfruit trees. By five o'clock in the morning, the music and the generator are still going strong when, half asleep under the mosquito net, I hear a new sound joining in, the church bells on the hill. Half an hour goes by and still they ring out. They sound crazy.

This is the *doble,* Lilia tells me, "the double," because today is the *Día general de las ánimas,* November 2, the day after *Todos los Santos,* or All Saints' Day. This is the day for the dead, she explains. If you have had someone die recently, or wish to remember people in your family who died a long time ago, you pay a boy to go up the hill to the church to pray the Lord's Prayer and ring *un doble.* There are two bells. Each has its own sound. When somebody dies, the Lord's Prayer is prayed along with this particular bell language three times. When someone from here dies in some other place such as Cali or Buenaventura, then it is played once. Today it will go on till six o'clock at night. When it finally stops, she tells me, you hear the bells inside your head for a long time. Around eight o'clock in the morning, the music from the *buzo* stopped. It has stopped, Lilia says, because the *buzo* has run out of liquor and taken a turn ringing the bells to gain a few pesos to buy more. Three years later the diver was drinking *biché* downstream at Piscinde and killed a man who had a reputation as a witch. But that's another story.

The church squats on top of the hill at the bottom of which cluster two-story wooden houses alongside the Río Sesé. Huge and shapeless, the church is an unpainted cement shed the size of an aircraft hangar mottled black and gray. It dwarfs a carefully fashioned wood house for the priest close by, also on the hill. But the priest rarely visits and there are no nuns resident either. His house is unoccupied and sagging. It won't last long. Inside the church, however, there are signs of care, beginning with the life-size wooden saints and a Christ with movable joints, bought in Medellin. A few years back they were repainted in lustrous color.

Men are rarely present in the church except for Easter, when a marimba—instrument of the devil and played only by men—is installed within. Men also feature in an alarming way when they spring out of the cemetery by the church brandishing leather whips and dressed in women's skirts on the night of Easter Friday. They wear white hoods and are called the *ánimas solas,* solitary souls.

Easter is also when the living return, making you realize that Santa María is as much a ghost town as a town of the living, ghostly in that so many of its people have emigrated to cities or sugar plantations of the interior. Once a year the living return, en masse, animating the absences their goings and comings and goings have made. Such animations are likely to cause trouble, even death. When I visited Santa María Easter 1976 in one of many canoes making their way upstream, we formed a fleet resplendent with cargoes of fine clothes, transistor radios, metal bedsteads, and tin roofing. In the morning a man's body was washed ashore, battered to death by his drinking companions. He had just returned from the interior with his money and finery, the Big Spender running head-on into the most basic contradiction the coast can offer, the envy aroused by success versus the need to show off your stuff when you return.

So what is the significance of this crowd of strong men sprung from the cemetery bent on flogging anyone brave enough to give them lip, this crowd of *ánimas solas* darting in pursuit of the slow procession carrying Christ's bleeding body at midnight over the slippery cobblestones on Easter Friday in Santa María, Timbiquí? And there are plenty who give them lip, too. Not the women up front so piously singing to the stars. Not the older men dressed as apostles with white caps and long white gowns carrying the coffin surmounted by candles and flowers, the body of the faithful following. No! The taunting comes from the faceless shadows. "*¡Chucurita! ¡Chucurita!*" cry the teenagers, daring the *ánimas* to dance. And dance they do! Like women! You hear them running and slipping on the wet cobblestones till day breaks and maybe a leg breaks too, as they lunge at those who mock them. The women are furious. The sacredness, as they see it, is undermined by these solitary souls of purgatory converting Easter into a carnival. But anthropologists would see the manifestation of conflict as a crucial design element. In other words, they would see it as part of the plan. But whose plan would that be?

It has been suggested that the *ánimas* and even the saints are substitutes for the cult of the ancestors common in Africa.[1] Who knows? To me, the *ánimas* come across as deliberately fuzzy and inexplicable. There is the *ánima* state of radical aloneness and anonymity, the *ánima sola* being the exemplar of this, but then there is that dense multiplicity of dead souls, a multiplicity that by far exceeds the dead of one's family to form an invisible crowd of the dead—which, to one celebrated observer of crowds and power, Elias Canetti, is the basis of religion itself.[2] These *ánimas* certainly are a puzzle. My guess is that they spill over and way exceed death so as to merge with the things of this world. Hence, *animation.*

Gustavo says the *ánimas* have their secret, and if you don't pray to them, the *ánima sola* becomes perturbed. María de las Nieves Venté Angulo is a big woman with white hair who spends all day stretched out on the floor of her tiny store as her legs give her a lot of trouble. She associates the *ánimas* with the prayers sung by the side of a dying person. The first prayer is the "Oration of the Guardian Angel," recited as the person is actually dying, *in agony,* as the Spanish has it. Then comes the "Celebration of My Soul" when death occurs. She assures me the *ánimas* are all around us as we speak, night and day, only you can't see them. But they can see us. Well, a few people can see them, but you can stop that if you want by pulling out your longest eyelashes. She once saw an *ánima* but was not afraid. Not in the slightest. It was dressed in white, early morning, down by the river, on Easter Thursday, casting a fishing net.

The *ánimas* bestow power on people close to them, for example, the power to predict death a few days before it happens. (Is this a power, or a curse?) These people see the spirit of the person about to die but can't discern who it is, only if it is a man or a woman. Such people seem to live as much in the shadowy realm of the *ánimas* as in the sunlit world of the living, and my guess is that women as they get older gradually gravitate to this world of the dead. They are constantly praying to the *ánimas* and are sure to have (an image of) the Virgen del Carmen, who attracts the dead, in their home so they can see the dead. They say their

---

1. See Thomas Price, "Saints and Spirits: A Study of Differential Acculturation in Colombian Negro Communities" (Ph.D. diss., Evanston, Northwestern University, 1955). Also see David Pavy III, "The Negro in Western Colombia" (Ph.D. diss., New Orleans, Tulane University, 1967).

2. Elias Canetti, *Crowds and Power* (1962), trans. Carol Stewart (New York: Farrar, Straus and Giroux, 1984), p. 42.

rosary, first to the saints, then to the *ánimas*. They have advantages, these people, in mining, in health, whatever. "Just look at the nurse!"

But the sound is what puts the world on hold. Sound that is arrhythmic, atonal, discordant, and mightily nonstop sound. The very name, the *doble,* indicates the existence of a form: *ding/dong—pause—dong/ding—pause.* But let me tell you, it certainly doesn't sound like that, and it certainly doesn't sound like the *vallenatos* that the diver who lives opposite played all night long, so long as the gasoline and the booze lasted. No! These bells for the *ánimas* sound crazy and disturbed, pretty much same as the wild horde of solitary souls dressed as women flashing their cruel whips all night long on the wet cobblestones. What the *ánimas* come to represent, both the ones you'll stop seeing if you pull out your longest eyelashes, as well as the ones scampering and slipping on cobblestones at night, is formlessness, or, to be more precise, the edge over which forms pass as living death so as to animate substance. Continuously. This same edge is the story of gold. The story of cocaine, too.

All day long the bells ring . . . wherever you walk, talk, read, look up at the sky or down at the earth, or take a shit in the quiet darkness under the house, pat the dog, play with Lilia's baby, eat lunch, this mad sound beside you, inside you . . . just a small village with a street of cobblestones and a string of wooden houses on either side. The sound becomes an intimate part of you, like your sweat or heartbeat, an elemental part of the universe like the rain and death's endless cycle through the houses into the street up to the church on the hill where the bells are knocking it out with the dead. They seem like they're talking, these bells, but also playing, turning speech into the language of things, like the birds wheeling in the sky over the estuary, writing their stories and looping their loops in synchrony with the passing landscape below. Is it that it never stops? Is it the irregularity—the irregularity chosen as such to mark death as such? *If it was the actual words, it wouldn't seem irregular, would it?* And what is it that happens to irregularity when it is repeated all day long? I am fifty-eight years old and this bell in my ear all day is without doubt the most sacred event of my life. A crowning performance. My past life stretches out before me like a ribbon. All my friends the world over since I was a child. They are here too. I write a letter to my friend on the other side of the Pacific whom I have known since I was five years old, knowing he never replies.

water in water

When I first heard about the *buzos* and later saw these strange figures in their blue rubbery suits emerging from swirling streams, I assumed they were the latest in high-tech mining, apart from the Russians with their bulldozers, of course. What a shock, therefore, to come across an 1856 account by Manuel Uribe and Camilo Echeverri describing gold diving by people of African descent in the interior of Colombia in the Department of Antioquia.[1] They noted three methods of summer mining practiced when rivers were low. The first, carried out only by women, required a wooden scoop around three feet long with a handle. Walking in the river, braced against the current with the scoop underwater and pressed

---

1. Manuel Uribe and Camilo Echeverri, *Estudios industriales sobre la minería antioqueña en 1856,* cited at length, pp. 224–46, without other bibliographic data in Vicente Restrepo, *A Study of the Gold and Silver Mines of Colombia* (1884), trans. C. W. Fisher (New York: Colombian Consulate, 1886), pp. 223–27.

into the riverbed, they would bring it full of sand and gravel to the surface to be washed for gold.[2] It must have been heavy, yet we are told this entire action took less time than required to describe it. The authors were surprised this was done by women, for it was considered one of the most grueling modes of mining.

Where the river was too deep to do this, tree trunks and branches were used to dam the river so that divers could access the riverbed downstream from the dam. A third method, just introduced at the time the authors wrote their account in 1856, involved a diver "with the head and the upper part of the chest covered with an impervious helmet, in front of which are two large glass discs to enable the wearer to see what he is doing."[3] This, of course, is the 1850s predecessor of the *buzo,* whom I encountered with such surprise in 1998, and the authors go on to describe how air was forced down a waterproof tube into the diver's helmet by means of a pump. However, according to Vicente Restrepo in 1884, after a brief flurry of enthusiasm, on the Nare and Nus Rivers, this method was abandoned.

It was killing work. But there were fortunes to be made. Early in the nineteenth century, a Swedish mining engineer and pioneer of the industry in Colombia, Pedro Nisser, described divers in rivers in Antioquia. When the Ponce River was low, they would go out in a canoe and install a makeshift dam they called a "horse," made of logs and palm leaves, securing it to the bottom with heavy rocks. This would lower the river by three to four feet and allow the divers to excavate a hole four to five feet deep in the streambed. It was said their *bateas* contained more gold than sand. Nisser thought the bed of the Ponce comprised the richest deposit of gold known to the world, but given the amount of rain, the river was rarely low enough, even for divers, to get at.[4]

Diving apparatuses go back a long way. Aristotle described devices allowing men to work underwater, while in 1242 Roger Bacon is said to have reinvented just such a contraption. There are engravings dated 1511 in Vegetius's *De re militari* showing a diver with a tight-fitting helmet and a long leather pipe for air,

2. Restrepo, *Study of the Gold and Silver Mines,* p. 225. Spanish edition of 1888 (Bogotá: Imprenta de Silvestre), p. 190: "Las robustas y valerosas negras de Antioquia . . ."

3. Uribe and Echeverri, *Estudios industriales,* p. 227.

4. Nisser, *La Minería en Nueva Granada,* pp. 44–45.

kept afloat by means of an inflated bladder. The diver's suit serving as prototype of those in use today was invented by Augustus Siebe in 1819.[5]

Some twenty to thirty years after Uribe and Echeverri's description of gold divers in the rivers of Antioquia in 1856, Luis Striffler described men diving for gold, this time in the Cauca River in the northern part of Colombia known as El alto Sinú. Striffler saw that many divers were at work here without artificial air supplies yet diving great depths, fighting the strong current, separating sand from stones, carrying *bateas* that they filled in the time their breath allowed. They suffered on account of pulmonary hemorrhages yet persisted, as it was so lucrative. "None of these laborers," he writes, "has ever thought of improving upon such crude methods." "They simply follow a routine. They are accustomed to do everything with their hands, and the use of tools never occurs to them."[6] An iron bar, a scraping hook, and a wooden bowl, or *batea*—nothing more apart from your bodily strength; for centuries it has been like this till the present day, and foreign observers always expressed surprise at the lack of innovation. When Gustavo, rather fragile in appearance, was working with a strange North American diver who appeared in a helicopter out of the blue at Santa María in the early 1980s, the stranger was outfitted with an Aqua-Lung. But Gustavo strapped a stone to his back and that's how he went down in the green water. Even the language remains "unimproved." In Uribe and Echeverri's account, published 150 years ago, four years after the abolition of slavery, one finds terms familiar today, such as the *coco*, or half-split coconut shell in which women deposit gold they may be lucky enough to find; and the *tonga*, which today is how women describe the hole they make in the bottom of the river when diving down to bedrock.[7]

There is a chain through time I am constructing here, a chain of divers, each link of which is connected by surprise. First, as my watercolor testifies, I was amazed to hear from Ricardo and his friends about the mini-dredges and divers up the Timbiquí in the early 1990s. But why was I so amazed and what are the

5. *The Encyclopaedia Britannica*, 11th ed. (Cambridge: Cambridge University Press, 1910–11), vol. 8, p. 327.

6. Luis Striffler, *El alto Sinú: Historia del primer establecimiento para extracción de oro en 1844* (Cartagena, 1886); quoted in Restrepo, *Study of the Gold and Silver Mines*, p. 222.

7. Restrepo, *Study of the Gold and Silver Mines*, pp. 224–34.

consequences of that? I still don't know, but I discern something radically exotic in this picture, incongruously composed of the modern alongside the prehistoric. The modernity turned out on further research to be an illusion, because the more I read and went back in time, the more of such diving I uncovered. Slaves in the Chocó province of the Pacific Coast are said to have tied stones to their backs in the rivers where the gold collected in deep ponds. The stones provided weight and stability against fast currents, my source tells me, yet a slip even in only thigh-deep water could be hazardous.[8] The circle was completed when I came across the statement by Robert C. West that "apparently the diving technique was widespread in aboriginal times in northwestern South America."[9]

Nevertheless, I couldn't shake off this sense of incongruity; diving under water, diving into and then under the streambed itself, either dying trapped below the riverbed or coming to the surface with lungs bursting and fists full of gold . . . It was all too, too grand, inexhaustibly strange and primitive in its mingling the human body in motion with the basic elements of *air* (to breathe with), *fire* (in the form of the machinery), *earth* (being the mud tunneled into on the riverbed), and *water* (the green opalescent water of the churning river)—all condensed and marvelous in the form of *gold*. As I see it, there are two steps and one trick involved here, the trick that determines the fate of humanity. The first step is to observe and then imitate nature. The second is to go beyond imitation to become one with what you are imitating, like the diver mingling with the elements as a fish and then as a mud crab burrowing in the dark. Here imitation undergoes a radical development. It passes from being outside to being inside, in fact to becoming Other. Imitation becomes immanence. Then there is the moment of the trick whereby in imitating and becoming Other, you stay right there, like water in water, for the sheer hell of it, for the pleasure at the loss of self and the transformations of Being—or else you use that moment to dominate nature and seek profit from it. The fork in the road.

The various "superstitions" about gold mining I have mentioned indicate acute awareness as to this trick. I am referring to the pact with the devil and the notion that gold mining is inherently transgressive. Nature can be imitated in or-

---

8. William F. Sharp, *Slavery on the Spanish Frontier: The Colombian Chocó, 1680–1810* (Norman: University of Oklahoma Press, 1976), p. 49.

9. Robert C. West, *Colonial Placer Mining in Colombia* (Baton Rouge: Louisiana State Press, 1952), p. 59.

der to dominate and profit from it. But only up to a point, because nature will return and exact revenge. What is here a question of superstition and magic is elsewhere an issue of acid rain, global warming, cancer, and so forth, a hideous, elemental payback, sorcery on a global scale.

Gold mining by such primitive means in Colombia and before that when it
was the Spanish colony of Nueva Granada and before that when it was Indian
country depends on the imitation of the elemental play of earth and water, which
is to say the force of the rain swelling the rivers tearing down the Andes. For this
is a country of mountain ranges, rain, and lots and lots of gold, which, being
gold, is both heavy and fine and hence sinks through water, through sand, clay,
earth, and gravel, to come to rest on its bed of bedrock. The rains burst over the
mountains, the rivulets stream down the mountain, washing away the sand, the
clay, the earth, and the gravel, and divers go down to the bottom of the rivers
filled by rain and scoop up the shiny stuff. "It's easy enough to understand," says
the Swede Pedro Nisser, in his 1834 booklet on mining in Colombia, "that a river
flanked by a mountain chain rich in gold and exposed to fierce tropical rains will
contain abundant quantities of gold."[10]

Not only were the Indians of Colombia the outstanding goldsmiths of aboriginal America, but it was from them that the Spaniards learned the technology of placer mining, so that instead of tunneling into the earth in search of
underground veins of gold, you get water to do the tunneling for you. What the
Spaniards added to the Indian manner of mining that existed before the conquest was mimesis on a grander scale. They diverted rivers and rain so as to wash
away mountains. They built dikes and dams with canals several miles long,
sometimes with aqueducts such as the one at the Valle des Osos fifty feet high
and five hundred feet long. Just as women pan gold by the side of streams, so
such "panning" is employed to wash away hillsides. In other words, placering can
be done directly in rivers and on riverbanks, or it can be done by a system today
called "ground sluicing" in which water is piped under pressure from rivers or
from reservoirs to the mining site. Ricardo Grueso once described to me a dirt
reservoir called a *pila* over a kilometer wide in the forest by Santa María, but

---

10. Nisser, *La Minería en Nueva Granada*, p. 36.

I never saw it. It is curious that what the Spaniards learned from the Indians about placer mining was what had been practiced anciently in Spain but forgotten. According to Gonzalo Fernández de Oviedo y Valdés chronicling events while living in Hispaniola in 1548, the ancient miners of northwest Spain knew far more about placering than the Spanish settlers in Hispaniola, the first Spanish settlement in the New World.[11] And Robert West tells us that in the ancient world, in *De re metallica,* Georgius Agricola described gold placering in Lusitania (modern Portugal and adjacent regions in Spain).[12] Spanish colonialism somersaulted backward in time. A long-forgotten European technology suddenly surfaced as the colonists copied their subjects. A grand mimesis.

Eighteen eighty-four: The British miner Robert White spent several years in Colombia looking for gold and studying ancient as well as prevailing modes of mining.[13] In the *Journal of the Anthropological Institute of Great Britain and Ireland* in 1884, he brings to archaeology an eye sharpened by the knowledge of a mining engineer. He was puzzled at the way these ancient mines combined so much skill with practices that didn't make sense, at least from his point of view. You get the feeling from him that these mines were more like some wild poetry expressed in brilliant earthworks in which an entranced mankind feels compelled to plunge into the good earth upon which we walk so lightly, creating sacred subterranean sculpture invisible to the naked eye. As regards quartz mines in Antioquia that he found remarkable, White notes that the Indians were able, using stone tools, to excavate what in his day could be done only with gunpowder. What's more, "their style of work was very peculiar." Instead of digging horizontal galleries, they sunk vertical shafts some three feet in diameter until they hit upon the lode, yet these shafts were not made to communicate with one another below: "They seemed to have aimed at making their operations as tedious as possible." Some shafts were eighty feet deep, so narrow that a person would

---

11. Gonzalo Fernández de Oviedo y Valdés, *Historia general y natural de los Indias,* 5 vols. Biblioteca de Autores Españoles (Madrid: Ediciones Atlas, 1959).

12. West, *Colonial Placer Mining,* p. 68.

13. The eminent Colombian geographer F. J. Vergara y Velasco thought highly of White's work. In his *Nueva geografía de Colombia* published in 1901–2, he says that White's "notable studies" helped plot the coordinates of the Chocó. F. J. Vergara y Velasco, *Nueva geografía de Colombia,* 3 vols. (Bogotá: Banco de la República, 1974), vol. 3, p. 1216. In his book on colonial placer mining, Robert C. West describes White as "intimately familiar with the northern Andes." West, *Colonial Placer Mining,* p. 69.

have to back up with their load. In some gold-bearing areas of Antioquia, because the excavations were so extensive, White felt thousands of persons must have been employed. He could discern no reason for what seemed to him a crazy system, other than what he regarded as a religious superstition to do with fear of taking out too much gold.[14]

Not only did the Indians take gold out of the earth in such bizarre and laborious ways, but they then put it back into the earth, burying their gold with the dead, deep in special chambers. Jean Genet had a similar idea when he suggested that the statuary of his friend Alberto Giacometti be buried in the ground as offerings to the dead. Robert White cites ancient graves in Colombia with gold ornaments worth up to thirteen thousand pounds sterling. Some grave shafts were sixty feet deep.[15] Truly, these Colombian Indians seem to have been obsessed with rummaging around in the good earth on which we tread so lightly. And having expended labor on the grave shaft, they would, in the words of our British miner, then ram the hole tightly full of earth. He makes it sound as if they were stopping it up like a cork in a bottle. Moreover, the Indians would sometimes use earth quite different than what they had just excavated, earth that today has a peculiar aromatic smell. Some grave shafts lead nowhere. They are fake graves.

Burying treasure with the dead makes you think twice about the value of value and value's dependence on death, on *ánimas* and animation. Is this payback, following the circle of endless return traced in Western culture by the devil in relation to wealth? And if so, might "payback" miss the point altogether because this sort of payback overshoots its mark by an exorbitant amount? All that hard work extracting gold from the earth only to bury it once more. What waste! What glory! Between life and death, gold comes into its own as the hard-won stuff validating the value of everything else.

---

14. Robert Blake White, "Notes on the Aboriginal Races of the North-Western Provinces of South America," *Journal of the Anthropological Institute of Great Britain and Ireland* 13 (1884): 245.

15. In the mid-1940s the archaeologist Wendell Bennett described graves from three to thirty-two feet in depth in the prehistorical Quimbaya region of western Colombia and noted that there were reports of eighty-foot depths as well. Bennett found large quantities of gold objects in the graves. Bennett, "The Archaeology of Colombia," in *Handbook of South American Indians,* 7 vols., vol. 2, *The Andean Civilizations,* ed. Julian H. Steward (New York: Cooper Square, 1963), p. 838.

How strange, then, that gold should also be that most utilitarian of objects, the humble fishhook. Robert White has said gold fishhooks have been found in the graves and are often found washed out of the sands of the rivers.[16] Eustaquia has found two in her long life panning gold. Juan Pablo says he finds them way upstream where nobody goes, one to one and a half inches long. Unbarbed.

Independently of one another, Pedro de Cieza de Léon and Fray Pedro Simón said Indian miners used human fat to fuel their lamps.[17] Were the Indians feeding them tall stories, and if so, why? Or did these men, among the first Spanish writers in the New World, invent this? Is there any reason why human fat is better than animal fat? Better for what?

Gold sits on the river bottom just above the bedrock. Water seems like its natural element. In 1834 Pedro Nisser wrote: "It's easy enough to understand that a river flanked by a mountain chain rich in gold and exposed to fierce tropical rains, will contain abundant quantities of gold."[18] I myself do not think it is so easy to understand. It is more like a miracle of coincident contingencies. With what, then, might the chain of surprises that began with Ricardo's stories, my painting, and the sight of the *buzo* in the blue rubber suit come to an end? Is gold what we want, by which I mean congealed amazement?

16. White, "Notes on the Aboriginal Races," pp. 246–47.
17. West, *Colonial Placer Mining*, p. 54 n. 9.
18. Nisser, *La Minería en Nueva Granada*, p. 36.

y cocaine n

julio arboleda's stone

Surveying the rivers of the Pacific Coast that run down the western slopes of the cordillera, mining engineers Henry Granger and Edward Treville were astonished in 1897 at the great bodies of gravel they saw, up to many millions of cubic yards, they said, which had been moved entirely by hand. They assumed that this had been done by slaves, sometimes with the aid of water pressure provided by canals over three miles in length or by small dams built to catch rainwater.[1] The coast abounds in powerful natural forces. What the rivers don't erase, the forest will cover in a year or so. But here with these great bodies of gravel, we have a miraculous glimpse into the shaping of nature by the human hand, a monument to

---

1. Henry G. Granger and Edward B. Treville, "Mining Districts of Colombia," *Transactions of the American Institute of Mining Engineers* 28 (February–October 1898): 39.

man's domination over nature through his domination over others, an archive of national history.

A few minutes downstream in a dugout canoe from Santa María, there was until recently a stone overgrown by the forest to mark the birthplace of Julio Arboleda on the ninth of June 1817. His parents, Matilde Pombo y O'Donell, from Cartagena, and José Rafael Arboleda y Arroyo, of Popayán, fled there during the Wars of Independence in 1816. A Who's Who of bigwigs in the province tells us that José Rafael gave generously of his wealth to the rebels against Spain and became a senator noted for his erudition and eloquence. Said to be adept in Latin and a skillful translator of Horace, he taught classes in literature at the University of Cauca in Popayán. He suffered mightily from chronic gastroenteritis—as one imagines did many people living in those places in those times—and he died in 1831 in Pisa, Italy, to where he had traveled in search of cure.[2] His son, Julio, was fourteen at the time. Linked to the Mosqueras, the Arboledas constituted the greatest slave-owning dynasty of Colombia, the two families being united by marriage in Popayán in 1730. While the Mosqueras, in the view of a prominent local historian, writing in 1979, were warriors, and therefore had a natural disposition to mining as a continuation of the wars of conquest, the Arboledas, by contrast, had a talent for business, "due to their semitic blood."[3] What a mythology is here packed into the San Vicente slave mine, precursor of Santa María!

A century before Julio's birth, his forebear Francisco José Arboleda was owner of many slaves and gold mines along the Río Timbiquí as well as others in the Chocó region and in Caloto in the foothills of the Cordillera Central in the interior. He owned extensive holdings of wild quinine, plus big spreads of sugarcane and tobacco in the Cauca Valley around Caloto.[4] The Arboledas were among the richest people in Latin America, if not the world, and it surprises me they would run away to hide in a place so forlorn as the headwaters of the Río Timbiquí. Perhaps with a retinue of servants, the jungles of the coast appeared less forbidding then than now? Maybe the rich were tougher then than today?

---

2. Gustavo Arboleda, *Diccionario biográfico y genealógico del antiguo Departamento del Cauca* (Bogotá: Horizontes, 1962).

3. Diego Castrillón Arboleda, *Tomás Cipriano de Mosquera* (Bogotá: Banco de la República, 1979), p. 4.

4. Arboleda, *Diccionario biográfico*.

What of the aristocratic Matilde Pombo O'Donell, having to give birth in such a place after the invigorating climate and medical advantages of Popayán? Today San Vicente exists as no more than a name and a crater. The diminutive stone commemorating Julio's birth was plowed under by the Russians' bulldozers, which stripped the land down to bedrock. By design or chance, the Russians had, of all things, chosen the eighteenth-century Mosquera-Arboleda mining site of San Vicente on the banks of the Timbiquí just below the village of Santa María as the center of their operation, right where Gustavo says there is a pond of gold with music coming from its enchanted depth, the "Pond of Death." Maybe that explains the shootout and hasty retreat of the Russians, leaving broken-down machines scattered in the river like dragonflies.

In the state archives in Popayán, I renewed my search for documents that would tell me about the slave mines at the Pond of Death. I had looked before without success, although there was ample material on the Arboleda's slave-based sugar plantations in the interior, in the Cauca Valley, which they had acquired when the Jesuits were forced to sell out by the Spanish crown in the late eighteenth century. But I found nothing on their mines on the coast. Maybe the mines were inconsequential or never existed? But Julio Arboleda's stone? That seemed real enough, even though I'd never seen it and now never would because the Russians were said to have plowed it under. And the music from the pond? What about that? Wasn't that real and what did that have to say about golden pasts and sudden death? Maybe Gustavo was hyper-suggestible, a mystical crank, but that did not disqualify his sense of the outstanding importance of this section of the river. To the contrary.

The days dragged on. Maybe it was only in my imagination, this legendary river of slaves and gold? Cardboard files were dragged down and carted in from dusty stacks. In the room in which I worked, three or four other scholars were diligently rummaging through signs of other pasts to flesh out their stories. It got hot and tiresome. I felt like the women panning river sand for gold along the banks of the Timbiquí. All I got was sand and gravel.

The underpaid archivists were patient and skillful. Without them I would have been beached up some other river in some other century. As we sifted through papers, I lost the initial sense that grabs me in the archive, that sense of time traveling to sacred destinations. "Say something," noted Walter Benjamin to himself in the 1930s while working in the nineteenth-century archives in Paris on his incomparable arcades project. "Say something about the method of composition itself: how everything one is thinking at a specific moment in time must at all costs be incorporated into the project then at hand."[5] I felt guilty at being bored. I wondered if Walter had felt bored too. After all, he is the author of those priceless notes on boredom that also appear in the arcades project.

Yet all the time he was sitting there in conversation with the past, Benjamin was developing a theory of history that refused to abandon the raw materials, the documents themselves, for the sake of telling a good story—although his love of stories was also evident in the vast number he read and the tenderness with which he wrote on the archaic figure of the storyteller whose stories, Benjamin claimed, always merged myth with nature, as in the stories by Nikolai Leskov about whom Benjamin says: "The lower Leskov descends on the scale of created things the more obviously does his way of viewing things approach the mystical."[6] Yet if Benjamin's show-and-tell method of presenting history eschews story-telling, it was not the "facts in themselves" that were worshiped by Benjamin, but the juxtapositions such facts made with the present. "In order for a part of the past to be touched by the present instant," he cautions, "there must be no continuity between them."[7]

What's more, history decayed into images, not stories, and it was the task of the historian to locate those images—*dialectical images,* he called them—which would rescue the past because of their resonance with present circumstance. Why "rescue" and what does he mean? It is as if the present owed a debt to the past, any and every aspect of which was waiting to be redeemed—not in itself, so speak, but in combination with something tugging at it in the present. Such a rescue operation could acquire the properties of an awakening of consciousness that would come about by merely showing. This was the method of montage, like those photographic displays that put images of different things side by side—as in a movie—in the hope that a new understanding might spring forth, an understanding that has been characterized as combining shock with critical distance.

Essential to this montage was the merging of myth with nature that had so appealed to Benjamin in his study of the figure of the storyteller. Here, history as ruin or petrified landscape took center stage, as if the succession of human events

---

5. Benjamin, *The Arcades Project,* p. 456.
6. Benjamin, "The Storyteller," in *Illuminations,* p. 106.
7. Benjamin, *The Arcades Project,* p. 470.

we call history had retreated into stiller-than-stiller things entirely evacuated of life—like those monumental things, those great bodies of gravel, that so astonished the mining engineers, Granger and Treville; millions of cubic yards heaped in the jungle, moved by the hands of slaves and now covered by forest. Benjamin's close friend T. W. Adorno thought the appropriate figure for this sense of the past becoming one with nature was the antediluvian fossil. Thus, history and natural history merged with myth and image—as we might recall with Ricardo Grueso's tender fossils in the gold mines of the Timbiquí; how they crumble at the touch, messengers from the time before time when the Flood drove rivers of gold underground.

Eventually we did find documentation verifying the existence of the slave mine at San Vicente. But what can I tell you that you didn't know already, maybe not as to specific detail, but as regards the general sense of slavery, isolated jungle mines, rushing rivers, gold . . . then your mind leaps like the river filling in the gaps, trying to sense how people there felt in that unbelievable existence. At the best, the documents may vaguely suggest shapes of this and that, but not, to my mind at least, nearly as effectively as does Gustavo's music from the Pond of Death or Granger and Treville's amazement at the mountains of gravel—bodies, they call them—moved by hand.

The 62 slaves at or close to San Vicente in 1809 had increased to 135 when Julio Arboleda was born there in 1817 and doubled again to reach close to 300 slaves twelve years later. This means that this mine together with San José, ten minutes downstream by canoe, was among the largest in the vice royalty of New Granada.[8] An 1829 census of the mine shows almost half the slaves were under twenty years of age, and one-third were between twenty and forty years old. There were practically no elderly. The census displays the slaves in nuclear families, giving the man's name first, followed by a woman's, noted as "*su mujer*" (his

8. "Inventario y avaluo de la mitad de los bienes de la mina de San Vicente de Timbiquí" (1829), Archivo Arboleda, Archivo Central del Cauca. Also see the *Inventorio de 1809* in the *legato "Rafael Arboleda: Mina de Timbiquí"* with figures for "Mina de Sta. María," "Mina de San José," and "Mina de San Vicente." Also see María Romero Moreno, "Familia afro-colombiana y construcción territorial en el pacifico del sur, siglo XVIII," in *Geografía humana de Colombia: Los Afrocolombianos,* by María Romero Moreno, Luz Castro Agudelo, and Esperanza Aguablanca (Bogotá: Instituto colombiano de cultura hispánica, 1998), tomo VI, pp. 123, 133–40.

woman), and the names of the children, as if all from this one union, each person with the exact age in years and months. Physical defects are noted—e.g., Manuel de Jesús Gato, forty-four years and six months old, worth two hundred and fifty pesos, with half a toe missing; other slaves with stomachache, hernia, or fungal infections. Yet, all in all, people seemed surprisingly healthy, and I see little reason to doubt the veracity of the census on this point, as it was aimed at monetary evaluation, not a human rights investigation. But why no elderly? What a shock, then, to hear Ricardo Grueso say that the slave owners at San Vicente killed or abandoned slaves when they were too old or infirm to work. He swore it was true, laying his head down sideways on the table to show me how they were guillotined. I still can't believe it, but that would certainly explain the strange demography and good health displayed by the several slave censuses.

Ricardo also threw light on what geographers such as Agustín Codazzi (in the mid-nineteenth century) and Robert West (in the 1950s) had pointed out as regards emigration downriver of the newly freed slaves from the mining areas at the headwaters of the coastal rivers. For Codazzi, this was a tragedy for the newly independent republic of Colombia because it meant a profound depletion of the gold-mining workforce. But Ricardo was adamant; the newly freed slaves didn't just "emigrate"—they fled and went into hiding, knowing at any time slavery could be reinstituted. And that's why they didn't work for no white man. That's what Ricardo says and it makes a lot of sense, his history in the present.

Oh! The *chigualo*? The funeral for a child at which people other than the mother are so happy, singing and dancing? That's because in times past, people comforted themselves with the idea—so Lilia explained—that at least the child had escaped slavery.

Note also that while only eight lines of text are necessary to describe the full complement of the mine's tools, the thatch-roofed church required an entire page of thirty-two lines including

boxes
silver reliquary
pulpit
altar
a statue of San Vicente worth ten pesos
[or one twenty-fifth of Manuel de Jesús Gato)

chalice
silver cross
silver platters
incense burners
portrait of St. Joseph
Our Lady of Bethlehem

The one stocks to hold prisoners was evaluated at four pesos, and there was only one chain, weighing fourteen pounds, and one pair of handcuffs—little by way of physical coercion, you would think, for so many slaves in so remote and wild a place. The slaves as a whole were worth six times the rest of the mine.

Army helicopters fly overhead as I search through these papers in the archive in the state capital of Popayán. It is cold and raining. I sit by the edge of the stone-laid patio just out of reach of the rain, but the wind catches the papers. They say it storms afternoons in July. I'd forgotten. Crisscrossing moody skies, the helicopters scurry like animals fleeing the storm, but these choppers never go anywhere, big-bellied birds of death groping their way through a war that long ago lost its way. How strange to be back here after almost thirty years, thunder rolling and the wind picking up these papers one hundred and seventy years old with names of slaves carefully written out in brown ink together with the value of saints and handcuffs. The paper is linen-based like all the colonial documents and seems like it will last millennia, not like the paper from the mid-nineteenth century onward that crumbles at the touch. A hawk flies before the storm. The director sits, long legs stretched, reading the local paper. She is new to this post. I want to tell her about the excitement here thirty years ago working through the Arboleda papers with Anna Rubbo, arousing all manner of suspicion from the secret police as a communist, from the janitor reading over my shoulder saying I was CIA, and from the director of the archive, himself an Arboleda, assuming we were spies searching for extinct gold mines . . . but most of all I want to tell her, so serene in her generosity and comfortable in her routine, of the shudder on having my eye fall on these documents she has found for me. For a minute, maybe shorter, the past brushes your cheek and you are there at the slave mines of San Vicente de Timbiquí in the forest in 1829. What is this shudder where the past meets the present moment? It has nothing to do with continuity. Its power lies in its juxtaposition in which those big-bellied birds—Black Hawks, they are called—

scurry before the storm. The director takes another drag on her cigarette, the local newspaper is tossed aside, and the hawk soars out of sight over the Andes.

The archive is located in a white colonial building that belonged to the Mosquera family, the same family that together with the Arboledas owned the slaves in San Vicente on the other side of the cordillera. Nobody lives in the house anymore. Old papers of state have replaced the people, but it is a sign of the Mosqueras' power, even in death, that the history of the province is archived in their house. With its white colonnades and generously proportioned low-lying buildings, the city is the most beautiful in Colombia, little more than a monument to the aristocratic pretensions of the slave-owning past. Time stopped here long ago. Petrified like a fossil, the city is surrounded by mountains and forest, home of the guerrilla since almost forty years. People are apprehensive. The city has been isolated by the guerrilla several times in the past few years, and any day it could be enclosed by them. Imagine! The center of what had been a vast and complacent gold-mining empire, converted into a guerrilla camp. How would the papers in the archive read then?

Surveying the rivers of the Pacific Coast that run down the western slopes of the cordillera (such as the Río Timbiquí), Granger and Treville were astonished at the great bodies of gravel they saw, up to millions of cubic yards, they said, which had been moved entirely by hand. I am repeating myself because I want to ask, What is it about the past that makes me want to cite it? Why am I so attached to these millions of cubic yards of gravel?

It is curious that many people on the Río Timbiquí, descendants of slaves, venerate the name of Julio Arboleda, given that he and his family took up arms against the abolitionists and that he himself added to that notoriety by marching his slaves from the interior over the mountains to the Pacific coast at Buenaventura so as to sell them in Lima, Peru, just before slavery was abolished in Colombia in 1851. He is said to be among Latin America's finest epic poets, and you find his work in anthologies of Latin American poetry. Marcelino Menéndez y Pelayo finds his works to be marked by an absolute abhorrence of tyranny.[9] The

---

9. Marcelino Menéndez y Pelayo, "Don Julio Arboleda juzgado por Marcelino Menéndez y Pelayo," *signatura* #80 (Archivo Arboleda, Archivo Central del Cauca).

airport in Guapi and the school in the all-black town of Santa Bárbara down-stream from Santa María are named after him, but he himself attended school in London.

Who is Julio Arboleda? One of the first things mentioned by Omar when cussing out the Russians was that they had obliterated the stone marking Julio Arboleda's birth. Coming from Omar it sounds like a lot of hype to me. He has a shrewd sense of how to exploit for his own benefit what we might call the official sense of tradition for which this stone marker could be made into a sensitive point of mediation with the white world and its generally ignored slaveholding past. I ask people in Santa María about Julio Arboleda. The wife of the man who fixed my bag said Julio A. was *una persona importantisima* who had done much for the pueblo. When asked if he'd had any connection with slavery, her face clouded. "Definitely not!" she replied. When I asked a young goldsmith, he had no idea who Julio A. was. By his reckoning, slavery was abolished in 1757 by one Justiniano Ocoró (born 1904) of whom there is an exquisitely maintained statue outside the high school in Santa María. At that school, where I am asked to talk to two classes, *nobody* in the class of fourteen-year-olds knew anything of Julio A. For good or for bad, he's disappeared. Nor could they tell me the date of the abolition of slavery. Of greater import, none had any idea of Artículo 55, the most ex-citing political development on the coast since the end of slavery. Proposed as one of the most innovative experiments in political theory this century, Artículo 55 proposes communal ownership by blacks to lands on the coast, thus granting to black ethnicity a political reality unknown in North or South America. This means that black villages on the Pacific Coast, and to some degree elsewhere in Colombia, can own and hence control their resources as corporations, such that any new mining enterprise like the French company or the Russians will have to take local interests to heart. Two students out of thirty in the class of sixteen-year-olds knew of Julio A., and they echo what my friend down the street says: that although he was born here, people want nothing to do with his memory be-cause when he left for the state capital of Popayán, he spoke badly of the people here. An old man in San José a little farther downriver from Santa María tells me: "*Era un hombre que nació en San Vicente. Después se fue a Popayán y negó a su patria!*" "I'm not from here!" explains Lilia. "I'm from Popayán!" Julio A.'s shame is not slavery but that he denied his place in the world, the place where he was born among these black people, Santa María.

mines

In our time: Enrique, aged fourteen, takes me to the mine where he works after school with his sister, Wendy Sulay, aged eight, and his brother Walter, aged ten. They are part of a group of some twenty children and adults, largely women, who divide the profits unequally, if there are any to be divided. The owner of the land and the owner of the water pump take 50 percent between them. The kids get a small amount of cash at the end of three weeks. If there is no gold, nobody gets anything. I am told it is not uncommon to wait years . . .

We walk past the outlying houses. Already it feels like we have passed an important division between town and country. Enrique bounces a soccer ball. We are joined by Javier, who teaches English at the school and wants to practice speaking it with me. Dairo, aged twelve, who refused point-blank a year ago to go back to school, is with us too. We follow the stream upward, passing through the shade of breadfruit trees with their sharply etched leaves, splashing through the clear water, feet searching for position on the round stones, Enrique leading, lithe and surefooted. The water dies out but the stones continue in the dry creek bed. We walk through a grove of plantains. An elderly woman with no clothes above her waist is crouched on the ground. Old felt hat and a necklace of beads, a bunch of plantains on the ground to carry to the village. Now it is slippery underfoot. A tree trunk obstructs the path. We pass a hole in the ground with beams poking through rotting vegetation. It is an old mine.

A little further on we come to the mine where Enrique works. First we see the wooden sluice standing in an orange sandy-bottomed stream running by the side of coconut palms and breadfruit trees. The mine is what is called a *pozo,* or hole, that goes straight down for about twenty feet. From the bottom, small tunnels are excavated horizontally in a radial pattern. The hole is elaborately buttressed by crisscrossing branches and tree trunks. The French method was to cut horizontal tunnels in from the riverbanks and rely on gravity drainage, but now with pumps you can dig straight down anywhere and then radiate out in a star pattern underground, although these mines extend nowhere near so long underground as the tunnel mines. For example, Leopoldo's tunnel mine, an extension of a French one, is some 1,300 meters long and at times 80 meters below the surface.

Enrique jumps down into the hole. Dairo follows. Trapeze artists making their way into the bowels of the earth. You can barely see the bottom. It's full of water down there. About one and half meters of water, says Enrique. Nobody is down there today. They are waiting for others to cut more beams. Enrique worked a full year in that mine and never once saw gold. His father was working in another mine for five and half months and at the end got a dollar and fifty cents. He's never going into a mine again, he says. But Enrique, Wendy, and Walter keep at it.

Dairo's father threw him out of their home a year ago for being disobedient, and he now lives with an uncle who teaches school and drinks too much *biché.* Every day he drinks *biché.* The uncle is small and beautiful, delicately featured with morose red-lined eyes, and he steers an uneven course up and down the street, swaying with the play of the cobblestones. Distilled under the stilthouses along the adjoining Río Saija, *biché* is scary stuff; potent as dynamite, cheap as air, it is, as its name suggests, rawness on its way to something else. In the bottle it smells like lighter fluid. Exhaled it gives off an aroma like honey mixed with vomit that hangs on to the person drinking it like a halo. Too much

and you get to be a *degenerado,* like Dairo's uncle. He walks unannounced into people's houses, breaks into their conversations with absurd questions, begs for rice and sugar, and refuses to leave. Although rich by local standards with a government check equivalent to 350 dollars a month on account of the many years he's been teaching, he's always broke and Dairo is always hungry, the only kid who asks me for money. His uncle's wife drinks a lot also and decided to live elsewhere, so young Dairo and his desperate uncle are left to cook for themselves.

People tell me his uncle is Gustavo's not-so-secret lover. Yet while Gustavo is noisy, demonstrative, and somewhat feminine in his gait and garb, pursued by raucous young boys teasing him to death on his way to pan gold with the women, Dairo's uncle is morose and withdrawn, a red-eyed phantom trailing honey and vomit. No wonder people say Dairo is an odd kid. And no wonder he is the only kid who doesn't go to school, where his uncle presides. A year later I heard he'd split and was working in a refrigerator plant way down in the mouth of the river, gutting and cleaning fish. It must be lonely down there in a decrepit building about to collapse into the gloomy estuary, no other houses around, just mud, soporific heat, mosquitoes, and the occasional surprise visit by the guerrilla hungry for fish. At least Dairo will probably get something to eat there.

Sometimes the village seems like the place to where the pied piper of Hameln spirited all those kids with his magic flute. Nothing but kids shrieking with laughter, swarming like sardines flowing in and out of the street. What joy. What light. What bubbling life. They are either going to school or coming back from school, neat and polished in their school uniforms and shiny black shoes. In the high school, boys and girls wear the same colors, a crisp white shirt and gray pants, for boys, a skirt for girls made of a light gray checked material with a thin red stripe. There is a lot of argument going on about changing this to blue jeans. A uniform is a huge investment. In 1998 there were eighty-four pupils in the high school and close to four hundred in the grade school. School sets the rhythm of the day, no less than the hopes for a future in the wider world.

When the children are at school, the village is somnolent, basking in the heat and ready to expire. All you can hear are the hot cobblestones grumbling and getting ready for the next bout of noisy rattling when the kids romp home from school. The teachers seem to find school too hot. Much of the time you see them chatting under a tree in the little park opposite the school, the park with the statue of Justiniano Ocoró, who left school at age twelve and, as they say, abolished slavery. The rector of the high school gets the equivalent of U.S. $750 a month (plus a mighty pension upon retirement); a teacher on a yearly contract in the grade school, U.S. $100—staggeringly high incomes compared with the rest of the river. Schoolteachers wear T-shirts with the name of their school and river emblazoned across them as names of football teams. In the canoe going upstream, a man carefully stows away a wooden plaque made by a prisoner in Santa Bárbara. The prisoner made it for his teacher in Santa María and it has a dedication engraved to her. To be a teacher here is to be a god.

Despite the effervescence that is the children bubbling with life, this is a ghost town in that so many of its people don't live here anymore and the ones who do are marking time, like so much of Colombia. When in mad discord the church bells ring the Day of the Dead, they ring as much for this emptiness as for the ghosts of remembrance. Take Yanet, aged thirteen, who lives with her mother, her mother's parents, and her four half-brothers and -sisters in a two-room single-story wooden house at the end of the village. It is dark as we talk and I scribble notes by candlelight, tracing out a spidery genealogy.

They have no money and live off plantain and boiled *yuyo* gathered from the forest. Yanet works for Lilia before and after school until eight o'clock at night, seven days a week. Instead of money she gets meals and her school uniform. Lilia is able to afford this because she runs a government-funded crèche, which is likely to be phased out as the present government cuts welfare in accord with IMF and World Bank promotion of market forces. Yanet's father lives in the port of Buenaventura, way up the coast. Her stepfather is separated from her mother and lives with another woman elsewhere in Santa María. Her mother's father, Apolinar, has four siblings in Santa María and five in Cali. Four out of five of her mother's mother's siblings live in Cali, the other in Buenaventura. The women in Cali work as live-in servants, the men in construction, if there is any, which there isn't. This is a hollowed-out village. The census I did in 1976, some fifteen years before talking with Yanet, showed that for every ten people born here, only four were still resident. The situation now must be even more extreme.

The village vomits out people. It has no future. It was once alive with Indians making golden fishhooks. Then it was an outpost of empire, an African slave camp sending gold to Panamá to await the Spanish fleet. Now it is a scar on time. Most of the coast has this eerie artifactual feel. Nobody would live here unless they were born here, like the Indians, or forced to, like the slaves, or shipwrecked, like the whites on the beach at Mulatos. It's high time everyone cleared out, which, in truth, seems to be everyone's dream.

Let me tell you about *yuyo*, what Yanet's family survives upon together with boiled plantain. As far as I know, *yuyo*, large-leafed and thorny, is special to the diet of the Río Timbiquí. Nowhere else on the coast, nor for that matter in rural Colombia, is anything like it eaten. And no peasant I know of in the interior eats greens. Moreover, the tiny thorns running along the surface of the leaves produce welts on the skin. Yet in Santa María *yuyo* is food. From conversation with Daniela Zuñiga, who as a young girl helped her mother cook for the New Timbiquí Gold Mines in Santa María in the 1920s, I got the idea that the French engineers used *yuyo* as a substitute for lettuce. It seems like the river was humming those days with flotillas of canoes carrying wines and cheese from France. No doubt I exaggerate. But what would a French lettuce look like after a month or more at sea and the rigors of the ascent up the Timbiquí?

This was a colonial fantasy I hung on to. It gave me pleasure to think of those robust French engineers so far from home, so willing to risk their health and possibly their lives for gold, but unable to do so without the customary pleasures of the table. It made them human to me. And it made them real. It brought their ghosts into the present, along with their stiff-necked presence in the occasional family photographs you glimpsed in homes along the river.

When I actually get to see *yuyo* and taste it, I realize I am way wrong. It is more like cabbage than lettuce and has to be boiled to softness otherwise it's too prickly. Here I am like an eighteenth-century botanist, or a privateer like Woodes Rogers in 1709, trying to understand something new in a new world by forcing it into my categories, lettuce or cabbage, as when Woodes Rogers saw his first sloth on the island of Gorgona and said it was a monkey, surprised it took all day to climb the mast that a monkey would scamper up in a minute. *Yuyo* has recently become a health-food specialty in Cali. Truly, ours is the time for the great awakening, the *apertura* of the coast, as the young interpreter for the Russians says.

In our time: Enrique, now aged seventeen, takes me to El Limbo. It fully deserves its name. Up hill and down dale we slither and slide. I find it almost impassable. I lose a shoe in a swamp. The forest presses in dark and dank with its brilliant shades of green. Sweat pours. At times we have to haul ourselves up with vines, finding toeholds in notches cut into slippery chonta palm trunks. Finally we break through the forest onto an immense beach of white and gray stones by the edge of a tawny river running fast and smooth in a graceful curve. There is an old man, don Julio, bent over by the weight of a bunch of plantains he is carrying toward a shelter of branches built on the edge of the forest.

Soaring opposite on the other side of the river is a cliff dripping water and exotic ferns with leaves shaped like tears streaming down its face. Twelve feet above the rushing river is the dark hole of the mine. A young man picks us up in a tiny canoe with an inch of freeboard. It wobbles with the slightest movement. If you grip the sides too hard, it leans into the river. Be still, don't show your fear, says the river. We drift with the current, get out, then have to climb the cliff on slippery wet indentations and inch along sideways till we get to the mine open-ing, where there is a slight protuberance that allows me to swing onto the floor at the entrance to the mine. Agida is there, smiling. "Watch out for the buggy!" she yells, and presses me against the dripping wall as a young man comes teetering out of the darkness with a wheelbarrow full of slimy gray rocks and mud. There is a pungent smell due, they say, to the freshly cut timber supports.

The principle of the human chain: Down below us braced against the current of the river are thirteen people passing buckets of stones and mud from hand to hand with lightning speed down the cliff to the wooden *canelón,* or sluice, stand-ing in water. Some people stand in the river; others cling to the cliff. What care they take! Even rubbing dirt off the rocks brought out of the mine so as to get every possible piece of dirt washed in the sluice below. How the women on either side of the sluice churn the gravel pushed forward by the force of the river, up to the elbows at times! How they move those *bateas* in the river, swirling the fine gravel for the final spin! The massive strength and endurance of those bodies, picking out the heavy stones, hurling them into the river. Agida at it all day long.

Of the seventeen people, ten are kids, ages ranging from six to thirteen. Three men chip away at the rock face three hundred feet within the mine, search-ing for what they call the *viejo canal,* the old riverbed, where the river ran in an-cient times before the Flood. Except for Agida, they are all kin-related. No gold yet, but I see hopeful glints in the *canelón* presided over by the owner's mother and wife. His name is Carlos Arturo Benté and he invites me inside the mine. "It's your home," he beams. "It's safer than an airplane!"

That night I go to Agida's house. It is full of children spilling out into the street watching TV. I find her at the end of the corridor in the kitchen preparing dinner after her day at the mine. It is pitch-black in there as she can only afford one electrical outlet, either the TV or a lightbulb, costing the equivalent of U.S. $3 per month for the electricity. It is pitch-black in that kitchen, like the mine.

Omar's mine, which is really his mother's, used to be a French mine. It's easy to find, ten minutes' walk from the village by a stream shrouded by bread-fruit trees from which the ear-splitting noise of the pump emerges, along with endless lengths of black-ribbed rubbery hose. As you enter the darkness with a carbide lamp brighter than any electric light, innumerable chip marks made by the pick enclose you. I stop, scared to go farther.

Years later I did enter a mine, its entrance a weeping hole in a cliff that formed the riverbank, the floor being no more than a foot above the level of the river rushing by. A small stream fed into the river with a little sandbank on which a group of muddy kids and women were waiting in the rain for earth to be carried out, it being their job to wash this for gold. The miners were too poor to have anything but candles, and because the tunnel took a right-angled turn, it was pitch-black most of the way. It became clammy and hot and progressively harder to breathe. I couldn't imagine what it would be like to heave a pick and iron bar all day at the pit face. My flashlight revealed intricate roof supports as we sloshed through the sludge. I felt I was choking and then saw the light after turning the bend. Two elderly skinny guys stood there scratching their heads, surrounded by boulders about two feet in diameter. An unholy mess. Somehow I had expected a nice flat floor and a neat right-angled wall of stone at which they would be chipping away. A real tunnel, you might say. Instead there was this gruesome disembowelment of mother earth with everything at sixes and sevens, oozing muddy water and nameless fluids.

As I turned to go back, I began to feel curiously at home and cozy in the mine, perhaps because I knew I was on the way out and could start to reflect on this as an experience that I now hand over to you. This is the basis of many theories of history, personal no less than worldly. At first the human being is so immersed in reality, in this case horrific, that she or he has neither consciousness nor self-consciousness. There is no Other, just the interior of the pitch-black mine penetrating your being. Then comes the second part of the story. Evolving differentiation enters the scene. Subject peels off from object allowing for consciousness of self. Aha! I am having an experience!

Plato said this occurred in a cave, too. But there was light in his cave, casting shadows that led people astray. They were having misleading experiences, he said, and it was his job to free them from illusion and lead them out of the cave. The great Hegel rewrote this story of experience with his parable of master and slave. While it is the master who makes decisions, like Julio Arboleda, the slave works at the rock face with bare hands or by the riverbank with a wooden bowl and enters into an understanding of the nature of nature that subtly intertwines being inside as well as being outside. The slave's selfhood emanates from this interaction with the physical world, framed by servitude to the master. But the master's consciousness sets him apart from nature, and he has experiences like looking out a train window or looking at gold.

In reference to this system of tunnel mining introduced by the French, and that subsequently spread to adjoining rivers like the upper Saija, the Guapi, and the Micay, Robert West wrote in 1960 that in inexperienced hands this is a most dangerous technique, and that frequent collapse of the tunnels has killed many due to faulty timbering.[1] I hear a villager died this way a year ago and that this is frequent. William Amú tells me that about twenty people have died from mining accidents in his memory over some forty years; Lilia says thirty, this out of a total popula-

---

1. West, *The Pacific Lowlands of Colombia*, p. 178.

tion of twenty-five hundred, a high mortality rate, indeed, far higher than the homicide rates in Cali, for instance, considered among the highest in the world.

I am outside one of the new mines cut straight down. The earth is shaking with the roar of the pump and water. Blue plastic sheeting lies everywhere. There are tiny shelters made of banana leaves, women underneath lying down half asleep or legs straight out in front, lit end of cigarette inside the mouth, waiting for the men to start excavating. Then they form a human chain, passing the earth dug from the mine in flexible rubber buckets, throwing each bucket from hand to hand until it gets to the two women at the sluice into which gushes the water the pump has extracted from the mine. Their hands move like lightning sorting big rocks from small, gravel from fine gravel, heaving buckets of stones out of the sluice, then stemming the flow of water so as to sift more thoroughly. Later in the afternoon they will wash the fine dirt using a *batea* to get the even finer, black pay dirt, called *jagua*. In many areas of South America today, just as in colonial times, mercury is used to separate gold from the pay dirt, with terrifying consequences for human health and the environment. But I never heard of its use here. Robert West reported in the early 1950s that most folk miners on the coast then used a trick acquired from the Indians, using a glutinous sap from trees like the balsa tree to create a surface tension to which the iron in the pay dirt clung, while the gold drifted to the bottom of the *batea*, but I never saw this.[2]

In fact, I never saw gold itself but on a couple of occasions, swimming like tiny stars in water at the bottom of a split coconut shell, which is how women keep it during the day out in the forest by the streams they are working. Why do they keep it like that, like little fish swimming in water? Why do we always find this intimacy of gold and water? Another time I saw a strong young woman, her five-year-old child watching from the bank, dive repeatedly with a stone tied to her back. In an eddy by her side bobbing up and down was a split coconut shell floating precariously on a torn-off piece of plantain husk. I keep thinking of the nonchalance and fragility embodied in this tiny craft destined to hold whatever gold she might find.

It sums up all I feel about Santa María.

---

2. West, *The Pacific Lowlands of Colombia*, p. 178.

Some thirty years ago the Gold Museum in Bogotá announced a great acquisition, nothing less than a miniature representation in gold of the story of El Dorado, the Golden King. It was a golden raft some eight inches long with human figures aboard, presumed to come from the vicinity of a highland lake close to Bogotá. The story is that upon his accession to the throne, the new king would paddle at night out onto the lake, naked, his body covered with resin and powdered with gold. While his people lit fires in the mountains around the lake, he slipped over the side such that the gold would stream in a gleaming shower to the bottom. Perhaps the Gold Museum should now include alongside this priceless piece a split coconut shell with a little water in it, but no gold, floating on the husk of a plantain tree?

entropy

Nowadays in Santa María you can go four years in a mine and get absolutely nothing—not four years before you find some, but four years before you decide to quit! And when you consider the back-wrenching effort, those years must seem like a lifetime. To mine underground breathing foul air, digging your tunnel, you need money for supplies. The banks won't lend without collateral, and there's none of that. So what is it that keeps you going? How many lucky strikes how long ago do there have to have been to keep you at it, year after year, tunneling through rock with nothing but a short-handled pick and a crowbar, eating plantains and *yuyo* from the forest? Even for the women panning gold who by comparison seem assured a far higher chance of finding gold in minute amounts, luck is what it's all about. But now the way I see it, luck becomes unbearably important. This must make for the most exquisite torture, for unlike other poverty-stricken villages and towns, a gold-based town has always this dream that just around the corner lies a bonanza. I ask Lilia why people keep doing the same old thing. She explains there's no market for agriculture here since everyone grows the same thing. There's no capital to start something different. And, well, mining is *costumbre, una tradición* . . . But of course there's one thing that can crash through all this and that's cocaine: like gold, immensely valuable, and also chance-prone in that being illegal and having its value dependent on the wrath of the U.S. government, it is a commodity subject to fluctuations not in price—that is assured by the policies of the United States—but in violence. Yet how long will it be before these coastal people start cultivating coca? As soon as the guerrilla encourage it or as soon as a *paisa* turns up with coca seed and a promise to buy *pasta*.

Who are these *paisas?* They are whites, legendary for their skill at business. Their indomitable work ethic encourages them to scorn blacks along the coast who have a more relaxed attitude toward life and are not consumed by the agitation and nervous energy that animates the *paisas* who have spread out from their homeland of the Colombian province of Antioquia to colonize much of western Colombia as small farmers or as agile entrepreneurs. All ten of the pawnshops in Guapi are owned by *paisas,* for instance. The first great coca cartels were created by *paisas* who brought the government to its knees through terrorism and at one stage offered to pay off the national debt in return for an amnesty. Every day brings more *paisas* to the coast. They own outboard motor agencies, cafés, hardware stores, and who knows what else. Years ago I saw two *paisas* on the wharf at Guapi feverishly loading boxes of what they said were ice-cream cones onto a launch with mighty motors astern.

When I first went to Santa María, kids would scuttle up trees and from their safe perches call down at me, "God bless you!" Last visit in 2002 several times kids greeted me with "*¡Olla! ¡Paisa!*"

When I last left Santa María and arrived downriver at Santa Bárbara, I kept thinking how audacious and independent the people of Santa María are. By comparison, Santa Bárbara, the municipal seat with fast boats to Guapi and hence the outside world, seemed sad and unworthy, a bunch of bureaucrats sitting around all day with nothing much to do but wait for the day to end and the next one to begin and complain some more. It is such a cliché and sounds so stupidly romantic to describe the people of Santa María as encrusted in nature, and maybe that's not quite the direction I want to take this thought. I am thinking more of money, the stuff that's in such short supply on the coast and especially so in Santa María, where people mine money, so to speak, but have none. Again it sounds silly, what an astute lawyer from this coast told me, that the major problem on the coast is lack of money. He didn't mean poverty, not specifically. He meant cash. His thinking seemed to be that if there was more money floating around, if, for instance, the government printed more and brought it in buckets by helicopter to fill the coffers of the one and only bank in Santa Bárbara, then the local economy could take off. Or something.

My mind floats back to the mid-1970s in the interior, in the slums by the sugarcane fields of the Cauca Valley with a coastal woman telling me with some despair and a great deal of poetry, "On the coast there is food, but no money. Here there is money but no food." But I don't want to end up with some smug trade-off between money and nature. I want to alienate money's alienation. Make its strangeness strange. I want to make going to a store and buying your daily food, for instance, seem like a miracle. For that's what a visit to a place like Santa María teaches you, beginning with the wonder that there is indeed anything for sale on the dusty shelves. I want to find a way to illustrate how the money form veils the things of the world. Yet surely this is obvious? Why bother with naïveté? Is it because we are heading into the strangest zone of all, the zone of the obvious, where things only become obvious once they are pointed out? I need to slow down the process of purchase and put it into slow motion. I need a way to spell it out so its sinks in as a physical sensation like being in an elevator that stops too fast, leaving your stomach behind.

And this is how this thought began, with this separation of the stomach from the body in flight, Santa María being the negative instance, the village of no money that shows up, therefore, the marvel of money. How clever and formidably tough in mind and body, not to mention soul, you have to be to live directly off nature like they do, yet at the same time these people are definitely not textbook cases of primitive hunters and gatherers isolated in a moneyless world. And what immense reservoirs of knowledge are needed to mine gold, tend the crops, give birth unaided by medical science, know the different trees, cut them into planks with a handsaw, build the houses, shape the canoes, know the moods and currents of the rivers . . . The list is a long one. And, of course, it's so much more than knowledge as information. It requires a feel for materials and an attitude toward both the body and inclemency, the mud, the rain, the fevers, the malaria, the hunger, the boredom . . . The list is a long one. The paradox still longer. The miners of money have none, and the lawyer sees the solution to the economy in buckets of cash.

When the French mining company controlled the upper reaches of the Timbiquí at the beginning of the twentieth century, they issued their own money called *cachaloa*. I have two such coins, light in weight and buckled with age. They remind me of play money, but then what money is not play? The *cachaloa* are of a diameter wider than most coins, almost one and half inches across. In large letters running along the circumference is stamped *N. TIMBIQUI G. M.* This stands for the name of the company in English, which is strange yet no doubt adds the requisite gravity, given that no English whatsoever is spoken in these parts. Along the lower circumference is stamped the Spanish, *ADELANTO*. The mix of languages and nations engraved on the coinage is a wondrous thing like the company itself with its British capital, French engineers, black workers, and its status as a quasi-autonomous sovereign state with a monopoly of the legitimate use of violence within a given territory of Colombia. The two coins I have, a fifty-cent *cachaloa* and a twenty-cent *cachaloa*, each had a hole punched in the center as if to be strung into a necklace. They were given to me as a gift by Gustavo in Santa María, who then stole my solar-powered flashlight. His sister, who lives next door to him in an equally precarious house, found the flashlight straightaway. He's known as a kleptomaniac, wandering into peoples' homes and taking what he fancies. Still everyone was embarrassed. Included with his gift was a tiny ten-cent coin issued by the Colombia state, dated 1938, also with a hole through the center, and a tiny silver jug about an inch high. The Colombian coin shows little sign of age, while the *cachaloas* are so weathered they look like they've been unearthed from a prehistoric site. As for the meaning of the word *cachaloa*, it seems to have come with the mining company. Lilia tells me it is still a term with some currency. It is a term of abuse. When two women are fighting over a man, she says, one may call the other a *cachaloa*, meaning a woman of ill repute.

So how do we who live in totally monetized worlds conceive of poverty among people who are essentially self-subsistent in the wilderness? Surely it would be wrong to equate poverty in this situation with lack of money? Remember my earnest lawyer friend saying the principal problem on the coast was lack of money? And he meant money as in cash, what the helicopter brings to the bank in Santa Bárbara and what the manager of the bank is constantly accused of stealing (although what happens is that no sooner is the cash money put into the safe, than it is whisked out and sent to Buenaventura to pay for all the stuff like cement, clothes, hens, and TVs that are imported into the coast). Is this chronic shortage of money why the New Timbiquí Gold Mines made their own money, like the companies trading in rubber and in tagua nuts ("white ivory" for buttons) such as the casa Márquez, the Benítez, and the Escrucería companies, each one of which made its own money too.[1] What does it mean to monetize an economy, exchanging raw materials such as gold or rubber for your own play money? Is this not a truly momentous act, like trying to alter the genetic constitution of a species by means of some virus or by radioactivity? Who knows what the consequences might be? And if money is simply a means facilitating exchange, could it ever stay just that, or does it inevitably lead to that curious alchemy whereby money reproduces more of itself as capital in some places and less of itself in others? I think back to Gustavo seventy years after their issue, bringing me a gift of two *cachaloa,* together with a tiny silver jug, and stealing my flashlight, the one item of use value to a local resident in this idiosyncratic little exchange system. Money is round and solid and is designed to circulate. A jug stays put and is hollow. These *cachaloa* used to circulate. Now they are in retirement. They are relics, of interest to an outsider such as myself. Only a swift movement fusing theft with gift could get them to circulate one last time and then stay put in the tiny jug that is my story.

This place is fucked up. That's what Marina's daughter tells me. She has come back from the interior with a university degree in economics and has a job in the municipal administration downriver from Santa María in Santa Bárbara. She is trying to figure out why the new computer doesn't work as we talk. She is part of a new generation. The only income here, she says, are the government salaries. This is what moves the commerce here and why there are stores with stuff to buy, even though they are pathetically stocked. And if stuff is sold, the

---

1. Claudia Leal, "Manglares y economía extractiva," in *Geografía humana de Colombia: Los Afrocolombianos,* by María Romero Moreno, Luz Castro Agudelo, and Esperanza Aguablanca (Bogotá: Instituto Colombiana de cultura hispánica, 1998), tomo VI, p. 417.

store owners remit their profits to Buenaventura and nothing remains here as capital. Everything leaves: lumber, fish, gold . . . and people. They educate their kids in the interior if they have any money or relatives living there. As soon as someone gets their pension or some windfall, they go to live in the interior. And nobody returns. There is so little cash circulating! The bank cannot cash a check! And why is Hector's sawmill not operating today? Because he has no cash to buy logs. And just as everything here leaves, so everything we consume comes from outside. Most of what we eat comes from outside. The plantains have been destroyed by plague and have to be brought from Nariño. Now that coca is taking hold, even the cultivators in Nariño are abandoning food crops. Vegetable and fruits are brought by boats from Buenaventura, as is the rice we eat. And here we are, in the bosom of a wildly prolific nature, the hottest of suns, the most massive of rainfalls, estuaries teeming with fish . . .

Three days before I arrived here at Santa Bárbara in 1998, a young woman was raped by four men at night where a small airport is being constructed, and hours later there were volleys of gunfire in this tiny town. Over five hundred shots! I am told. What is the world coming to? And an airport? What is the point of an airport? Marina's husband, who comes from many generations of people here, tells me the town is totally screwed. All people want to do is leave for the interior. The words clang in my ear. All people want to do is leave . . . Here is a no-place. A mistake. A temporary abode since 1851 between slavery and the no-place of freedom. All people want to do is leave. And when the young get into trouble with the law or with other gangs and drug dealers in the interior, they race back here to hide. A strange fate: the coast becoming a refuge for the crime consuming the cities. Now the commonest crimes here are possession of drugs and illegal arms. "What we need here," he continues, staring me in the face upstairs in the wooden house by the black river as we eat a dinner of rice imported from the interior and a small can of tuna imported from the United States, "is for a multinational to come and exploit the gold." I think back to the Russian fitter from the multinational mining company that recently invaded Santa María upstream asleep in his grave under wild flowers with his rotted liver.

The old woman sits day after day downstairs in her cavernous store in Santa Bárbara with its empty shelves sagging with dust and the same six shirts wrapped in cellophane that were here last year. Every day she maneuvers her big arthritic body down the steep wooden steps in the dark to the store, sits there not really expecting anyone to come and buy a shirt, and then struggles upstairs right on twelve for lunch and comes back down again to sit in the same seat in the same position looking out at the black river till night falls and the lamps are lit. Every day. She knows I am interested in anthropology. She has two whalebones found at the mouth of the river and wonders if I would like one as a gift.

moonshine

One river north of the Timbiquí lies the Saija, famous for its heady brew of FARC guerrilla and coca fields since the late 1990s, together with paramilitaries massing there since late June 2002, so as to kill the guerrilla and acquire their coca. As I write these lines, the river is in turmoil and people have fled, anticipating a pitched battle. But for many years before that, the Saija stood out for something different, and that was the production of moonshine, a potent sugarcane brandy by the name of *biché* distilled under just about every house along its banks (all houses being built on stilts). *Biché* was by far the main source—indeed, the only source—of cash income other than that sent back by emigrants. Like gold and cocaine, *biché* is good value, only it's a lot cheaper. After merely one swig, the river starts to dance and the glare of the sun cascades through your brain like a whip. People start to sway. If Timbiquí was the river of *gold,* Saija was the river of *biché*, just as both are now becoming rivers of *cocaine*. So what do these three products—gold, *biché*, and cocaine—have in common?

Compared with food products or livestock, all three are enormously valuable in relation to their volume and weight, and thus it does not matter that they are produced or found deep in the rain forests far from urban markets. The insuperable problems that plague people in Santa María who might dream of cultivating plantains or corn for cash sale are of no concern with these commodities.

Like cocaine, *biché* is illegal; the difference being that the U.S. government doesn't give a damn, so the repression is a lot less. *Selladores* determined to maintain the state's monopoly on liquor production and distribution came up the river many years back and smashed the primitive distilleries. Yet production resumed and today, thanks to its high alcohol content and its cheapness compared with the state-distilled brandies, *biché* enjoys a wide distribution far beyond the confines of the coast. It is really a wonderful thing these people have hit upon; a way of making money even in so distant a place. And unlike cocaine, *biché* knows no monopolization. Just about every household possesses a distillery. Moreover, there is no violence associated with *biché*. So, here we have a puzzle— and a welcome puzzle, at that—a high-value product but without violence or monopoly that provides income for coastal people. A cause for celebration.

Economists no doubt would search for rational reasons to explain this difference—"rational" meaning explanations in terms of market principles such as the profit motive and the laws of supply and demand. We could play a game like scissors, paper, rock, each item different to the other in terms of advantages, the three forming a system: scissors cuts paper; paper covers rock; rock smashes scissors. Thus: *biché* is illegal but free of violence and monopoly and is potentially infinite in supply; gold is nonviolent and legal, but there is none left and for all its legality, along with alcohol and drugs, it is mythically weighed down with evil too. And *cocaine* is illegal, violent, and extraordinarily prone to monopolization. Round and round we go comparing and contrasting, searching for the bedrock of explanation. But I think *biché* goes far beyond the laws of supply and demand or the search for profits, just as do cocaine and gold, for that matter. Indeed, what *biché*, gold, and cocaine share is that they each challenge everything the market stands for *and this is why they are valuable*. They make a mockery of the notion of "laws" of supply and demand. They decidedly sabotage the notion of "demand," riddling it with complexity and phantasmic properties unknown to conventional economics. They are the luxuries for which people are prepared to be decidedly foolish about, the mad poetry of love and despair that beats aching notes in every human heart desperate to go that little bit further, that brimful that pours over the edge of caution and common sense . . . In short, *biché* is a wonder. My first sip of it was in 1975 from a hip-flask-sized bottle whose elegance testified that in a previous life it had indeed contained a perfume called La Maravilla, the name that was applied to *biché* itself. I still think of it as just that, something no doubt that would have caught the eye of the surrealists in Paris as doorway to the Marvelous, not to mention Convulsive Beauty.

the accursed share

Men never pan for gold except for Gustavo and seven other elderly men. Instead, they work at the rock face in the underground tunnel mines or alongside women in the mines that are like wells going straight down into the earth twenty feet or so. Underground in the tunnel mines, you can go for years without finding gold. Take bug-eyed Omar of beetling brow. He's still investing money on top of the six million pesos he's already put in, so I'm told (around U.S. $10,000). He used to have a shop as well. Now it's practically empty. A few dried biscuits and an erratic cooler with some beer when the Russians had electricity fed in to keep the villagers happy. He works the mine double shift and often sleeps there. Everyone hates him. Why does he work the mine at night? "He's crazy about money." There's a story afoot that from one day to the next he went mad and turned against his wife, his family, and his friends. They say he's bewitched. A Faustian character, he puts the desperation of the Russians in perspective. He personifies the drama of gold, sacrificing everything and anybody to his mad pursuit. But unlike the Russians, so far from home, who are being sacrificed by the company, Omar is sacrificing himself and anyone close to him, as can be discerned, I think, not only by the undying enmity he provokes, but by the meanness he seems to activate and inhabit, drawing it around him like a moth-eaten cloak.

There is another way of looking at this association of the devil with gold, of course, and this has to do with giving oneself over, living on the edge. Omar is doing just that by deliberately spurning the code, abusing family and friends, flaunting the laws of give and take. That is one edge gone over. He really doesn't give a fuck about other people. Just as common is the flip side of this, the Big Spender, the man who works for years finding absolutely nothing, ensconced deep in the mine to emerge blinking into the light one day with a bonanza and spend it in a week on booze, women, fine clothes, sunglasses, and electronic equipment. This man is the despair of the Dutch and German NGOs trying to stimulate community development on the coast, and he is pretty much every-where. Here the devil, master of guile and mimicry, appears as the man with the keys to the palace of excess, which William Blake equated with wisdom. This gold cannot be hoarded. It has to be spent and spent lavishly. Either way, the way of Omar or the way of the Big Spender, gold belongs to the devil and has thus served worldwide as the basis of value since the beginning of time, if not longer.

A variation on the Big Spender would be Juan Pablo. Last time I saw him, he was dead drunk. Five days on *biché*. He is a musician and a *labrador*, a person who can work wood to make a dugout canoe, paddles, and, in his case, a marimba. He lives four hours away (his speed), alone in the forest in the steep foothills, earning some money by hunting and by making canoes. You can't get too close. He radi-ates heat. I ask him why he talks funny. "I was born alone," he replies. I could plot a constellation around this man: a halo of drunkenness, sweet music, working the wood of the forest for fine craft, at home with animals, intense gregarious-ness, intense solitude. I have heard it said that he, too, has a pact with the devil.

"I was born alone," he said. What he means is he raised himself. When he was around ten years old, his parents were sick and went to stay with a daughter in Cali and never returned. He had to get food and on the weekends would hunt and fish. His father had made him a twelve-note marimba when he was small and he learned music on that. Now he plays a flute because this is an instrument you can walk through the forest with. The instrument of the loner. Not like the marimba. He made the flute from PVC and gets half-notes off it. He is now sixty-five years old with the slender body of a youth. He eats no meat but lives by selling the meat of animals he catches in traps and fish he nets with an *atarraya,* the blossoming Spanish net that spreads like a parachute when, after much practice, you throw it out onto the river. He has come to the village this night to pay the equivalent of forty-two dollars for such a net made by Yanet's grandfather, who took almost a year to complete it. He leaves at five in the morning. A night visitor. People fear his witchcraft. He lives in another world. But Lilia tells me it is not all that uncommon for kids to be abandoned like he was and fend for themselves. My thoughts shift to Dairo. This other world of Juan Pablo's I call the "back" of the village, the back of the coast, a sort of no-man's-land for me at least where the hot heaviness of the coast gives way to the steep mountains and cold nights of frost, where there are still fish to net and animals to hunt along winding paths between upstream gold villages, where the rapids are so common that canoes are of no use. Here is where the guerrilla from the interior are gathering, swarming like larvae, slowly descending the Pacific side of the high cordillera. Likewise here is where the poor white peasants—our infamous *paisas*—are coming to cut the forest and colonize. A talented sorcerer could do well here, you might think, right on the junction of the archaic and the monstrously modern. Sixty-five years old, lithe as a cat, comes in the dark of night and leaves before sun up. I was born alone.

It is common knowledge that "you can't speak of saints in the mine, only of the devil." This is because the devil owns the mine and must be paid off. Let's say 20 percent, says Omar, making it sound as businesslike as it should, while telling me there are no superstitions in mining. Ricardo Grueso also says it's bullshit. Pure mythology! He snorts. He sticks to his story of the Diluvio Universal. The Flood. A young woman down the street puts it somewhat differently. She says a horde of gold is always protected by something, by a spirit, a *duende,* or some say by the devil, and in the mining of this gold, someone is going to be killed or else the miners will encounter some terrific obstacle. "You see that bitter fellow across the street, always sitting on the stoop of that house filled with screaming argumentative people, he's actually made a deal with the devil and to pay for the gold he has found he has to kill people. He killed my husband's father ten years back, placing poison in his *biché,* and he killed my neighbor's daughter a few years ago

The Accursed Share

while she was giving birth, using a toad with its belly slit open." What a way to die. And she tells it so calm.

I wake up in a peasant village in the interior of Colombia and see a dog-eared book in the corner written by two professors from the United States aimed at teaching peasants how to reason better. The first lesson is to set priorities.

At 7:30 in the morning little Walner, aged seven, pushes aside my mosquito net to tell me a man has come asking for me. His name is Epifanio and he is known as a *brujo*. Everyone is afraid of him. A great man with words, he tells me for a mere one hundred thousand pesos he can give me a bottle of herbal medicine that will block anyone who wants to do me over (*que quiere tumbarle*). As an extra he will throw in some *bejuco de sangre* for the member so it will be hard under any circumstance. The bell tolls up in the church. It will ring all day because today is the day of the *ánimas*. I tell Epifanio I need time to think. He looks forlorn, the classic outcome of the *brujo* with the intrigued but skeptical gringo with money to burn. A friend points up the hill to the church and the cemetery. She tells me he has put plenty of people away.

Every two years or thereabouts, a person here is murdered by poisoning. This is roughly the same rate as deaths due to mining accidents and far higher than the country's homicide rate, among the highest in the world, counting homicide due to guns and physical violence (but not including sorcery). Just last month someone was killed this way. It's less than it could be because people are very careful with what they eat and drink. Also used are toads and "special bottles," perhaps like the one Epifanio wants to sell me. Many times I can't figure out if the poison that people talk about is real poison or a magical medicine, and my working hypothesis since years is that's just how it should be; left in doubt and confusion, the confusion of the division between mind and body, spirit and matter, same as the confusion between form and substance.

Is this the same confusion that links gold to the devil? There can be no praying concerning the mine, nor in it, no saints there either, and no mention of God or the church. Instead, there are visions of an Antichrist emerging as the sound of machines that Gustavo calls "music" from ponds in the river or from dark recesses in the mine as a hen with chicks. The devil can cast a long shadow with lingering suspicion that fortunes are made and perhaps can only be made by making a deal with the forces of evil deploying magical potions so as to kill other villagers. All this points to the sense of gold being "off bounds." But what do I mean, then, of the confusion of spirit with matter and of form with substance?

The Antichrist exists at one extreme as a formless chthonic power embedded in nature, in the earth, in water, and, of course, in gold. Music that is devoted to breaking rhythms, as with the madness of the howling bells or the machine music emanating from the pond, is an apt expression here of that plasticity of form, of some power that is just that—pure power, tempting form like shadows do leaping across a flapping screen, a flowing, as of sound through water.

At the other extreme, this multifarious metamorphosing force is figured as the devil in the Christian pantheon, yet the fact he appears commonly in animal form, as a black bull, a fox, a hen with chicks chirping deep in the rocky fastness of the mine, or as music, serves as a reminder that the Great Imitator slides ineluctably into natural force and, if I may say so, is an exquisite expression of the mimetic principle of nature itself. This, then, is what I mean by confusion—as between forms themselves and then also as between form and substance.

To transgress is to break a rule, and not just any old rule but one of such importance we call it a taboo because it is a barrier of attraction as much as repulsion. Then all hell breaks loose as a sacred barrier has been violated and pollution issues forth, which can be likened to the concept of miasma, a contagious and destructive force explicit or implicit in many societies, the word itself coming from pre-Socratic Greece. To break the rule means to create and enter into a space, like the mine, in which the rule is suspended and comes to exist in a ghostly, negated form, of which gold is but one, albeit splendid, manifestation. The problem is that the space thus created is uncontainable without rituals of purification as practiced in ancient Greece, or by the Nuer of the southern Sudan, for that matter, who have entered the anthropological record on account of the assiduousness with which they practice such rites.[1] To the contrary, in Santa María there is no recourse to purification; no sacrifice, no libations, no cleansing baths. The village is caught, it would seem, between the profane norms of a worldly economy greedy for gold and a sacred economy that defines their livelihood as transgressive and self-destructive. I don't want to exaggerate this. Everyday life proceeds without great drama or clash between sacred and profane. But under the surface, this pattern exists and it has everything—but everything—to do with the value of gold. For the village, the state of emergency in which they live is not the exception but the rule, and this has to be the case, gold being valuable precisely because it cannot be purified of the attraction and repulsion embodied in it. Gold, we might say, is congealed miasma—as is cocaine.

To transgress is to suspend the rule such that it is heightened in its dissolution. The magical medicines also exist in this state of suspension. This is the Other side of the law; its dark side, the side of sorcery, the moon, and of the left hand. "The rule proves nothing; the exception proves everything."[2] What is more, the unofficial *justice* system based on magic is the unofficial *medical* system as well, such that the heady pharmacopoeia of "special bottles," toads, and poisons is both an instrument of law and an instrument of medical practice. There is no body that does not extend into mind, just as there is no body that does not extend into nature as well as into cosmic space and fate itself. Nature is a moral cat-

1. E. E. Evans-Pritchard, *Nuer Religion* (New York: Oxford University Press, 1956). Fieldwork done in 1936.

2. Carl Schmitt, *Political Theology: Four Chapters on the Concept of Sovereignty,* trans. George Schwab (Cambridge: MIT Press, 1988), p. 15.

egory as well as being plain nature. Hence the heady "confusion" of mind with body, no less than of the rule with its exception, which replenishes the rule. Epifanio has his bottles and toads, these substances that reek of the exception. And as he talks of these wonders, many learned, so he claims, from forest Indians and from people of African descent living in the legendary lands of magic to the north, the Bajo Atrato in the Chocó, what then of those other magical, time-compacted substances, gold and cocaine? Here come the bells, again, those crazy, wailing bells, making sacred space inside your head.

A dog growls in the doorway of the house where I am staying in Guapi. I have never heard this dog growl before. I look out in the street. There are two armed soldiers walking by on patrol in standard-issue camouflage. Strange how the dog picks up what most of us feel but do not express. What would happen if we all growled when soldiers walked by? A whole town growling! How wonderfully appropriate to growl back at the state, mimicking it, growl for growl, watching it magnify in the fullness of biological prehistory, writing being but another form of hair rising on the back of the neck. Slap up against the wall of the forest, you get an acute sense of the thing called the state. To me this is more than a heightening of contradiction exposing something hidden. I think of it as natural history, the natural history of the state.

Writing is sixth sense, what dogs are supposed to have, same as what fills the space between the words. People say dogs whine the night before someone is going to die. Perhaps that is related to their being used to sniff for bombs. How they pull at the leash! In one of his stories for kids on Berlin radio in 1931, Walter Benjamin described the famous earthquake in Lisbon of 1755, advising his young listeners not to be too frightened: "For the moment," he said, "the senses of some animals are still superior to our most sensitive instruments. Dogs, especially, are said to display unmistakable signs of agitation days before the eruption of an earthquake, so people keep them as helpers in the lookout posts in earthquake-prone regions."[1] My friends in the white-walled colonial city of Popayán in the interior tell me that just before the earthquake there in Easter 1983, the birds stopped singing and the dogs began to whine piteously and lie down, as did the cattle. At night sleeping after the earthquake, you could hear the earth growling, like stones crunching. Way away in the forests of the Putumayo, I heard tell from poor colonists who had passed through Popayán during the earthquake how a huge black dog had been seen by the graves opening in the cemetery. That was no ordinary dog is what they were saying. Yet it would short-circuit the story to say it was the devil because it's the dog quality of the dog that's important, the animal representing the prehistoric fate of mankind erupting from graves falling in on crumbling cities—more like the dog was a messenger of all that horror as the earth spewed forth its dead, paying anew for the sins of mankind. And when people tell me about the frightening eruption at dusk of the guerrilla into the village in Santa María deep in the forest last year, they make a special point of two things: the beautiful girl warriors and the huge dog they had with them, three feet high and coffee colored. In medieval times, saints might be depicted or etched into stone treading a dragon underfoot. But in secular art, so I am informed, the dragon was replaced by a dog.

Unleashing dogs on Indians was, like the use of the horse, a principal weapon of conquest by the Spaniards in the sixteenth century. J. H. Parry tells us of mastiffs—the name alone makes my hair stand on end—weighing up to two hundred and fifty pounds. Is that possible? Could a dog be *that* big? Two hundred and fifty pounds of vengeful teeth ripping Indians apart in one leap? These are the canine ancestors of those you see today sniffing in airports, leaping at baggage

1. Walter Benjamin, "The Lisbon Earthquake," in *Selected Writings*, vol. 2, *1927–1934*, ed. Michael W. Jennings, Howard Eiland, and Gary Smith, trans. Rodney Livingston et al. (Cambridge: Harvard University Press, 1999), p. 540.

carousels, and asleep at the feet of guards in black Armani-like outfits in the door-ways of pharmacies in Bogotá and Mexico City. "Their dogs are enormous with flat ears and long, dangling tongues," says a sixteenth-century Native American text found in the Florentine Codex. "The color of their eyes is a burning yellow; their eyes flash fire and shoot off sparks. Their bellies are hollow, their flanks long and narrow. They are tireless and very powerful. They bound here and there, panting, with their tongues hanging out. And they are spotted like an ocelot."[2]

What beauty there is in these monstrous dogs of prey! And note that other mimesis, not just the one that converts cruelty into hollow-bellied fire, but the fear on the part of at least one conquistador that the Indians might raise dogs to attack the Spaniards! Gonzalo Jiménez de Quesada, fabled conqueror of what is today called Colombia, told his king in the early sixteenth century that as the Spaniards had made gifts of dogs to Indians, there were now many villages with five hundred to a thousand dogs. He envisaged a day when the country as a whole might rise up "because they could use their packs of dogs against us."[3] A whole town growling! How wonderfully appropriate to growl back at the state, mimicking it, growl for growl, watching it magnify in the fullness of biological prehistory, writing being but another form of hair rising on the back of the neck.

We think of these dogs as auxiliaries or mercenaries recruited to the cause of war, paid in good red meat, visits to the vet, and maybe an endearing name as well. We think of them as but another security device somewhere between radar and a machine gun, and thereby we overlook the message they transmit and the mythology their pointed ears and wagging tails transmit. But now I hear the whole town growling. The famous "sixth sense" at work again, this time sensitive to the magic of the state. This magic comes across clear as a bell with that mortal god Leviathan, an Old Testament monster, which Thomas Hobbes used to describe the modern state. Hobbes was searching for something transcendent with which to understand the anonymous violence that allowed the state to make might right. It seems strange that he finds this transcendent force in the animal world, albeit mythic. But, then, are not all animals mythic when you look at them right?

2. Quoted in J. H. Parry, *The Discovery of South America* (London: Paul Elek, 1979), p. 150.
3. Quoted in Parry, *Discovery of South America*, pp. 234–35.

Stripped-down Hobbes is useful, in this way. The state is created out of the state of nature when men came together in social contract and laid down their arms. A grand melodrama this: nature one moment; state, the next. What I think is important is that the passage from the state of nature to the nature of the state is never complete. Each aspect bears the trace of the other, and the narrative is constantly stopped and doubled back on itself. It's this *doubling back* that I have chosen to examine.

One thing seems sure. Even obvious. But it surprised me. And that was not only the presence of soldiers in the sleepy towns of the mudflats and mangroves of the Pacific Coast, but narcotics smugglers and guerrilla as well. It was certainly no news to find soldiers, paramilitaries, or guerrilla in, say, the Putumayo, on the other side of the Andes stretching down into the Amazon basin. Coca has been commercially cultivated there for export as cocaine to the United States and Europe since 1980, and for at least three decades that area has served intermittently as a base for the FARC guerrilla. But here on the Pacific Coast, we thought we were on another planet, so removed from the centers of power, so difficult the climate and so intense the malaria. A warring nature kept war at bay.

Yet by 1995 I was hearing about narcotrafficking centers along remote rivers and settlements like Satinga and López de Micay into which nobody from the outside, including soldiers, would dare to venture without permission. But over and above and in apparent contradiction to this surprising news (and there is more to come), I was struck by how close and obvious the state can be in such a remote place long before cocaine came our way.

The first person who took me into the rivers and estuaries of the Pacific Coast was a lean young fellow with huge sideburns, temporarily released from prison so as to make this journey, gratis, for the young foreigner with letters of recommendation to the state hospital. His name was Plutarch. The state abetted my every move, even to freeing its prisoner. This is also the beginning of a story, the story of the voyage into the unknown, traveling by water ever farther into the swamp into the equatorial forest.

At first I thought my surprise at finding the state so starkly in your face amid estuaries and dank forests at the farthest reach of the nation-state was that I subscribe to a picture of power in which there is a center and a periphery, the state, of course, being the center, progressively attenuated as you move away, passing eventually, you might say, into nature, along with the crabs scuttling out of sight into mangrove roots and the rain dripping down the back of your neck. This is why I am taken aback by stately presencing in the bosom of nature. Take that all-too-easy target, that overdetermined symbol of stately being, the police, just about the first thing you come across when you arrive at Santa Bárbara, little capital of this vast municipality and the main settlement of the Río Timbiquí. White, pimply, and sweaty, the police lounge under the almond tree in front of the concrete two-story police station polishing their black boots, dominating the public space, fussing, cleaning their guns, flirting with girls, sending little children off on errands. Their gaunt aluminum boat has been dragged up onto the concrete causeway, derelict in its disutility astride a trailer with fat tires aching for a rumble in this roadless province. From its rear like a prolapsed rectum hangs a massive Mercury 115-horsepower outboard in permanent disrepair because nobody can find the spare parts for these outdated U.S. motors, one sweep of which would set awash all the dugout canoes from here to eternity. Standing back we can see that here, on the concrete causeway, curved and contoured to fit the muddy riverbank, the state meets the world. It is, of course, an unconscious arrangement delicately poised between people at play, people at work embarking and disembarking from their canoes, and the black sweep of the river curving in front of the green flare of the forest beyond. Here is where most everyone comes to bathe from the earliest streaks of dawn and where young men in great numbers exhaust themselves playing football. To be truly stately, these wretched policemen should be tall and hard as ramrods like the presidential guard in Bogotá in their nineteenth-century red, black, and gold uniforms with shiny helmets from the Wars of Independence. Yet is there not something even more heroic expressed by these sad roly-poly bodies that speak eloquently to the disturbing mix of loyalty and opportunism that life in the armed services requires for the protection of the state, the same state that issues them weapons so pathetic nobody would care to attack them so as to acquire their arms?

Maybe we need to think some more about the cosmic geometry of power and influence I rely upon, the solar system of center and periphery? What if the periphery is now the center, for instance, as with the state power exercised by the state's not-so-secret agents, the throat-slitting paramilitaries concealed in the bureaucracy, or the guerrilla concealed in the bosom of nature?

It has been observed that the guerrilla in many ways mimic the state despite the fact that the guerrilla would seem, on first consideration, the state's antithesis. Yet this insight as to the mimetic symmetry is incomplete. Behind it lies a tectonic shift in the mutual recognition of nature in culture and hence the resurgence of the archaic in the modern. The mimesis between the state and its enemy comes about because nature (the guerrilla) and culture (the state) have been forced into a new constellation of mutual acknowledgment of how each contains vital aspects of the other being mirrored back and forth—as when the dog growls and the writer writes, hairs on end, sixth sense invisible in the space between words as graves open and the earth shakes and beautiful *guerrilleras* with huge dogs lope through the forest. Like the dogs, the writer whines the night before death but this dawn never breaks.

The unconscious but continuous symbolic discharge of the state infusing the everydayness of life needs to be distinguished from another mode of stately presence that is achieved through stark contrasts, such as the fact that one feels more exposed and vulnerable to the state out there in the rivers and forests than in the inner city. This is another truism, easily forgotten. The isolation also means humanity cherishes itself more. The river, for instance, is like a telephone line, or the plaza of a village, people laughing as they greet each other, the one up high on muddy stilts leaning over a split-bamboo verandah, the other afloat coursing like a hare downstream or straining against the stream, knees braced, searching with the pole for hold on the rocky bottom. Everybody knows everybody's business. Even a policeman from the interior, body and mind ignorant of local ways, could fathom out what's going on sooner or later.

In fact, one can complicate this further. Out in the sticks, one personally knows the judge, the policeman, the tax collector, the government nurse, the government doctor, and the government teacher, and is likely to know them intimately and through a variety of perspectives that come from sharing overlapping familial and small-town relationships. And yet it is precisely because of this closeness, I believe, that the rule of law and adherence to bureaucratic culture gathers force. Far from diminishing the mystery of the law, personalization augments it.

As I write this, a picture flashes before me of Omar bursting with rage from his dark doorway at Santa María. He is screaming at other members of the Communal Action Committee, an organization with state authority complete with what is called in Colombia its "juridical personality." They have taken the village's radio telephone from him together with its bamboo aerial. Getting hold of a battered typewriter within minutes, he starts typing out a *denuncia* in flowery legalese with the *inspector de policía* looking over his shoulder. Truly the pen is mightier than the sword, even though the typewriter and the machine gun sound similar.

Here at the end of the earth in the midst of a teeming nature, the one means of livelihood everyone wants more than anything else in the world is a job with the government. I doubt I can make this as desperate as it deserves. My thoughts fly to Oblomov, lying in bed day in, day out, paralyzed in his existential funk in one of the memorable nineteenth-century Russian novels relating to bureaucratic miasma in tsarist Russia. A friend born in Santa Bárbara, capital of the Timbiquí, but now living in Bogotá tells me his town produces nothing. Maybe he has an old-fashioned view of production. It's an enchanted city, you might say, lost around a bend in the river, a bunch of two-story wooden houses and a handful of police astride a huge concrete wharf, a no-place doing nothing, producing nothing, yet pumping out the sickly aura of governmental light and lethargy. The state-inspired agricultural projects aimed at developing the local economy, as with coconut and African palm production, lie in ruins; the coconut palms went down with plague; the processing plant for the African palm was placed too far away and the product went rotten.

Fact is all these towns are sustained by the cash income people receive working for state bureaucracies. My friend has one of the best of such posts and stands as the great success story; but what he also indicates is that as soon as someone has money, they leave the coast to live in one of the interior cities. In 1993 with the neo-liberal reforms, María Zuñiga, who was born on the river and lived there most of her long life, told me that the payroll of civil servants in Timbiquí had been reduced from one hundred and six people to seventy-six! And a good thing, too, she added, noting that not-so-many years ago there were just four people, and their secretaries, of course: the mayor, the treasurer, the judge, and the *personero*, the public defender. With her usual forthrightness, one of my schoolteacher friends, born and resident in Guapi and mother of ten, declaimed, "Here nobody works or wants to work. Everyone wants to be bureaucratized," meaning become a teacher like her or get a post in public administration or the health service. *Burocratizarse* was how she put it, full of sweet despair. It means to bureaucratize oneself, or to be bureaucratized, and to me suggests a profoundly bodily and not just a political act, comparable to developing pubic hair or something.

Omar, for example, had made it, big-time. There he was all on his own, up in the last village at the headwaters of the river. No friends. Deserted his family. Brooding and malevolent with the red eyes of a witch. Off to the mine every day. Even sleeping there with the drip-drip of the watery walls for company. And all the time he had a government position as well, "collector of national taxes." God knows what taxes there were to collect up there. When after thirty years he qualified for a government pension, having tried to lord it over the village for much of that time, he was able to retire to the interior and now awaits his pension of four hundred dollars a month in Cali. This is unimaginable. In these villages, women panning gold gain around a dollar a day, and days pass when they find nothing. And the very notion of "retiring"! On the other hand, I should point out that Omar left eight years ago and is still waiting for his pension.

I don't know what Omar did for his tax-collector job or whether he did anything at all. But I got some insight into taxation on the beach at Mulatos right on the coast in the year 2000 when three characters turned up one Sunday afternoon with pistols in holsters demanding the same sort of tax Omar was meant to be collecting way upriver. The young woman in charge of the tiny hotel told them the owner was in the interior and as far as she knew there were no taxes owing. The men crowded into the dark kitchen pointing to the grimy state certificate on the wall, their hands never far from their holsters, but she defiantly stood her ground and refused to pay. She was brave, Serafina. My heart leapt for her dignity. One man said he was a policeman. Last I saw of them they were halfway up a ladder staircase leading into someone's home waving their arms threateningly at the bewildered people inside. "If they came to my place and did that, I'd kill 'em," the young boatman told me, fingering his gold chains.

The dependence on these state posts is incredible, not just at the personal level but for the coast as a whole. They seem just about the only and certainly the major source of cash money for entire towns and villages thus kept afloat in coin of the realm and the hope, always the hope, not to mention the quiet desperation, that more might follow. And one cannot begin to do justice to the importance of the pension. Take Santa María, with its 2,500 people in 280 households, over half of whom must be less than fifteen years of age, which leaves, say, 1,000 adults, many of whom are only partially resident. It has the following personnel on the state payrolls: twenty-two tenured schoolteachers plus eight working on yearly contracts, one nurse, one health promoter, one *inspector de policía*, and twenty "community mothers," each responsible for a crèche in their own home. There are unpaid voluntary state posts as well: two *policía civil*, five members of the *junta de acción comunal*, and thirty people in the *defensa civil*. Discounting these unpaid positions, there is roughly one civil servant for every twenty adults. If we include the unpaid positions, it would be more like one in ten. Now to appreciate the importance of this, you must understand that many (some say 30 percent, others say 60 percent) households have no cash income whatsoever other than what comes from panning for gold in the river, barely enough to buy rice for a meatless, fishless dinner and a swig of *biché* in the street when the sun also rises to shake off the cold and sleep. The village is by-and-large cashless— except for what the state pays as salary and the odd remittances from relatives who have escaped to the interior. In the twelve months of 1998, the outboard motor agency downriver sold but one motor to someone in Santa María, and that was to a teacher with lifelong tenure.

This dependence on the state for cash makes for a dizzying surrealism. Start with the story of the mayor who secretly sold the new equipment destined for the hospital before it had even been uncrated. Or that these three coastal municipalities—Timbiquí, López de Micay, and Guapi—have been designated by the central government as the most corrupt in Colombia, the one judge in the town says. He should know. I remember a friend being told that if he didn't pay that judge under the table, he'd never win his case . . . A helicopter pounds overhead at Santa Bárbara. "Here comes the money," shout the nurses in the hospital, meaning their pay. And rush outside. Only to see it veer away at the last minute. It's like someone stuck a needle in a balloon. We relapse into ourselves amid the smell of ancient chemicals and piles of threadbare sheets and mothers with sick kids who look like they've been waiting years, faces fixed in masks of patience.

When I got to the village in 1998 after a three years' absence, the river was running high and we made excellent time, even though Saturnino's canoe was excruciatingly unstable. Every time it leaned to one side, you involuntarily leaned to the other and the canoe would roll back on top of you. Never had the world's axis been so twisted as we butted the current, dragged the boat over rapids, and defied whirlpools in deep bends where cliffs rise from rushing water. Assassination, guerrilla, youth gangs, kidnapping, death squads, *limpieza,* UZIs, AK-47s, marijuana, cocaine, heroin, *bazuco,* beepers, Nikes, mobile phones, and dark-tinted SUVs had no place here. There was one of the highest mountain ranges in the world between us and *that,* and those mountains were covered with slime, rain, the deadliest snakes in the universe, and endless forests no Nike or death-squad SUV could master.

What a shock, therefore, when I heard soon after I'd arrived that the guerrilla now "come frequently." The last time was eight months ago. That sounds like a long time. Might they not be back soon? Or does it mean they have no intention of returning? These are not academic questions, especially for a foreigner.

There were twenty-three of them, men and women. They built a camp on the other side of the river and wandered through the village for three days trying to recruit anybody over the age of eleven. Nobody wanted to go with them. A flirtatious teenager pretended she was interested but got scared and hid. Each day they came back looking for her. They held a meeting in the village saying their mission was to help the poor. A medical doctor explained he'd given up the soft life to join *the cause*.

"Go ahead," the villagers were assured. "Ask us anything."

"Why do you kill peasants if you aim to help the poor?" asked one villager.

"It's the government which kills them, then says it's us."

They took goods from the tiny store, and, so I was told, when the owner asked to be paid, they said they'd burn his house down if he asked again. But maybe the owner is just saying that so he won't be accused by paramilitaries or the army of collaboration. The small-store owner in rural Colombia is just about the first target of the paras and the army when in fact such a person has no choice but to collaborate. By killing store owners or frightening them into flight, the paras choke off supplies reaching the guerrilla in the hinterland.

The guerrilla came another time to Santa María as well. Two black men and a light-colored woman. They rented a house at the end of the village and said they had come to set up a business cultivating marijuana. People could join them for a fee equivalent to twenty-five dollars, depending on the result of a medical exam administered by the woman, who was a doctor. She showed them a video-tape of her home in Bogotá. It was a mansion. All its fittings were of gold. People still talk about it. More than two hundred people enlisted, even though they had to pay the doctor for medicines if she found them unwell. Luckily she would accept personal jewelry and most women here have exquisite gold earrings made of gold dug with their bare hands. The guerrilla told the villagers to clear the airstrip the Russians had built because by this time it had become overgrown and said they would return by helicopter. Two years later, when I got there, the villagers were still waiting, as were people the length of this and adjoining rivers as well. They were not guerrilla at all! They were daring scam artists. Later I heard the "doctor" was assassinated by the guerrilla south of here in Iscuandé, which

seems like a silly place for her to have gone, as it's notorious for coca and guerrilla. "*Ratatatat,*" Mario, aged nineteen, told me with a big grin. No! The coast is
no longer boring.

It is not just exploitation of the locals that the fake guerrilla and the Russians had in common, but the element of duplicity as well. Only in the case of the
Russians, the intrigue was more *about* them, while with the fake guerrilla it was
by them. In the case of the Russians, there was and will forever remain stories of
dissimulation about the quantity of gold they may or may not have extracted,
and whether it was really gold they were after or uranium. But the two incidents

also seem quite different. The great exploiters, the Russians, turn out with the passage of time to have left a legacy of warm memories in the village, not unlike Julio Arboleda and the French. They were being screwed, like the villagers, yet, unlike them, were lost in the forest, far from home. They used their formidable technical skills with the lathe to help villagers, and they became friends, even though there was a powerful element of legend in this as well as ambivalence— their massive drinking orgies, their eating raw fish, being shirtless and smelly . . . The fake guerrilla, on the other hand, entered as saviors and left as thieves, and what is most surprising to me, and hence salutary, is that without so much as blinking an eyelid, the villagers believed in them. How could such cautious people be so naive as to think that the guerrilla would act this way *and* be willing to pay to join them to the extent of the women parting with their jewelry? "Their poverty!" says a friend downstream. But surely poverty makes you suspicious? Yet it takes a certain amount of naïveté to be a social being, let alone a writer, naïveté being the antenna down which the words come as lightning in social storms.

Justice and cocaine: It is really quite extraordinary how these two hang together or how history has brought them together in our time. What do peasants want? Right now? Justice and cocaine is what they want, right now. Hence the success of the guerrilla. The guerrilla bring justice, big-time, and cocaine, meaning income, also big-time. On the other hand, the state brings no justice, prohibits cocaine, and is seen as utterly corrupt. First thing you'll hear about the FARC guerrilla in southwest Colombia the past fifteen years or more is how they have completely stopped theft in areas under their control. "You can leave clothes hanging on the fence to dry." "You can let the chickens wander wherever they want." As for adultery, getting drunk, or smoking crack: "Three warnings and you're dead." The days of the *ratero,* the thief, are over, my friend. Nothing could be more important to people than stopping theft and violation, and the guerrilla are right on the money in having seen and acted on this. FARC leaflets I have seen where poor white colonists are coming into the coast from the mountains are resolute in their warnings against deforestation. You can fell trees to build a home and furniture but there will be no commerce in lumber. Violators will be heavily fined and the money turned over to the community. As a conservation measure, the guerrilla have enforced a moratorium on all shrimp fishing in the estuary of the Timbiquí during February and March. If you're caught, they take the motor and burn your canoe, dousing it with your own gasoline. The mayors and treasurers of many of the eleven hundred Colombian municipal governments are hauled to secret meetings in the forest or in the mountains where they are lectured and threatened for stealing community funds and for other forms of corruption.

When the guerrilla left Santa María after another visit of three days in April 2000 with dire warnings about another Vietnam-style war in Colombia as a result of impending U.S. intervention, they demanded that in their absence five men draw up a list of thieves in the village. When they returned, they were going to take the people named on the lists and force them to build trails through the forest so as to enhance the mobility of the guerrilla. Imagine yourself in the place of these five men having to come up with a list of names of their neighbors.

July 27, 2000: Last month a man called Puro, short for Purificación, was killed here. He lived on his own in the forest and was found dead by a woman miner on her way home to the village who at first thought he was asleep and drunk on *biché.* Then she saw the gunshot wound. He had a reputation as a sorcerer and people were a little scared of him, even though he was gentle and liked to play with the children of the village. He had one enemy in particular, and people soon put it together that this man, fearing Puro's sorcery, had snuck up one afternoon and killed him. The *inspector de policía* wrote out a *formulario* and sent it downriver to Santa Bárbara, capital of the municipality, but no police arrived because—so it was explained to me in the village—since 1997 Santa María, like many parts of rural Colombia, has been designated by the army as a "red zone," which means that it is subject to military law and no municipal police enter. (The *inspector de policía* is not part of the police.) Since the army is hesitant to enter so far in the forest, Santa María exists in a vacuum of lawlessness. Puro had no family here other than a daughter who works as a servant downriver in Santa Bárbara. There is nobody to date who might take the law into their own hands. The suspect is a young man known as a thief and generally disliked. But there is no official proof because there has been no official investigation. I wonder if he will appear on a list when the guerrilla return.

By July 2000 everything had changed. Even this forgotten coast where never a coca plant had sprouted was being sucked into the vortex of violence and drugs. "On a scale of one to ten," a pontificating young lawyer from the Río Saija told me in the interior, "the danger for you going to Santa María is nine!" FARC guerrilla were said to be in several locations, especially where coca was being cultivated at one point along the Saija (one river north of the Timbiquí) and along the Río Patía (two rivers south). It seemed only a matter of time, brief at that, before everyone would be growing coca. By July 2001, a year later, one person in Santa María had started planting coca and teenagers had been recruited to harvest the coca crop the guerrilla were raising on the Saija. This was progress. At last the deluded gold miners mining no gold would break the habit, just as they had swarmed to the fake guerrilla with its promise of marijuana. Never did the U.S. War on Drugs seem more idiotic, as if on purpose aimed at stimulating the spread and even raising the price of cocaine in addition to furthering bloodshed, corruption, and devastation of both the natural and social environment. Nothing was what it seemed, and surreal fantasies and rumors provided the basis to most everything else. Still, some things were real enough. In April 2001 the paramilitaries came over the top of the mountains separating the coast from the interior and massacred colonists and long-term inhabitants along the headwaters of the Río Naya to the north. At first it was said some sixty, or eighty, people were slain. A year later I heard it was eighteen. In any event, the aim of sowing terror was achieved, and but two months after the massacre, refugees from the Naya were arriving as far south as Timbiquí. A month later there were paramilitaries there as well.

The effervescence of what I call the "breakthrough economy," which is the economy of prohibition and transgression—first you make the rule, then you make a lot of money by breaking it—was now running in high gear as even the wife of the colonel in charge of drug policy in the U.S. embassy in Bogotá sent drugs stateside in the diplomatic pouch. There was a tonic feel to Guapi, too, lonely outpost of the Pacific Coast. All of a sudden there was DirecTV and SKY TV bringing more than one hundred channels from Europe as well as from the United States and Latin America. All of a sudden there was ornate furniture shipped in from Cali, fragile glass-fronted cabinets as high as the ceiling—God knows how they had been carried from the wharf—huge oval-shaped dining tables in heavy carved wood with glass tops capable of seating a presidential cabinet meeting with stiff-backed upholstered dining chairs; double beds in beautiful solid wooden frames, one for each child; exquisite dressers for each child, each drawer running smooth on rollers in this humid, wood-expanding climate; and an explosion in the number of 200-horsepower outboard motors that could make the run up to Central America. In García Márquez's *One Hundred Years of Solitude,* it would be magical realism. To be in this league, you had to have solid support. You had to be in with the army and police and the politicians all the way to the presidential palace, it was said, and you had to be deeply involved with the guerrilla too. The cultivation of the basic staple, the plantain, had virtually ceased and was being brought in at inflated prices from clean-living Ecuador, the Switzerland of South America, safe haven of the U.S. imperium complete with its dollarized currency and spanking new U.S. Air Force base on the Pacific coast at Manta to make strikes into Colombia.

The Colombian state was pretty much a farce, a theatrical affair of puppets and illusions, a house of mirrors for adroit swindlers to crawl around in and reap profits from the bloody conflict and its tireless staging of facades. Lethargy and incompetence saturated every office you entered into no matter where or at what level of administration, like a disease blending sadness with crushing boredom. In the office of the lawyers directly responsible to the governor of the province, the officials spend most of their time searching for lost files. And I thought I was the only person who did that. As you talk across a desk with the attorney general, who has been kind enough to grant you time, a mousy fellow runs in and out of the office. He rustles in a mountain of papers on top of the desk, moving adroitly either side of the AG, mixing hysteria with stoic indifference. Continuously interrupting our conversation, the AG tries to recollect where the missing files might be. "Try there! Try here!" he barks. But the mousy fellow never finds what he is after, despite the whirlwind. Another man with an oversize suit and nervous twitch holds the doorknob as if his life, and that of the entire Colombian state, depends on it, as well it might, his pronounced twitching shaking his head from his forehead down to his chin like a seismic counter registering the earthquakes shaking the ship of state. The moth-eaten carpet and clerks propped up on their elbows, half or fully asleep, others bent deep in furtive whisperings, oblivious to the hordes of petitioners waiting at the door, confirm the feeling that this is as much a dream state as a state. The Governor's Palace, a graceful colonial-style two-story building constructed around an elegant patio, has in recent years suffered a modernist intrusion in the form of a mirror-covered cube, several stories high, stuck in the middle of the patio. Containing dark, low-ceilinged offices, this is where the governor sits, along with his entourage. As you walk along the verandahs of the old building, you see yourself elongated and malformed in the mirrors.

By midday the attorney general has without notice abruptly left for the day to attend to a personal business deal several hours away to the north along the FARC-controlled highway—and this in a week of unbelievably high crisis for the government, the FARC having threatened all the mayors of the forty-four municipalities of the province with death if they did not resign their posts immediately. This included death threats to the judges and prosecutors across the province as well. Only three or four mayors remain at their posts. The army commander has called the others cowards. "First comes the Fatherland," he bellows, "then Democracy, and lastly one's own life!"

The following day four hundred FARC guerrilla fighters with mortars made from metal gas cylinders normally used for kitchen stove use but filled by them with nails open fire on the mountain town of Toribio in Indian country, held by a garrison of some twenty police and an Italian Catholic priest. Two days before, the people of the region had held a protest against the FARC, demanding they be left alone as neutrals. This was their reward. The police fought twenty hours straight then surrendered when out of ammunition. The army never made a showing. Not once. Just left the police to what seemed certain death along with the physical destruction of the town. When asked why the army did not help, the commander—the same one who called the mayors cowards—replied he could not go in until his security was guaranteed.

A day or so later, the U.S. embassy sent in several advisers from Bogotá to discuss the problem of the resigning mayors. After hours of discussion, they suggested the mayors stick to their posts and wear bulletproof vests.

Behind the guerrilla come the paramilitaries. And they, too, depend on drugs shipped statewise. The guerrilla can be tough on civilians, the paras even more so, spectacular massacres of defenseless peasants being their stock in trade. The guerrilla were here a second time, two months back, I was told in 2000 in Santa María. There were about twenty of them and they said they'd be back soon with two hundred more. They said they wanted to arm the young and train them to defend the village against the paras, whom, they said, are likely to come this way soon! (How right they were.) The guerrilla had come early morning, just two of them, as scouts, and then called the rest. It's at dawn or dusk when they come. They had been in a firefight way up on the other side of the cordillera near Argelia, suffered casualties, and now needed a doctor, the only one in the region being at the mouth of the river. A girl guerrilla confided how cold it was at night in their camp in the mountains, two days' march from here, so cold they sleep five together for warmth and even so shiver all night. They paid a man to take them downstream in his canoe, but he is scared now that if the paras come, they will kill him as a collaborator when in fact he had no choice. Assembled in the tiny plaza by the guerrilla, someone from the village asked about the peace process. "What peace!" they replied. "*¡Eso es la paz!*" and fired into the air, saying they had to prepare for another Vietnam War.

A woman in the village tells me that when the guerrilla return, they will entice or force the young to join them. The young are intrigued by these strange visitors. But she is deathly scared. "There's a psychosis of fear throughout the village," she says. And I feel it too. She wants to send her eldest son away to school downstream but hasn't even the money for that, far less move her family to Ecuador, which is what she'd really like to do. I look down the street. Nothing but drizzle and the clang of stones as someone walks in the dark. The coast is no longer boring.

Along with several *narcotraficantes* in 1999, the Dwarf was staying in the Hotel del Río Guapi, three stories high with tinted glass, tiled bathrooms, wicker chairs, AC, and even a reception desk. You can imagine how such a place stands out. Only three blocks away, the wooden shacks lean out over the swirling river, where the cement steps leading down to the water are awash with green plantains, chontaduro nuts, canoes fighting for space, and huge women under straw hats almost three feet across sitting on upturned plastic buckets gutting fish with broken machetes flashing in the cruel sun.

It was 1999 and the first cocaine traffickers had arrived. Like his two bodyguards, the Dwarf came from the state of Córdoba, the heartland of Colombia's paramilitaries, far from here on that other coast bordering the Caribbean. Each bodyguard carried his own *nom de guerre* too, El Flaco and Gomelo. Why these ridiculous names? I thought to myself. To make themselves even more sinister by means of cartoonlike names such as the Dwarf, Skinny, and the Flake? After all, humor is actually very close to violence, as in cartoons, and there is nothing more chilling than absurdity blended with terror.

Not that I knew anything about these strange goings-on, me, stuck up the headwaters of the Timbiquí blissfully ignorant of what was all too obvious to everyone else. Indeed, most every night the Dwarf and his buddies would be at the hotel carousing with the police. In the morning he'd take off in a fast launch for the village of El Charco up the Río Tapaje. It was a beautiful river—she added—but is now full of chemicals from the cocaine labs. It is also the river that runs past a Spanish galleon rich in silver and gold, so they say, the shipwreck that led to the founding of the strange colony of white folks known as Mulatos. But who cares about sunken treasure now?

I first heard of the Dwarf two years later when I felt a tickling of my ribs as I was about to board a flight from Cali to Popayán, it now being too dangerous for a foreigner or indeed anyone with money in the bank to travel by land because the FARC had control of the highway. There was only ten minutes in which to talk.

"I heard you were running with the paramilitaries?" I blurted.

"He was my boyfriend," she told me. "At first I thought he was a *narco-traficante.*"

"Isn't that weird," I asked, perhaps a little jealous. "Isn't that weird to have a narco for a boyfriend?"

"Not really!" she said without expression. "If they get killed, it would be in Cali or Medellin. The paid killers on motorbikes—the *sicarios*—they haven't gotten to Guapi yet." Love is a funny thing. Here she was giving me the scoop, yet what I was most aware of was her face as a silhouetted image buried deep in my heart, framed by lemons heaped in the incandescent aluminum cooler in the restaurant in the Cali airport where we were sitting.

In July 2001 the Dwarf invited her to El Charco to stay for a while. After a few days he went upriver. At night. The launch was fast and well equipped with lights that rotate from side to side scanning the river. She soon realized he was more than a cocaine trafficker. He was a leader of a paramilitary group within the Bloque Calima that holds jurisdiction from Calima, close to Cali, all the way south from Buenaventura to Guapi, where it connects with the Bloque Nariño, which extends to Ecuador.

"I wanted to converse with you for such a long time," she said. My heart leapt. "Why?"

"Because it's so different to what people think."

"How so?"

"Because before they do anything, they advise the authorities, like when they're going to kill someone . . ."

"What authorities? The police?"

"Yes! And the state prosecutors."

"And the authorities get paid off?"

"Of course!"

"And the army . . . ?" I asked, nervously glancing at my wristwatch as the plane was about to leave.

"Well, in Guapi it's the navy. They have a base there, and we were in contact with them on a daily basis, either with a messenger or by radio using a code."

We hugged and I saw her walk straight to a car that had been waiting at the entrance to the airport. In the plane I kept seeing her face against the lemons and wondered why she had wanted, as she put it, to converse with me so badly. Late that night I called her on her cell phone and suggested she catch the bus to where I was staying in Popayán at my expense so we could talk without being hassled. Her response was immediate. "¡Sí, señor!" Like her mother, she made decisions on the spot.

Next morning she turned up with her more than handsome brother and two small boys about five years of age. One was her son; the other was his. I took her to the archive to show her what I was working on and to introduce her to the director, who helped me so much in finding early-nineteenth-century documents concerning the slave mines of San Vicente along the Timbiquí. The director was thrilled to meet someone from the coast and led her on a tour through the dark recesses of the Spanish colony as preserved in the crumbling linen-based documents bound in heavy leather volumes.

We found a place to sit outside where nobody could overhear us by the arch bridge just below the statue of Julio Arboleda outside of the majestic Banco de la República. It was lunchtime and two welders were playing football on the

grassy flat by the stream next to their shop. Every now and again, a shady character or group of young men would walk slowly by, making me nervous. We started
at the beginning but I got lost in details and made notes that I completed at night
alone in my hotel room, watching her story fall into several stages:

Discovery & Awakening
Dispenser of Justice
Fear of Guerrilla Attack
Return of El Tío, War within the Paras
Withdrawal
&
The Pieces Come Together

Discovery & Awakening: In July 2001, a few days after the Dwarf left her in
El Charco and proceeded upriver to supervise his coca fields, she received a
strange call on her cell phone. It was from a man called Bocanegra, which translates as Blackmouth. He was upriver, mad as hell.

"Where are the medicines?" he demanded. "Where's the *panela,* the canned
food, and the gasoline?"

Mystified, she asked why he was calling her.

"Don't you know?" he bellowed. "Aren't you with the Dwarf?" And he explained to her that the Dwarf was leader of a band of paramilitaries, most of
whom were stationed at the coca fields upstream from where he was calling.

As the days went by, she learned a good deal more. Under the Dwarf, there
were two commanders in charge of some fifty paramilitaries upriver by the coca
fields, and another fifteen in El Charco. There was the military commander,
namely, Blackmouth, and a finance commander, whose *nom de guerre* was
Kalimán—a supernaturally empowered character in a wildly popular 1970s radio
program listened to by adults as well as children. Kalimán, the radio serial version,
not the paramilitary, was from the Middle East and blessed with extraordinary
mental powers and telepathy as well. He was known as *el hombre invencible* (not
to be confused with William Burroughs, who, down on junk and finding himself
as a writer in Morocco, liked to fancy himself as *el hombre invisible* when walking
through the market). Many of the phrases became clichés enlivening everyday
speech, peasant and working class. When the Banco de la República in Pasto in

the southern highlands was broken into by means of a tunnel laboriously excavated over months from the kiosk just outside, selling cigarettes and candies, the night watchman was reported as saying: "I suspected it from the beginning"—*Lo sospeché desde el principio*—a phrase no episode of *Kalimán* could be without.

Blackmouth's job was to drill his troops (some of whom had been trained on a hacienda adjoining the busy road between Cali and Buenaventura) and to be responsible for all weapons and uniforms. On the other hand, Kalimán was responsible for the *gramaje,* or tax, that the drug traffickers from Cali and Medellin had to pay the paramilitaries for each kilo of semi-prepared cocaine known as base that they bought from the local peasantry. It was up to him that the salaries equivalent to U.S. $350 a month, twice the country's basic wage, were paid on time.

She also learned about coca production, how the local peasants not only cultivate the coca plants—*la peruana* is the variety preferred because it matures in seven months—but have to prepare in situ what is known as base from the harvested leaves, and this is done, she explained to me, by soaking the leaves in gasoline, leaving the mix covered, while stirring occasionally. After three to four days the leaves are squeezed, the gasoline evaporates, and the paste is allowed to dry so that when you test it with a lit match, no sparks are emitted. I could see she was proud of being on top of all this detail, which I, too, was voraciously trying to assimilate, especially the thing about the sparks. In my mind's eye, I could see them sputtering in the dark recess of some jungle hideaway with Julio Arboleda right behind me pretending to see nothing, his gaze fixed on something invisible yet transcendent on the remote horizon to which nobody middle class and upward in Popayán would dare travel to nowadays on account of the FARC.

Dispenser of Justice: The paras offered her a job as their accountant, a job she kept for the three months she was with them. Her responsibilities included keeping track of supplies from Guapi and Buenaventura that had to be gotten upriver to the paras at the coca fields. Her mother was furious with her, and her father called just about every day he was so worried.

The most curious thing was the way people in El Charco came asking her to solve their problems. They assumed she was a paramilitary and hence a power in the region. One fellow came with a sad story about some land he'd let a neighbor use in 1998, but now the neighbor refused to vacate it. Could she force him out, please? Another man had a son aged twenty-four addicted to *bazuco,* a residue of cocaine, who was stealing left and right. Could she kill him, please? She went and talked to the son. He stopped smoking at home, cut back on his intake, and a few weeks later came to her, asking if she could help him get his TV set back from his father's lover, who had taken it to her house. Another time she was abused by a drunken wharf laborer she caught stealing beer from the cargo brought in by the coastal boats. Next day she called a meeting of the five men responsible for loading and unloading cargo and told them they had to cease stealing. The man who had abused her groveled at her feet, pleading forgiveness. Another time the paramilitaries upriver killed a local man—an "accident"—and refused to hand over his body to his family at whose request she intervened and got the body returned. So grateful was the father that he offered her a million pesos (U.S. $500).

Fear of Guerrilla Attack: She heard people in El Charco saying the guerrilla were going to take over the town. She had trouble sleeping. One night a canoe came round the bend in the river with five armed men. Terrified, she stayed awake the whole night smoking cigarettes, wondering if they were guerrilla scouts. Next day the Dwarf sent down three men to guard her and he himself gave her a crash course in the use of small arms. He taught her to dismantle and put together a Browning blindfolded. The catch is more complicated, she explained, than the Italian model she was first offered but is more secure. I was being initiated.

Return of El Tío: At the end of two months, she decided to leave, but he wanted her to stay and offered to pay her, handsomely at that, the equivalent of U.S. $600 a month. "But they would never pay me that much," she said. "The Dwarf is not the one who pays! The paymaster comes from Buenaventura and is strict. He paid me only 400 dollars [in pesos] for two months' work and after that 175 for the third month."

It seems time was running out for the Dwarf. He was chief of the Río Tapaje, but word came down he was overspending and shouldn't have been in that river in the first place. One day El Tío, leader of the southernmost group of paras, turned up with a bunch of men and disarmed the Dwarf along with ten of his followers in Satinga near the mouth of the Tapaje. The Dwarf retaliated with threats. El Tío returned with almost one hundred men, heavily armed, including an abundant supply of grenades, and opened fire on the Dwarf and his thirty men, capsizing them into the water. There was nothing left for the Dwarf to do but claim it was all an unfortunate misunderstanding and that he would pull his men out from the coca fields of the Tapaje.

Withdrawal: "A map! A map! I need a map!" The Dwarf was hysterical. None of the paras knew where they were, how to get there, and how the different rivers, swamps, estuaries, and *esteros* linking the rivers through the swamps related to one another. It was up to her to get them a map and orient them as to their new territory. "Is this for real?" I asked her. "That they didn't even know their way around?"

The deal with El Tío was that he would resume control of the Tapaje while the Dwarf could have the rivers north of there; namely (in order north to south), the López de Micay, Saija, Timbiquí, and Guapi. They must have known López de Micay and Saija had long had guerrilla units, and that coca was being cultivated by the FARC up the Saija.

The Dwarf and his group withdrew to the town of Guapi to lick their wounds. Some went away on vacation. Others took sick leave. Their number dropped to about thirty, yet the Dwarf, restless for action, decided on a little excursion up the Timbiquí. With his reduced group, he occupied a house on the riverbank ten minutes by launch upstream from Santa Bárbara, made every passing vessel subject to search, and an Indian was killed as a result. It was another "accident." The victim had—in her words—acted stupidly under interrogation. Word spread quickly and the rumors were alarming. Another paramilitary massacre seemed imminent, especially by the time the rumors reached the interior of the country from where the governor of the province, the first Indian governor ever, sent an army helicopter to Santa Bárbara, where, surprisingly, the local authorities, police and mayor, said there was no cause for concern, and the situation calmed down. ("The paras and the police—they work together," my boatman had told me earlier, locking his forefingers together.) Shortly thereafter the paras left the river. They had been there three weeks only. That was October 2001.

The Pieces Come Together: What I had been told earlier by people upriver was that there had been a great deal of consternation in the lower Timbiquí. The paras would descend on Santa Bárbara at night, demanding food and liquor, and there was a lot of action in the red-light district as well. After the paras killed the Indian, the army gave them three days to leave.

I'd always assumed the bad guys were well organized and knew what they were doing. But now I had to think again. On the one hand, it all seemed so amateurish. On the other hand, this blundering seemed guaranteed to create even worse fear. Was this view I was being offered from the inside a comfort or cause for more concern?

Early June 2002, five weeks before she and I were sitting talking by the arch bridge in Popayán, the Colombian army entered the Río Saija and forced the guerrilla to flee, incinerating their camp. Three weeks later, the Dwarf with some seventy men entered the breach created by the army. Of course I didn't know it was the Dwarf. It was she who told me all this later, making the chaotic reality assume a semblance of order, one crazy step leading to the next. It was by virtue of her having been part of it that allowed me to see it with some depth and a human, all-too-human, reality. It wasn't only the particular things she was telling me. Just as important was her presence uniting me to that other reality, making it less abstract and less phantasmic, indeed, less terrifying. What before had been ominous shadows of death and dismemberment streaking up rivers and clawing across the cordillera, paralyzing one's will and ability to think, now seemed emptied of its mythic power, the paras' main weapon.

I felt I was far more in control of the facts than I had been a week earlier, when, after a year's absence, I had returned to the area a few days after the paramilitary incursion into the Saija. It was a dangerous time. I accompanied skittish government human rights officials expecting a terrible crisis of displaced people. They spent hours locked in discussions with the mayor of Timbiquí in Santa Bárbara, and as night fell they fled in their launch for the relative safety of Guapi.

I stayed. And for me the strangest thing in Santa Bárbara was not the displaced persons, of whom there seemed few, but the occasional white man walking around calm and self-possessed. "Look!" says Buena Gente excitedly. "Look! There goes one!" and he grabs me by the wrist and hauls me out-of-doors to see a recently arrived *paisa* who was said to be cultivating fields of coca up a branch of the Timbiquí not even one kilometer out of town, a *paisa* who steadfastly refuses to look at us so boisterously looking at him as if he were a freak in a freak show. There were three of four others like him, bringing in coca cuttings to plant along with money to hire locals by the day to do the planting and harvesting. Doña Mercedes shows me another such "freak" standing confident and strong looking on the street corner as she tells me things look normal, but they're not. Everyone lives *muy atensionada en la incertidumbre,* waiting for hell to break loose. I notice her store now has no outboard motors or power saws for sale. The economy must be dismal. Her husband is living in the interior because of threats of kidnapping.

"How amazing these 'freaks' must be," I say to myself, "to come here like this so brazen, not knowing anyone here, and prepared to take on the violence of the guerrilla, paramilitaries, and, lets not forget, the Colombian government as well."

And talking about the Colombian government, where is it? Well, the mayor can do nothing to stop the coca because, quite apart from the fact that he may be paid off, his cousin tells me the coca guys have told him he'll be killed if he interferes. And in the inimitable Colombian lingo you hear so much nowadays, he is supposedly also an *objetivo militar,* which means that the guerrilla have put it around that they are going to kill him. As for the police, my friend draws her finger across her throat; they daren't interfere either. So as doña Mercedes says, everything looks normal. Just another Colombian Potemkin village where the police are busy polishing their crumpled black boots and rearranging their sandbag barricades.

Given the confusion and double-talk, let alone the memorable image of that finger drawn across the throat, I wondered what the government human rights people had picked up from their hours of discussion behind closed doors with the mayor and his assistants. I also wondered what use their information could be, for mostly everyone repeats the same tired language. You quickly learn a sort of "human rights crisis talk" of paternalistic gesturing laced with legalisms pumped up with workhorse phrases about the "situation being *muy delicado*" or "*muy complicado,*" how the Church is doing a great job "with the base," and so forth. There was indignation about lack of governmental support. "As soon as we're back in Bogotá, we're going to contact the office of the United Nations and get them to send observers. That's the only way you can get the government to wake up . . ."

God help us, I thought. One has to resort to these childish maneuvers to get one part of the government to chase the other, and everyone knows through the haze of confusion and rumor that at the most real level of all, far from the United Nations and Bogotá, everyone is corrupt or corrupted, and it will remain that way so long as coca is illegal, the freaky white guys stand tall on the street corners, girls fall in love with narcos and paras, while the Dwarf or his successor is having a high old time back there with his police buddies carousing in the wicker chairs behind the tinted glass of the Hotel del Río Guapi, where the ever-diminishing tourists from Bogotá stop over on their way to the island of Gorgona to go look at whales.

cement & speed

Upstate New York where I live near Rosendale in the summer, you find the remains of nineteenth-century stone kilns in which limestone was burned to a fine powder for cement. Abandoned limestone mines run for miles through the hills. Every so often you find a weathered blue sign by the road like this one:

DISCOVERY OF CEMENT
At Bruceville, Nathaniel
Bruce burned in a blacksmith's
forge some native rock and
discovered cement in 1818.

State Education
Department 1939

Actually cement was "discovered" in many places and at different times in Europe and North America from the late eighteenth century onward. And it was not really discovered but rediscovered, because it was used in ancient Egypt as well as in ancient Greece and Rome. This repetition and the centuries of forgetting between its ancient and its modern discoveries seem more than fitting for such a material, mimetic in the following ways: (1) Its modern "discovery" mimes its ancient past; (2) the name given it around 1800 as "cement rock" reminds us today of the obvious yet forgotten wonder of synthetic materials that mimic natural ones; and (3) to be specific, the fact it can be molded and shaped as liquid stone allows it to mimic many forms—as modernist architects such as Corbusier made into a virtual religion. One hundred years ago, this Rosendale cement found many buyers and was famous for its durability. Real rock, we could say. It took thirty days to harden, I am told, was the cement used to build the Brooklyn Bridge, and for a long time it was stipulated in New York State law that a certain percentage of cement used on state freeways had to come from Rosendale. Hard as stone, they said. But Portland cement, patented in 1824 in England and developed in the United States by midcentury, hardened in thirty hours. Not so hard, but it did the job and destroyed the market for the cement from around here. The cement industry disappeared, but the stones of the kilns remain like crumbling altars in the hardwood forests of ash and maple. There are myths as well. People around here say the White House in Washington stores its files in the unused mines that honeycomb the hills.

Cement is made by burning limestone in stone kilns. Andean Indians, however, put limestone in their mouth, not to make cement, but to add to the coca leaves they chew so as to more speedily release the effects for which cocaine is famous. In the mountain peaks above El Bordo in the Cordillera Central of Cauca, Colombia, sits the tiny village of Almaguer, whitewashed adobe huts running along a steep ridge under a blue-domed sky. It was one of the very first gold-mining settlements in the New World, but nobody has mined there in a long time. Indian women sit on the ground there on market day in irregular rows in the midday sun. The sky is dazzling up there and the air bone dry. They are selling coca leaves carried over the hills in woven cloth bags that seem like they will last forever. Next to each bag are cakes of lime to chew along with the coca. Down in the valley, young men in civilian clothes with acne and long hair stop the bus with machine guns looking for cocaine. They open up your 35-mm film canisters. It is 1976, long before the war started. I'd never even heard of cocaine outside of the dentist's office. When I got off the bus in El Bordo down in the valley on my way to Almaguer, a chubby young man asked me if I was CIA. What was I meant to say? Yes? No? Way up the mountain where the sky touches your face, a strangely dressed man kept following us on the mountain paths, always a few hundred feet behind on those winding trails. Something was brewing up there. But all you need is limestone, aka cement. The coca is everywhere.

When the Colombian government, urged on by the United States in the 1980s, blocked the importation of the chemicals needed to process cocaine from coca, the chemists soon came up with a substitute. What do you think it was? Cement! Soon cement trucks were heaving their way across the mountains and down into the jungle. An army colonel said not so long ago there was enough cement carried into the Putumayo to pave that enormous province several times over. Since the army controls all the checkpoints, the colonel must know what he's talking about. Since the army controls all the checkpoints, you would think maybe they would have stopped all that cement. But who can argue against cement, the backbone of modernity?

Cement is intimately related to water. It needs water to harden. This seems counterintuitive. The first-century Roman architect and builder Vitruvius understood stone as composed of four elements: air, earth, fire, and water. As a builder, he wanted a substance like stone but malleable. When you stop to think about it, this is like something out of a fairy tale: *like stone but malleable.* Smashing up limestone into small particles and mixing them with sand was not good enough, for there was neither unification nor hardening. That could only come with intense heat, which left the stone porous: "The water and air, therefore, which are in the substance of the stones, being thus discharged and expelled, and the latent heat only remaining, upon being replenished with water, which repels the fire, they recover their vigor and the water entering the vacuities occasions a fermentation; the substance of the lime is thus refrigerated and the superabundant heat ejected."[1] I quote at length because this is such a vivid example of the ancient four-element theory of being that preoccupied the pre-Socratic philosophers. It

---

1. Stephen Sass, *The Substance of Civilization: Materials and Human History from the Stone Age to the Age of Silicon* (New York: Arcade, 1988), p. 130; R. H. Bogue, *The Chemistry of Portland Cement* (New York: Reinholt, 1955), p. 5.

is vivid in that it makes stones seem alive and capable of amazing metamorphoses once they have been processed by man, pulverized to a powder and heated. You start with stone. You make a powder. And then in the process of building, you add water and end up with a new form of "stone" in accord with the shape desired. It sounds like magic but we call it technology.

In Guapi, on the coast, cement buildings stand out as signs of the modern and the good. What a contrast such buildings make with the older wooden houses! Cement comes on oceangoing boats from Buenaventura, while lumber comes from the trees upriver, although wood is becoming scarcer and certain types of hardwood, such as *chachajo,* are almost impossible to find along the mid- to lower reaches of the Río Timbiquí, for instance. The older wooden houses in Guapi and Santa Bárbara are often huge, a few almost the size of a city block, two tall stories in height. Inside, the houses are dark and musty. The floor creaks underfoot. The walls between bedrooms are opaque to head level and then become slats to assist the circulation of air, such that at night when a light is burning, striated rectangular shadows like a Piet Mondrian painting splay across the interior walls and ceilings and out onto the street. When you sleep, you hear

the person in the next room sleeping, an occasional creak or a whimper. The staircases are the steepest I have encountered, steeper than the seventeenth-century houses in Amsterdam, for instance. Most wooden houses are badly in need of repair. Rarely are they painted. The color is a patchwork quilt of grays and browns, of old and new planking wherever a new side has been built or a patch made. The planks are not tightly joined, one next to the other, like weatherboarding. Instead, their edges abut one another, leaving a slight gap. As you walk the street, it seems like the walls of the houses are passing you on either side as a moving series of verticals and horizontals, depending on how the planks have been nailed. Improvisation is ubiquitous, each wall a different mosaic. This suggests flexibility, which is indeed true, as put to the test by earthquakes, which frequent the coast and are more destructive of cement buildings.[2] The downside with wood is fire, which swept through Guapi in 1933 and 1967, burning much of the town to the ground, and devastating fires like this have occurred in all the towns of the coast.[3] But cement is fire resistant and lasts far longer than wood. In 1955 a new batch of Catholic priests trained local men in reinforced concrete construction and built a huge Gothic church with flying buttresses and a lacelike cement brick superstructure for ventilation. Like all cement buildings here, it has become mottled with fungus so it seems even more worn down by the Tropics than the older wooden buildings.

After the church was built, the cement workers went out to sea in their pea-green boats where they built the prison on the island of Gorgona. Then they went back to Guapi and built the Banco de la República.

> the church
> the prison
> the bank

Every so often in Guapi, I come across an elaborately carved wooden bedstead—made by the prisoners in Gorgona years ago. This is no bed for mortals

---

2. Gustavo Wilches-Chaux, H. Meyer, and A. Velásquez, "La Costa Brava," in *Colombia Pacífico,* 2 vols., ed. Pablo Leyva Franco (Bogotá: FEN, 1993), vol. 2, p. 491.

3. Wilches-Chaux et al., "La Costa Brava," p. 491.

but for gods. The carving craves wood, eats wood, makes love with the wooden-ness of wood till it fuses with it and becomes one with the wood it chisels at and deflects into flower petals and whales by whose side scamper dolphins across ocean waves lit up by flights of angels. This is the ancient art of mimesis, with a vengeance, wood on the move, woody metamorphoses speaking poetry as the prisoner with all the pressed-in time in the world eases his chisel softly round the bends. In my friend's cement house with its grand echoes and hard-tiled floor, her bed is the one objet d'art of which the house can boast. When you open the bedroom door, the bed radiates, like lifting the lid of a pirate's treasure chest.

This cement that is so expensive and comes from so far away, from the in-terior and sometimes from neighboring countries, is also poured out in immense quantities for landing stages and steps for canoes and larger boats. You only have to see how treacherous a muddy bank becomes after a few weeks of use to appre-ciate solid cement underfoot. Slimy black river mud and mottled cement unite in one happy interface. One descends from concrete to mud and one ascends from mud to concrete as part of one's amphibious being.

Even though there are hens here, eggs come from the interior of the country, like cement. The hens lay only if fed corn and that's not easy to come by. On the cement landing steps at Santa Bárbara, I see black hens in crates unloaded from Buenaventura. And here I am in the bosom of nature, together with imported hens.

It will take four hundred bags of cement each weighing a hundred pounds to replace the gravel steps on either side of the church on the hill at Santa María. One dugout canoe poled upstream by two men can carry ten bags from Santa Bárbara and takes two days of Herculean labor.

Speed: Talking with kids at Guapi, I was amused to realize the way they referred to motorized river craft was by a number—*nueve nueve, quince, veinte y cinco, setenta y cinco*—meaning the horsepower of the outboard motor hitched to the stern. There are many canoes still with the beautiful pointed ends fore and aft, but the squat-ended, high-sided dugout with the motor screwed astern is now a major feature on the rivers, despite the fabulous expense of the motors and gasoline, which, like cement and black hens, come from the interior.

At the wharf at Santa Bárbara, launches come in at great speed. Their bows point way up in the sky. The stern is sunk deep in the water. The *motorista* cuts the motor and puts the boat in a tight curve as it settles into the water and coasts to the cement steps. Often the boat carries a government employee or a small group of such. The ones from the interior assume a look of superiority that belies their trepidation as regards the new world enclosing them as the launch loses speed and nature reasserts itself in a tepid, rocking motion and the clammy heat gels. With its supernaturally endowed speed across the surface of the water, this boat is their sign of power, their privilege, and their escape from all that now threatens. The motors and their speed seem to be saying, "Look! Out there mud and mangroves, mosquitoes, rain, and unremitting poverty, a forlorn world buried in amphibious horror! But with me and my birdlike speed skimming the waters, you are not only removed from the raw nastiness of nature. You turn it into a spectacle like the view from a train window. What does *place* mean now? *Place* has become an unraveling ribbon of time, and the ribbon is yours to put in your pocket as a trophy."

But the motors lie. The godlike promise of speed's glory is torture. The human body disintegrates into a shuddering mess, and the rain darts like hot needles into your eyes so you are forced to look down at your feet all the time. Passengers become inert matter, turned inward into their agony waiting with animal-like patience for the journey to end. Your actual physical body that you thought you knew so well becomes a dumb insensate part of the surge of gray river water. Yes, the motors lie. Far from being removed from the raw nastiness, far from having nature as spectacle, you enter deep into the shuddering resistance of nature.

Otherwise, life is slow. In fact, it's stopped. Maybe you could even say life here is going backward. Think, therefore, what it must be like, to hurtle through the elements like this, defying basic laws of physics and God. Prometheus unchained. Then the motor cuts and it's all over. The boat sinks down with a sigh. You hear the sound of the river once again. You stagger up the steps in the sun's steamy glare, a few greetings, and it all comes to a standstill. The waiting that is life begins once more. A meal of rice and warmed-up tinned tuna, if you're lucky, and a night of Peruvian TV adulating the president, the white race, and explosively fragmented ads for beer in the English language. Then the generator cuts out at 10:30. No postal service. No telephone service since many months, and even when there is one, there is none, it being so inefficient.

But speed. Yes! That we do have. It's addictive, the poetry of the gods, bow lifting, the spray cascading in the fan-shaped wake, wreaking havoc on lesser vessels, the noise preventing all speech, the thudding on the hull as we skip from wave to shuddering wave out in the open estuary. All this is new. And escalating. Like the arms' race or the 20 percent inflation the country's suffered under for as long as I can remember—inflation being the central bank's way of raising taxes in a country where the rich are untaxable (but not unkidnappable). No sooner have we gotten used to the 9.9, than it's the 15 horsepower, and after that the 30, and so on it goes now to 200 horsepower, and instead of just one huge motor, you install two! When I first traveled from Guapi to Santa Bárbara in 1971, and felt very lucky to arrive alive, the trip took the best part of a day with a 15-horsepower motor. Now in the store owner's double-engined open boat carrying twelve passengers, all without life jackets, it can be done in one hour! This must be the closest thing to flying possible, while still technically in the water.

Farther north, the Embera Indians of the Chocó and southern Panamá have stories of phantom gringo boats with zombie crews, creatures of diabolic realms that spell great danger. Shamans make models of such boats to use in curing séances. The model works by sympathetic magic. In copying the phantom boat, you get its mysterious power. Now with the benefit of our 200-horsepower engines, we too have become zombies stock-still in our faster-than-light phantom gringo boat.

As we head out of the estuary, the hull thumps on the waves. The boat shudders with each concussion. Sometimes we surf on the waves as we round the point near the reef. Big-beaked birds fly in formation low over the sea under the canopy of a gray sky. We are on parallel tracks for a while, the birds and us. We move in a straight line, but the horizon has a different trajectory. It circles us, leaving the coast a tiny smudge without the slightest distinguishing feature. We are no less empty than the emptiness we smash through.

Why the speed? Is it required for some practical reason, or is it for the thrill, which turns out to be an ordeal, the thrill of being modern as well as the thrill of speed itself? Once you've tried to sort through this, you'll find you're asking a quite different question. Especially on the coast, where life is so slow. Speed takes you to the very opposite of speed. It takes you to the river's own power, to two women in white dresses standing precariously balanced, their bodies tensed and slightly bent, poling downstream a dugout canoe filled with green plantains like giant fingers beautifully bunched amidships, maneuvering their slender vessel through rapids. At times the canoe moves like a shot from a gun. One slip and its all over. Other times it seems suspended as on a glass surface. Like insects, its long poles scratch the surface, and the whole scene seems to move with them and not just the canoe. The river slips past and takes slices of the world with it. A movie screen. Or it may be way out in the calm of the estuary, paddles slowly dipping as if there's all day and tomorrow too, slipping across the surface of deep muddy waters.

But the vessel was once even stiller and slower, standing upright in the forest around Santa María where the best and last trees for canoes exist. It was cut down by hand, hollowed out and roughly shaped by ax in the forest where it lay, then dragged to the village. Enter the *labrador*. The woodman. There are around fifteen in Santa María. For this mining town is also a world of wood. Even the basic tool of mining is made of wood: the *batea* in which Lilia's newborn now lies, just the eyes peering out of swaddling clothes. The wood for the *batea* comes from what is left over in the making of a canoe, and *bateas* come in two sizes. The larger is for panning gold. The smaller, more ellipsoid but still basically a saucer of wood, is used as a baby's cradle. So:

trees

    canoes

        gold

           child

                a circle or an ellipse

The *labrador* uses nothing but an ax, a machete, and two kinds of small planes, one for flat surfaces and one for the interior curves. Nearly all craft on the coast have been made this way, tree trunks become boats, every tiny angle and indentation bearing the mark of the hand of its maker. Vicente Angulo looks at me young and strong as he puts the finishing touches with nothing more than a machete to a beautiful paddle seven feet long, made of one of the hardest woods, *chachajo,* his face in a grimace, belied by an expansive smile. "You've no idea how much work it is with an ax. How it gets to you, aching deep in your body. How much we'd give for a chain saw." But there is only one power saw in the village. The man who owns and lives off it is very thin, very nice, has a crumpled leg, and his tumbledown little house on stilts is stuck way out beyond the tail end of the village. In fact, he is not from the village. He comes from way downriver. How much *chachajo* or *palo de mulato* for canoes would there be left if everyone here had a chain saw?

I met a man who owned a sawmill. It was way downriver in the estuary where the bigger boats dock against piles of dark weathered lumber, one plank slipped flat on top of the next so as to form an improvised wharf from a mountain of rotting wood. He was a big man with a generous nature who had long ago given up physical labor. His wife and children lived in Cali, and he stayed most of the time with his mother, who lived on the river in an empty two-story wooden house with a steep staircase and creaky interiors. For him, the coast was memories and a place to exploit. His existence here was an enforced one, sweetened, no doubt, by the fact he had one of the better-paying "jobs" with the municipal administration as well. What surprised me was that while he could identify cut lumber easily, he could not identify the living trees from which the lumber came.

Men paddle standing up with those long paddles like Vicente Angula was making. Women's paddles are half as long, and they paddle with long, slow, elegant strokes, sitting on tiny wooden seats with tiny backrests. Sometimes you see them paddling with a baby at the breast.

There would be no 200-horsepower motors without cocaine, and cocaine is what allows cement to rise in the streets of the coastal town like dream castles. I cannot think of anywhere else in the world—or at least in my world—where speed can actually be experienced like this: *fulsomely*. It is common enough to hear of speed in relation to electronic mail and transfers of cash, air travel, and fax machines. Yet such speed remains at a stage of remove. The human body remains encased in a standard environment as in a capsule. Not so, however, on the water with two giant Yamaha outboards at full throttle.

A Lesson in Natural History: It was only on the coast that I became aware of the change in time. The incoming president of the Republic, a man named César Gavíria, had at one shot introduced neo-liberal economic policy and U.S.-inspired daylight saving time to relieve pressure on the nation's electricity supply, and somehow, with the defeat of Marxism and the triumph of free-marketeering dogma, this all seemed tied into the arrival of the gold-digging Russians. As the machinery clambering up the Río Timbiquí indicated, it was the time of the "economic opening," President Gavíria's "*apertura económica.*" So, we ask, was this bold attempt to change the time the last flicker of the authoritarian state surrendering its power to the market? Or, better still, did it not illustrate the thesis that the free market is only free to the extent that the state legislates basic categories of experience, including the Kantian ones of space, cause, and time itself?

The radio, TV, banks, government offices, and commercial airlines fell into line. But on the coast, most people, including the church in Guapi and the schools there, followed the old hour so that there were two times ticking away an hour apart and even more opportunity for creative games with time. And when people tried to confirm which time was meant, they would ask, "*Hora Gavíria?*"— Gavírian time?—testimony to a love of confusion no less than admiration for the man who had tried to change time. For even behind the anonymity of the clock face and its immaculate working lurks the invisible hand of a person, but it needs a joke to reveal its unconscious presence. To cap it off, there was a rumor along the river that Gavíria himself was a partner in the Russian mine and had visited there at least once by helicopter.

Changing the clock for daylight saving time is routine in many First World countries. It means adjusting the workday more finely to the daylight hours, in other words, more efficiently exploiting the energy of the sun so as to more efficiently exploit the energy of people. On the coast this change created two clocks that confused time itself, locked into the heady drama of the cosmic struggle between a mere man and the sun itself, or at least between the modern state and our ancient friend, the sun. What is at stake in this drama is the domination of nature, including man's inner nature, the sense of time in relation to the dawn's spreading light. "The sun gives without receiving," says Bataille.[4] Speed, gold, and cocaine all partake of that logic, that love of giving over and over again without restraint. But only divers do it right. Blood pours from their noses. Their life is on the line. The risks are huge. The rewards might be huge too. Their hands become their eyes as they pull the sun down through the water into the opaque green murk at the bottom of the river and so transform it into gold.

4. Georges Bataille, *The Accursed Share: An Essay on General Economy,* vol. 1, *Consumption,* trans. Robert Hurley (New York: Zone Books, 1988), p. 28.

my coca

miasma

Finding our way through mud and mangroves, I become aware there is no border between land and sea. What exists is not a coast but a blur. The mangroves
claw at the mud, like me, matter falling through time with a strange comfort in a
sucking motion where being coagulates in a unity of sticky shadows. This morass
is definitely the long-sought in-between of sludge rising and falling with the tide,
home to all manner of life-forms, the lunar zone of rot and decay in whose slow,
eternal rhythms clouds of shrimp waft and crabs hide. Gold and cocaine cause a
similar ferment that we choose to call corruption. Mangrove swamps offer comfort here, being nature's own corruption, where death and life sustain one another in extremis, and matter—formless matter—spreads itself like a snail's silver trail in the moonlight.

Because of the incessant rain and mad energy of the rivers, the soil of the increasingly deforested mountains washes down to rest here, graveyard of the nation-state. One day all that will be left of the west will be the bleached bones of mountains of bedrock where gold once lay with its fossils, and the remainder, the vast remainder we remember so well as forested dips in an ocean of jungle and blue mountain ridges, all this once-upon-a-time will be silt suspended in these mangroves, a nation decomposed into globules midway between being and nothingness, where the Pacific calls and gulls plunge, visible as sprays of water just beyond this zone of fertility, the beginning as well as the end of life.

If I seem like a mad poet on the loose, desperate for new experience, dreaming of exaggerated realities, let me cite Robert Cooper West's article in the *Annals of the Association of American Geographers* in 1956, where he states that the tidal forests of the Pacific Coast of Colombia running four hundred miles "contain the most luxuriant mangroves in the world." The red mangroves grow over a hundred feet high. And West also emphasizes the instability of the coastline, in constant flux, "one section now retreating, another advancing." Nor does he hesitate to describe the mangrove swamps as "creepy," and that they have an "evil stink."[1]

Being creepy and of evil stink evokes what Georges Bataille once called "shipwreck in the nauseous." This is in his discussion of horror at putrefaction of the corpse. It was his contention that humanity is marked by wild contradictions, which thought, as a reflection on life, has a lot of trouble registering. At stake in what makes humans human, he thought, is not only language but humanity's separation from animality on account of the invention of prohibitions, notably those surrounding erotic life, work, nakedness, excretion, the incest taboo, and the horror and respect for death as marked by aversion toward the corpse. So we might surmise that where these prohibitions become shipwrecked, so, too, language will start to creep and crawl. The bottom line is the extremity of attraction combined with repulsion engendered by life in death as with those "unstable,

---

1. Robert C. West, "Mangrove Swamps of the Pacific Coast of Colombia," *Annals of the Association of American Geographers* 46 (1956): 98, 113, 121.

fetid and lukewarm substances where life ferments ignobly. Those substances where the eggs, germs and maggots swarm not only make our hearts sink, but also turn our stomachs. . . . I will rejoin abject nature and the purulence of anonymous, infinite life, which stretches forth like the night, which is also death. One day this living world will pullulate in my dead mouth." And what is sacred, he goes on to note, "undoubtedly corresponds to the object of horror I have spoken of, a fetid sticky object without boundaries, which teems with life and yet is the sign of death."[2]

Thus does the miasma crawl out of and over the swamp: an antique word this *miasma*, treasured as much for its age and incarceration in time as for its meaning, which now has to include its musty origin. To resurrect this word seems a miasmatic act in itself. *Miasma:* from the Greek meaning a contagious and dangerous pollution as due to transgression of a supernatural sanction, and more recently meaning an infectious or noxious emanation; "a vapor as from marshes, formerly supposed to poison the air," as a current *Webster's Dictionary* would have it; emanations from rotting matter of noxious particles causing malaria, as the *OED* has it. Note the "formerly supposed," and note also the current displacement of the word *marshes* by *wetlands,* as these lands are now subject to political debate as developers contest environmentalists for whom marshes, now, are not only not bad, but are fast becoming sites of veneration. Just like the word *sacred,* meaning holy *and* accursed, the abject status of the marsh assures that it belongs irretrievably to the long-sought zone of the double gesture, where things spin on a dime in a riot of self-negation. Where the developer sees money by ridding the marshes of their miasma, the environmentalist sees ever-fewer life-enhancing places demanding protection. Yesterday's marshes seem far behind us as dystopias spreading pestilence, eerie and phantasmic. To hear the word *wetlands* today is to unconsciously register this displacement, together with its previous state of miasmic abjection. The first example Robert Parker provides in his book on miasma in early Greek religion is contact with a corpse.[3] Freud describes the effects of the breaking of a taboo the same way as

---

2. Georges Bataille, *The Accursed Share: An Essay on General Economy,* vol. 2, *The History of Eroticism,* trans. Robert Hurley (New York: Zone Books, 1991), p. 81.

3. Robert Parker, *Miasma: Pollution and Purification in Early Greek Religion* (Oxford: Clarendon Press, 1983), p. 4.

"holy dread."[4] The swamp then is just that: "holy dread," and to break a taboo is to become a swamp discharging contagious emanations.

"Formerly supposed" lies snuggled in our dictionary no less than in day-to-day conversation, in deeds no less than in words, especially money-making deeds involving drainage and improvement. Have we forgotten that most of Europe's current agricultural land, for instance, is land that was drained by large landowners and by the state from the late Middle Ages onward, especially in the eighteenth century, reducing the wild land available to the poor? Nowhere is this more poignant, more complex and contradictory, than with the Irish bog. To step into a bog is to step into suspended life-forms, not to mention the dreamlike stories connecting fairies to the bog and the bog to human sacrifice. The bog is an active, prehistoric force that has at different times spread over great areas of land. Yet the very same life of the bog assumes death together with petrifaction in its depths. To the outsider, this soggy medium that provides fuel for the fire is a mass of contradictions. In the form of peat, the bog is a cheery, life-maintaining thing, to be sure. Yet as a muddy prehistoric substitute for the oak forests that once covered the island, and as the remnant of what the wealthy landowners have otherwise appropriated or drained through centuries, the bog is a poignant sign of destruction, exclusion, and poverty.

As a source of metaphoric power, *miasma* exudes prehistory in the form of the "bog people" celebrated by poets, such as Seamus Heaney, and by scientists, such as professor P. V. Glob of Denmark in his remarkable book *The Bog People: Iron Age Man Preserved*, first published in Danish in 1965. What I think is significant about this plainspoken book is how its indissoluble mix of science with myth is made possible by the conceit within which it is written. For like *Alice in Wonderland*, it is ostensibly written for children—for young girls, to be precise—although it is in many ways an adult's book. The conceit is established by the prologue, entitled "An Answer to a Letter," replying to a group of British schoolgirls enquiring about bog people such as Tollund Man and Grauballe Man with whose discoveries professor Glob had been involved. According to its pro-

---

4. Sigmund Freud, "Totem and Taboo" (1913–14), in *The Standard Edition of the Complete Psychological Works of Sigmund Freud*, 24 vols., ed. and trans. James Strachey (London: Hogarth Press, 1953), vol. 13, p. 18.

logue, the entire book is nothing more than a long letter of reply, first to his own daughter, Elsebeth, and through her to other young girls and those, "like you, who wish to know more about antiquity."[5]

To my mind, it is this amalgamation of the adult's imagination with the child's imagination of the prehistoric that brings the mix of science and myth to perfection so that you can't tell one from the other. This is a startling manifestation of something even more eerie than the bog itself, namely, the articulation between literality and metaphor that makes language work. We might say, therefore, that the weirdness of the bog is nothing more and nothing less than the weirdness of language, so slippery yet firm, where space gives way to time and time gives way to its punctuation. More specifically, the provocation of meaning created by this sliding back and forth between literality and metaphor is itself not merely an articulation of the child with death, of the girl child with prehistory, but occurs, so to speak, *as a process of depetrifaction*, the very process we might now call *miasmatic*, remembering that both petrifaction and miasma owe their existence to the swamp, as we see with Glob's bog people, preserved over millennia.

This very same paradoxical mix of hardening and spectrality is conveyed by the Irish poet Seamus Heaney in his poem "Bogland," describing the bog as a "kind, black butter, melting and opening underfoot." Yet can this particular ground be opened, even by a poet? Like treacle, the bog closes in on him faster than he can extract images from its depths, for this is ground, admits the poet, "missing its last definition."[6] But does not the bog petrify and preserve creatures from prehistory as its own poetic act? Such is that ancient dame from the beginning of time, the Bog Queen, petrified and perfect, found by a turf cutter's spade, reminiscent of Walter Benjamin's "language magic," when, before the Fall, there was but one language unified and immanent in person and things: "My body," says this creature of the bog,

> was braille
> for the creeping influences:

---

5. P. V. Glob, *The Bog People: Iron Age Man Preserved* (1965), trans. Rupert Bruce-Mitford (Ithaca: Cornell University Press, 1969), p. 17.

6. Seamus Heaney, "Bogland," in *Opened Ground: Selected Poems, 1966–1996* (New York: Farrar, Straus and Giroux, 1998), p. 41. Thanks to Drew Walker for bringing this poem to my attention.

dawn suns groped over my head
and cooled at my feet[7]

Like the Bog Queen herself, the body of the poem transforms the body of
the reader as Braille for the creeping influences. Frog's spawn and spawn of the
Bog Queen mingle in Heaney's verse, the frogs being especially notable, "the
great slime kings," in the poem "Death of a Naturalist."

Flax had rotted there, weighted down by huge sods.
Daily it sweltered in the punishing sun.
Bubbles gargled delicately, bluebottles
Wove a strong gauze of sound around the smell.
There were dragonflies, spotted butterflies,
But best of all was the warm thick slobber
Of frogspawn that grew like clotted water[8]

Like the mangrove swamps of the Pacific Coast: heightened life, heightened
death, together.

Invoking the hollow glass ball or snow globe as among Benjamin's favorite
toys, with its snowflakes falling over the sleeping city when shaken, Adorno illus-
trates the philosophic counterpart to this when the toy is turned upside down
and back again. As a method, it is close to a conjuring trick, depetrifying certain
things, awakening them from their death sleep, thereby allowing others to emerge
as prehistoric, bringing history and natural history into the one brooding presence. Let us immediately acknowledge the presence of the child in this two-beat
method of interpretation, as indicated by the toy itself, or by the girls via whom
Glob writes for adults about prehistoric bodies in the bog, and let us proceed to
the miasmatic depetrifaction of awakening with which Glob's book opens, the
scene of discovery of the Tollund Man in the Tollund fen in Central Jutland in
Denmark in the spring of 1950. Evening is gathering. It is still, broken by shafts of

---

7. Heaney, "Bog Queen," in *Opened Ground,* pp. 108–9.
8. Heaney, "Death of a Naturalist," in *Opened Ground,* p. 5.

declining sunlight and the calls of birds. "The dead man, too, deep down in the umber-brown peat, seemed to have come alive. . . . His face wore a gentle expression . . . as if in silent prayer. It was as though the dead man's soul had for a moment returned from another world, through the gate in the western sky."[9]

Note that Glob's method here is not so much historical, dependent on the idea of history as a chain of cause and effect working through homogenous clock time, but is instead a perception sensitive to a 2,000-year-old slice of past time leapfrogging into the present. The 1950s swamp of Jutland becomes, in effect, Alice's descent into prehistory, where humans and animals talk to one another, and the child—forever innocent both morally and philosophically—is called upon to mediate the tricks that language plays on its rules of reference. Whether swamp or child, there is a dreamy otherworldly feeling evoked as time is telescoped like this, complete with its messianic standstill ("His face wore a gentle expression . . . as if in silent prayer"). And what makes Glob's bog people relevant for my purpose is the perfection with which they have been preserved. Even the eyes—especially the eyes—are jellylike aqueous substances, and it needs be that the smile is here too; that seraphic smile of wisdom drawn taut across the pensive face of Tollund Man that so perturbs us with the specter of living death. What is especially illuminating in this regard are the black-and-white photographs of these prehistoric bodies. Somewhere between statues and live people, their status defies the division between life and death that these photographs, so to speak, permanently suspend. Indeed, despite the poking through of skeleton, the figures in these photographs can seem more alive than live people, and the alternating current of interpretation set up by Adorno, as regards Benjamin's glass ball of shaken snow, is unmistakably registered by the eerie quality of flesh and almost translucent bone and tendon these bog bodies exhibit as they flit between a miraculous preservation and an always-there of imminent decay. Three-quarters of a face may be a congealed mass of bubbling tissue with an eye socket barely visible, while the muscles of the arms and flexed leg bulge with life, tendons predominant as the prehistoric flesh recedes. The statuesque element is striking. This is earth saturated with the bodies of saints and martyrs.

---

9. Glob, *The Bog People*, p. 18.

What you have to do is hold contrary states in mind and allow the miasma to exude. Imagine the immaculately preserved bog bodies at the bottom of the bog, and then side by side with that imagine the depetrifaction attempted in 1971. All you can see of this action at first is mud and water with bits of gravel glinting in the sun. Maybe it's not gravel but floating petals. A man is running. Long-stemmed delicate weeds curve from the edges of the frame. Now he is swimming, his hat miraculously floating above his head, which disappears under the water, if water it be. His swimming proves it is water. His name is Joseph Beuys, and it is said he has "an affinity for the boggy parts of northern Europe, a predilection for peat and a mysterious love of Ireland."[10] The man is leaping with all four legs into black pools. His clothes give him away. He is too, too one of us. There is something of the banker here. Yet also the clown. His face is a different matter. It is etched in smooth stone. Way out on the horizon stand trees, each one a sentinel of the swamp in which cavorts the man with the black felt hat, stone face, and black waistcoat. The story is told and may be even true that he was in the Luftwaffe during the Second World War, crashed his plane over Asia, and was rescued by people who live in felt huts and eat curds and whey on the top of the world. Years later he came to a Manhattan art gallery in an ambulance and stayed under a felt blanket in a room with a coyote for seven days. He called this *I Love America and America Loves Me*. Banker and clown, too, too much like any one of us, his message—for he undoubtedly has one—concerns the proximity to nature we have lost, harmony with elemental forces, and all that rot the bog burbles on with. But the photographs give the game away. By which I mean, the hat floats steady while the eyes underneath stare at you just above the finely tailored water line, arms and legs racing like pistons across the mud, or is it water? "Bogs are the liveliest elements in the European landscape," the downed Luftwaffe pilot is quoted as saying thirty years after the Fall. "Not just from the point of view of flora, fauna, birds and animals, but as storing places of life, mystery and chemical change, preservers of ancient history."[11] People think of him as a shaman. He slides through the time machine of the bog composed equally of life and death, slipping and sliding, running fast fully clothed though craters of chunky in-betweenness. Benjamin had his snow globe. Beuys, his swamp.

10. Carolyn Tisdall, "Bog Action," in *The New Avant-Garde: Issues for the Art of the Seventies*, text by Grégoire Müller, photographs by Gianfranco Gorgoni (New York: Praeger, 1972), pp. 39, 130–34.

11. Tisdall, "Bog Action," p. 39.

Years later in 1985, Beuys completed a set of objects he called *Lightning with Stag in Its Glare, 1958–1985*. The objects had been made at different times from 1958, but only in 1985 did they come together in the specific setting called *The Workshop*, a large room with light-filled windows forming one side. As with Albrecht Dürer's engraving of a workshop of stone four hundred years earlier, entitled *Melencolia I*, tools lie scattered. On a solid workbench under the windows are vices and lamps, heavy-duty electric cables, power points, and protective visors. Beuys's "stag" is an ironing board fixed to chunky lumber forming squat legs, and around this stag scattered on the floor in their dreaming spontaneity lie all manner of what I call "primordial animals" cast in roughly textured bronze

Joseph Beuys's "Primordial Animal," from his installation Lightning with Stag in Its Glare. © 2003 Artists Rights Society (ARS), New York/VG Bild-Kunst, Bonn.

with cruel tips of sharp metal tools protruding from their "mouths." They are made but unmade as well, halfway between the child and the adult, caught midstream in the act of creation, asking us the way out. Is this a playroom or the cemetery for lost objects that never made it to the world of categories? With regards to Dürer's *Melencolia,* Benjamin had observed that the petrified deadness displayed by the workshop meant its objects were drained of life and emotion, ensuring them, no less than the angel staring blankly at the stone floor, an enigmatic wisdom and another form of life. Benjamin could just as well be speaking of the ungainly objects scattered across Beuys's workshop floor: shapeless sprawling organic-looking things resembling large turds in shape and size, holding meaning in suspense, so perfect are they in their enigmatic incompleteness. They are terrible and terrifying things that are not things at all, dying seals, perhaps, that for miles filled the seas, leaping and twisting, some coiled in on themselves, others their spines arched in play or agony, frozen there on the floor of the workshop by the ironing board on its way to becoming a stag. Surrounded by primordial animals, the stag stands petrified by the glare of the lightning, like deer in the car's headlights. But remember the man leaping on all four legs into black pools.

"Ours was the marsh country," says young Pip, and therewith begins Dickens's *Great Expectations* mid-nineteenth century in a lonely village nobody visits by the swamp at the mouth of the river Thames running along the northern border of the county of Kent. Alone, Pip stands face-to-face with the emptiness of the world. He has just discovered a graveyard hidden under nettles a mile from the village with the tombstones of his mother, father, and five infant brothers. Beyond the graveyard stretches a dark wilderness intersected by dikes and mounds and the low leaden line of the river with the wind rushing in from the sea. And it is at that moment that the shivering, crying little boy is accosted by a creature erupting from the graves and threatening to cut his throat—a man in coarse gray with a great iron on his leg, "a man who had been soaked in water and smothered in mud, and lamed by stones, and cut by flints, and stung by nettles, and torn by briars." This is the Bog Queen's consort: a convict, sentenced to transportation to Australia and just escaped from one of the death ships known as prison hulks moored in the marshes. To make sure young Pip will keep his existence secret, the convict warns him there is a young man lurking nearby who has a "secret way pecooliar to himself, of getting at a boy, and at his heart, and at his liver." A little boy may think himself safe and warm in bed with the door locked, but the killer "will creep his way to him and tear him open." The convict disappears into the marsh. "I wish I was a frog," he says. "Or a eel."[12]

Pip's eyes follow the man making his way back across the marsh under an angry sky scored red and black. On the edge of the river far away, Pip makes out two black objects: one is a beacon for sailors; the other is a gibbet with chains hanging off it that a long time ago held a pirate. "The man was limping on toward this latter, as if he were the pirate come to life, and come down, and going back to hook himself up again. It gave me a terrible turn when I thought so . . ."[13] In his dreams that night, Pip sees himself adrift on that same river, passing the hulks on a strong spring tide, hailed as he floats past the gibbet to come ashore and be hung. Two centuries earlier that gibbet with its chains swinging by the marshes and the sea beyond was waiting for pirate men like William Dampier, Bartholomew Sharp, Basil Ringrose, and all that pack of merry boys, who at different times had headed west across the Atlantic past these marshes to careen at the island of Gorgona perched ten miles off those other swamps of the Pacific Coast of what is today known as Colombia.

Many pirates on the Spanish Main were runaway convicts. From the beginning, England had used the Caribbean islands as dumping grounds for what one historian describes as its "refuse population," meaning servile labor from the prisons in the mother country not thought fit to be tried for their lives, that is, hanged.[14] Some seventy-five thousand people are thought to have been hanged in England between 1530 and 1630. But after that, rates declined for a century as such persons were transported.[15] In 1665 the Council of State ordered the apprehension of all lewd and dangerous persons, rogues, vagrants, and other idlers who had no form of livelihood and refused to work, to be transported by contractors to the English plantations in America.[16] This date corresponds to the golden age of piracy, and Pip's dream has a basis in this history gathered under the sign of the gibbet. Once meaning a gallows, the gibbet in eighteenth-century

---

12. Charles Dickens, *Great Expectations* (1861) (New York: Dodd, Mead, 1985), pp. 2, 5.
13. Dickens, *Great Expectations*, p. 6.
14. Haring, *Buccaneers in the West Indies*, pp. 126–27.
15. V. A. C. Gatrell, *The Hanging Tree: Execution and the English People, 1770–1868* (Oxford: Oxford University Press, 1996), p. 7.
16. Haring, *Buccaneers in the West Indies*, pp. 126–27.

England was reserved for notorious criminals who, once they had been hung dead, were then tarred and hung in a cage of iron chains at the scene of the crime. With pirates, the gibbet might be placed between high and low water. Aimed at denying the victim a grave and at providing a fearsome image of the law, "the body would of course decay over time; birds would tear the flesh, pieces would fall to the ground."[17] Picked clean, the skeleton would swing creaking in the wind.

Through death erupting from the marsh, congealed life in petrified objects is awakened and living things present themselves as prehistorical. Think back to the black gibbet, along with the beacon, by the winding river's bank, rusty chains swinging. Limping toward it, the escaped convict seems to Pip as if "he were the pirate come to life, and come down, and going back to hook himself up again."[18] The cyclical repetition involved here—coming to life, coming down, going back—this repetition of being hung by the state, hung over and over again, this dying and returning from the dead, only to die once more, seems clumsy and overwrought, drawing attention to itself as trying to indicate something inexpressibly more, as does the reversal itself, of death passing to life, followed by life passing back to the death it came from, hung on the gibbet for all the world to see, only nobody lives there and who knows what passing ship might espy this tragic sign and why this now functionless gibbet has been left to stand? The petrified object has awakened under Pip's scrutiny of the convict, now become ancient, "as if he were [a] pirate." Such is Pip's view of the hobbled convict as urhistorical, tracing his flight into the marsh under a sky scored red and black. Only the pieces of eight and stories of buried treasure linger in this piteous dog-eat-dog maelstrom of Dickens's England, unspoken indications that Pip's future may not be so bleak. Hence, great expectations.

But by Pip's time in the mid-nineteenth century, pirates of that sort were the stuff of boyhood legend, as with Long John Silver of *Treasure Island,* written a few decades later. Yet if real pirates belonged to the past, children's literature re-

---

17. Ruth Richardson, *Death, Dissection, and the Destitute* (London: Penguin, 1988), pp. 35–36.
18. Dickens, *Great Expectations,* p. 6.

suscitated them by forming an archive not so much of history as of prehistory, featuring pieces of eight, parrots, eye patches, cursing out your mother, drunken brawls . . . and rebellion against all forms of authority, as Sigmund Freud pictures for us with gusto in "Totem and Taboo" with the pack of merry boys murdering then eating their tyrannical father. Only in Freud's story, the pack then abandons its animality and incest, settles down to law and language, and adopts a decent family existence of heterosexual couples. While in piracy . . . obviously another route has been chosen and the pack of merry boys enjoy their *temporary autonomous zone* in either the adult version of piracy or the Peter Pan version of the lost boys who will never grow up.[19] The two versions combine in the adult's imagination of the child's imagination as with William Burroughs's lost boys let loose as pirates alongside Indians from wild Darien, queer boys whose capacity for hanging and being hung is second only to the orgasms thus produced in the body of the hung alongside libertarian visions of socialism enshrined in pirate communes.

When the gentleman pirate handsome young Captain Strobe was hung in front of the courthouse of Panamá City in 1702, there was a curious smile on his face and a yellow-green aura surrounded his body. Rescued dangling on the gibbet in the hot sun by a hit squad and fed opium, he awoke with a throbbing erection. He knew where he was: forty miles south of Panamá City. "He could see the low coastline of mangrove swamps laced with inlets, the shark fins, the stagnant seawater."[20]

This is the same place in the imagination where the marsh is fused with the dead in the opening scene of *Great Expectations*. Marsh and death act in concert to access the archaic that the storyteller needs to drive the otherwise realist narration of which Dickens is master. "Death," says Benjamin, "is the sanction of everything that the storyteller can tell. He has borrowed his authority from death. In other words it is natural history to which his stories refer back."[21]

---

19. I take the idea of the temporary autonomous zone from Hakim Bey, *T.A.Z.: The Temporary Autonomous Zone, Ontological Anarchy, Poetic Terrorism* (Brooklyn: Autonomedia, 1985).

20. William S. Burroughs, *Cities of the Red Night* (New York: Henry Holt, 1981), p. 27.

21. Benjamin, "The Storyteller," in *Illuminations*, p. 94.

Gazing at the graves of his family, this is the scene that Pip describes as generating his "first most vivid and broad impression of the identity of things." It is the marsh that initiates this breakthrough in the child's understanding of the way of the world and his place in the scheme of things. "Ours was the marsh country," begins Pip, taking care to set the scene, "down by the river, within, as the river wound, twenty miles of the sea." A strange geography and an even stranger statement with its *withinness* and with its *windingness.* And if it is tempting to think of Freud here, the little boy's discovery not of the primal scene but of the death scene as primal, with the graveyard replacing the family home, stark and terribly fixed with its stones marking out the mother and father in one line, the children's gravestones in a neat row in front of them, then we might also want to consider the terrible cry of the man who "started up from among the graves," threatening to cut the little boy's throat.[22] This staging in the bed of the dead, father of phallic arousal and castration in the one action, aimed here at the throat, organ of speech, restages the child's entry into the "symbolic" register, meaning the acquisition of language understood not as cries, terrible or otherwise, but as a social convention of patterned sounds with no literal relation to what they signify, such that in the words of one student of such matters, "the symbol manifests itself first of all as the murder of the thing,"[23] following which symbols refer not to things but to other symbols posing as things . . . Murder provides harsh judgment here so as to forcibly remind us of the artificial character of the symbol, but murder suggests a more striking truth still. For murder ensures that the thing symbolized lives on "inside" the symbol, like the river winding its way in and out through miasmatic marshlands. Could it be that murder has to be continuously staged and restaged precisely because there is such a compelling counterforce welding the symbol to the materiality of that which it symbolizes? There must be some sort of trick here, and that is why we encounter the dramatic flourish of the *murder of the thing* because far from eliminating the thing, murder ensures its perpetuation by strengthening the feeling of presence of the thing erased as visceral memory traces and ghostly returns, real and unreal at the same time. Language founders *and* thrives on this ambiguity so long as we

---

22. Dickens, *Great Expectations,* p. 2.

23. Jacques Lacan, "The Function of Language in Psychoanalysis" (1956), in *Speech and Language in Psychoanalysis,* trans. with notes and commentary by Anthony Wilden (Baltimore: Johns Hopkins University Press, 1968), p. 84.

are capable of blinding ourselves to it, to the hole, as Anthony Wilden puts it,[24] through which "meaning pours"—back into the swamp—as when at the outset to the tale we witness Pip stumble across his dead family, creating, by his own admission, his "first most vivid and broad impression of the identity of things."

"I wish I was a frog. Or a eel," says the convict slipping into the darkness of the swamp.

---

24. Wilden, in Lacan, *Speech and Language,* p. 217.

swamp

Getting there, 1998: Waited all day. Mabby recognizes a boat tied to the wharf belonging to a man from the Río Timbiquí called Demosthenes who'd come to Guapi to pick up an outboard motor axle for his father. By now it is late afternoon and starting to spit rain. Again. And that gray sky hanging low. Why is it always gray? Finally Demosthenes arrives, but Mabby says it's too late, too dark, and too dangerous. I waver. He seems so calm and capable, I change my mind and decide to go. A mad rush. I wrap yards of plastic around my pack knowing it will have little effect. Now it's Demosthenes and me and a dark spitting sky. The river runs fast and black. I put my fingers in the shape of a square and pretend to take a picture as a way of saying good-bye to her standing resolute on the pier, solid as a rock, silently admonishing me, trying to smile. Hubie told me in Germany how Mabby held a huge party for Plutarco's fiftieth birthday party in their house in Guapi a few years back and how, when the guests refused to leave at six in the morning, she went into the bedroom and came out with a gun. And she's a *motorista* in her own right too. When Plutarco is on the high seas or up a river, I notice she's always receiving radio-telephone calls from him and telling him what to do. I recall how she prays with her teenage daughters in an echoing circle in their concrete house before sunrise and late at night. Their Bible was almost too heavy to carry and in the stark simplicity of that house at that time it emitted an aura like a lighthouse. Demosthenes opens the throttle and we tear away in the gathering dark, the rain like needles in our eyes.

I have to sit so far forward to balance the boat that I can't speak with him, and anyway the motor is too loud to talk. There was an ancient Greek Demosthenes with his mouth full of pebbles who had to talk without choking himself or allowing the pebbles to drop from his mouth. Yet "verbal reverberations keep us safe," comments Susan Howe from whom I learned about this other Demosthenes.[1] But what is it that keeps us safe: the verbal or the reverbatory? Here the only reverberation is the motor and the hull shuddering across the dark water with our darker thoughts. So many things pass by in a blur that I want to ask him about. Walter Benjamin had some intriguing ideas about verbal reverberations too, as did Joseph Beuys, who spoke of words as verbal sculpture, but I believe Beuys would have preferred the notion of words as pebbles. Yet it is Benjamin who will stay in mind on account of his citing the brilliant Johann Wilhelm Ritter: "It would be beautiful," remarked Ritter early on in the nineteenth century concerning Chaldini's "sound-figures," those patterns formed in sand on a sheet of glass at the touch of different notes, "if what became externally clear here were also exactly what the sound pattern was for us inwardly: a light pattern, fire-writing. . . . Every sound would then have its own letter directly to hand. . . . That inward connection of word to script—so powerful that we write when we speak . . . rooted in the fact that the organ of speech itself writes in order to speak."[2]

Benjamin loved this example because he was fascinated by any instance of what he took to be even a hint of writing in nature. It must have been intoxicat-

---

1. Susan Howe, *Pierce-Arrow* (New York: New Directions, 1997), p. 13.

2. Quoted in Walter Benjamin, *The Origin of German Tragic Drama* (1963), trans. John Osborne (London: New Left Books, 1977), pp. 213–14. Benjamin also cites Ritter as one his favorite authors in his memorable essay "Unpacking My Library." Referring to Ritter's book, which in English would be translated as *Posthumous Fragments of a Young Physicist*, 2 vols. (Heidelberg, 1810), Benjamin writes that he considers its preface as "the most important sample of personal prose of German Romanticism." Benjamin, "Unpacking My Library," in *Illuminations*, pp. 65–66.

ing for him, this notion of music translating itself into the horizontal movement of sand across glass, forming whorls and ellipses; the analogy with the opening and closing of the vocal cords shaping words and sentences; the sympathies and correspondences binding sounds to letters; and finally the billowing proposition that speech is the external expression of an inner fire-writing.

He would have also loved these names: names like Plutarco and Demosthenes. How might we trace their genealogy like ivy clinging to the walls of history? Then there is Mabby. Her father wanted to call her Mavis, a Hungarian queen he found in a book. The nun at school said that was no name and changed it to Mavi. So now it's Mabby. But Demosthenes, he is neither writing nor speaking, just reverberating. And traveling fast across dark waters.

Is this travel? It seems more like a physiological test. Put a human being in a wind tunnel and observe what happens to the eyes, streaming, and the ears, pounding. Observe what happens to the sense of the earth and other elements as you become a fish skimming into the night as the seer and the seen become one. When Ricardo Grueso, yarning about his years on the high seas and threading his canoe through the *esteros* of the mangrove swamps, argued in favor of traveling by canoe powered by paddle only, everyone in our circle, seated outside his home in Guapi, scoffed. A hopeless romantic, to be sure. It's nicer, he said. You have a chance to see everything. His maritime life must have just preceded the arrival of the outboard motor. In his youth they used to make journeys in sailing canoes called *ibaburas* some fifty feet long. With a crew of five, they could carry twenty-five tons, had beds to sleep in, and a roof to sleep under. William Prescott describes how in 1526 Bartolomé Ruíz de Estrada, Pizarro's pilot, striking out from the coast to the deep sea slightly to the south of these parts, was surprised to come across a strange vessel like a caravel of considerable size with a sluggish sail. Coming closer, he saw it was an Indian craft, consisting of trunks of balsa wood lashed together with a raised floor of reeds for a deck. The Indians on board had gold ornaments, fine woolen clothing, and a balance to weigh precious metals.[3] Were the *ibaburas* modeled on these Indian craft?

The currents and winds generally flow from south to north along this coast. To sail from Guapi north to Buenaventura, Ricardo told me, took him two days

---

3. Prescott, *History of the Conquest of Peru,* pp. 244–45.

with a sail, eight days with paddles alone. Coming back, against the current and wind, took him a month. Now people take off in the dark in open launches on the high seas and get to Buenaventura in three to six hours, twelve in a trading boat, rarely wearing life jackets, surfing sideways along the swells. Ricardo was a paradox. Truly a mechanical genius, here he was advocating paddles over engines. Demetrio Góngora told me Ricardo once got stuck out on the ocean with a motor that had insufficient oil. So he used his shit as a substitute for oil and got the motor to work. That's what Góngora said. Maybe that's analogous, in the realm of storytelling as history, to Ricardo's advocacy of the paddle?

We pass sawmills and fishing villages. The word *village* is comforting. It sounds *European*. But these were ramshackle clusters of wood-plank homes with greasy walkways hanging precariously over muddy banks into which the dwellings were sinking. With refrigerator plants installed, such villages at the river's mouth expand and become more numerous. Two to three decades ago, there must have been few houses here, even though a notable feature following the abolition of slavery in 1851, so it is said, was the migration of people downriver from the mines at the headwaters.[4] We pass canoes in the estuary laying out nets in the driving rain. One canoe has two women. Another a man and a woman. They are dressed in the usual skirt or pants. Sodden. None of them has anything like a raincoat. A thin kid aged about seven without a shirt stands stock-still in the center of a tiny canoe with another kid seated, paddling in the stern. There seems no more than an inch of freeboard. The kid standing has his arms so tightly clenched across his chest and into his armpits trying to keep warm that he seems like a statue, taller than the canoe is long, gliding across this immense river mouth through the pelting rain, pelicans diving, the great Pacific calling.

In the distance I see bombs of spray, luminescent in the gathering darkness, as big-beaked pelicans here called *gavanes* dive into the water, then emerge to fly parallel to the surface. Rather than risk going out to the ocean, Demosthenes looks for a channel through the mangroves. There are many such *esteros*, each with its own name. They form networks in the swamps like clots of blood

---

4. West, *The Pacific Lowlands of Colombia*, p. 104; map, p. 105.

vessels. High tide is approaching, so there is likely to be enough water. Last time I came through the swamp in 1992, we were coming the other way, screaming south from the Timbiquí with Plutarco at high speed and two children dying from burns lying under plastic raincoats and attended by a doctor with a pink-and-green life vest and dark glasses now and again feeding them saline solution. There were four police with us as well. In his black jumpsuit and gold chains, Plutarco never slowed down, weaving in and out like a kid from New Jersey on the Outer Drive along the Hudson. Now and again we saw a blue sail, stationary, on the horizon.

But now I am alone with Demosthenes. He throttles back till the motor is barely turning as we thread our way through the channels. On all sides in back and front of us stand tall mangroves. They rear at the sky then clamp down on the muddiest mud you could imagine. The quintessence of mud. Demosthenes asks me to go farther forward to level out the boat because the water is shallow. I am shivering, clothes saturated with rain despite my oilskin jacket. He stands awkwardly peering ahead into the gloom, semi-crouching with his hands on the body of the motor behind him, tilting it forward out of the water when he thinks it will strike bottom. He has no paddle. Why does he have no paddle? It goes along with having no life jacket. Without a paddle, we could not proceed if the motor failed or the draft was insufficient.

Think of being stranded here and as soon as you put foot outside the boat, sinking to your neck in that mud, eye to eye with those mangrove roots and only crabs for company, flashes of red streaking like fire over black mud. But of what are these crabs afraid? Of us? Jesús Alberto told me of the strange creatures he called *pejesapos* that grow up to a foot long, live in the mud, and have a sharp dorsal spine that stings so badly he was in bed for two days. There are lots of them lying quietly in the mud. Just the spine protrudes. "This is why there are no tourists on the coast," he added. "So what happens to the women who go into the swamp for shellfish?" I asked. He shrugged. "They must be immune." "Don't be silly," Lilia told me. "They wear rubber boots!"

As we inch our way forward in the suffocating quiet, I hear a distant crash. It blasts a hole in time into which I fall, thinking of the arrival of those other Europeans, of Pizarro in the sixteenth century losing his way in this labyrinth. How could you not be confused in the swamp—four hundred miles of it, they say—thinking of gold and where the next meal was coming from? What must it have been like coming as a slave from Africa to mine gold at the headwaters? Falling through time, I feel more connected to the strangeness of the world yet cannot understand why.

Filled with memories of traveling along another coast, the coast of West Africa from where the slaves came, a coast "where the merry dance of death and trade goes on in a still and earthy atmosphere as of an overheated catacomb," the author Joseph Conrad pictures the rivers there as

> streams of death in life, whose banks were rotting into mud, whose waters, thickened into slime, invaded the contorted mangroves, that seemed to writhe at us in the extremity of impotent despair.[5]

We drift. Night falls like a wet blanket. The motor starts. We *put-put* through the swarm of unicellular life-forms fading into oblivion, the cold sky descending into our marrow. The motor stops. We drift some more, then *put-put* into an unimaginable solitude, for it is here you become one with the mud from which spring the mangroves so stately to reign over their silent kingdom. I keep thinking of sinking in the mud, my way of wondering whether mud is solid or liquid or nothing at all, the decomposing west, once a land, with a flag and everything, rushing down these mad rivers to its final rest in this majesty of mud symbolic of sexual organs and soaks. Or is sex itself made of these things, drifting into solitude?

We break through to a wide lagoon. As we proceed, it turns out to be a loop in a larger loop of something that eventually takes us to "the river." But now there are no rivers and there never were. It's water and mud and trees all mixed, and words no longer correspond to things like they do in ordinary language and in geography textbooks. Slow down! You've arrived! It's the Timbiquí River. Can't you see those huts up on stilts, black aeries against a blacker sky? Each one with a steady blue light shining from it like a shrine? TV. Demosthenes speeds up. We are flying in the pitch dark. We should be on TV!

---

5. Joseph Conrad, *Heart of Darkness* (1902) (Harmondsworth: Penguin, 1983), p. 41.

We cannot see. The boat is shaking from the speed. All is black. We stop at a bunch of houses on stilts with dark figures sitting on canoes and cleaning nets in a soft golden light streaming from the houses. This is Corozal, a village of fishermen and fisherwomen with a freezer for storing fish and to where people moved after a tidal wave wiped out the fishing village of Chacón. I am shaking with cold. Demosthenes yells for a paddle "because the river is dry" and starts off again, one hand on the tiller of the motor, the other on the paddle in the water to test the depth. It is totally black: the sky, the river, and all the shapes and shades of blackness in between.

the right to be lazy

In 1849 the Colombian government hired an Italian cartographer by the name of Agustín Codazzi to map and tabulate the resources of the new republic wrested from Spain. He measured angles, drew lines, counted miles from here to there, and adjusted mountains, rivers, towns, and swamps to the cardinal points of the earth. He counted everything that moved or crawled and was capable of carrying a gun. He took in tow a small army of watercolorists to paint the peasants and Indians and scantily clad Negroes as if he knew that in thus typifying them, in thus casting them into molds and types, he was all the more making certain their demise. Counting and mapping was the same. It was like taking a snapshot. As soon as the clicker clicked, it was all over. Why did they do it? Why was a map necessary?

There were military questions included in the survey Codazzi had agreed to undertake.[1] There was interest, for example, in how topography and climate would affect troop movements between localities. Hence distance and the time required for *marchas de tropa* were described, measured, and published in tables, which, however, did not indicate that over the more difficult trails the surveyors were carried by peons. (Imagine an army marching to war singing martial airs while sitting in cane chairs facing backward on the sweaty backs of peons.) However, there was in my opinion more at stake than military intelligence or commerce. The map was preeminently an emblem of statehood; to make the map was to make the state—in an act that appeared to be one of domesticating the chaos of nature and obtaining some leverage over the dense inwardness of local knowledges concerning geography, topography, chorography, flora and fauna. No map or associated survey actually achieves these things. It appears to. That's all. And it does so by the crudest magic, transposing the unruliness of the experience of nature onto a piece of paper marked north and south, east and west, where the sun sets. Was any abracadabra as crude as this? What seems crucial here is what this tells us about the state; how it needs this theater with its magic, but needs it disguised as science, and how important the domination of nature is to such theater.

True, there was the stated issue of alienating lands that had been reserved under the Spanish crown and making them accessible to the market by means of accurate surveys. True, there was the stated issue that good administration requires a good map. And it is also true, and no less vague, that "for various reasons of utility and public convenience," the country should be "explored, recognized, and examined so as to provide a description of its physical, moral, and political relationships."[2] But what fool of a businessman would place maps and statistics above a warm human contact, as every foreign embassy official knows?

Codazzi was stimulated by the far-seeing and energetic Tomás Cipriano de Mosquera, owner of many gold mines on the coast. A chinless man of slight

---

1. Efraín Sánchez, *Gobierno y geografía: Agustín Codazzi y la Comisión Corográfica de la Nueva Granada* (Bogotá: Banco de la República, 1999), pp. 238–40; Andrés Soriano Lleras, *Itinerario de la Comisión Corográfica y otros escritos* (Bogotá: Imprenta Nacional, 1968).
2. Law 15 of May 1839; quoted in Sánchez, *Gobierno y geografía*, pp. 82–84.

build with a whopping mustache, Mosquera was three times president of Colombia, and I doubt if ever there was a president of Colombia as deeply immersed in international wheeling and dealing as he was. His connections with Europe and with the United States were legion, as testified by his command of English, French, and Italian, his frequent voyages to those then far-off places, and of course the various trophies and signs of the exalted life, such as the hunting dogs he brought back from France to use in his favorite hacienda, Coconuco, outside of Popayán.[3] Anxious for the nation's commercial development by means of external no less than internal trade, he was himself a keen geographer.[4] So keen, in fact, that he disputed the map that emerged from the Codazzi Chorographic Commission and had his own book on the geography of Colombia published, in English as well as in Spanish.[5] "Codazzi sent me his work, which I submitted to various corrections," Mosquera said, damning the work with faint praise, "so that it could be used as a basis for topography and initiate map-making."[6] It must have been an anxious moment. Who really knew the new Colombia? Who would best represent it?

It is tempting here, so terribly tempting, to succumb to the fullness of the land, against which the map must appear artificial, compromised, and incomplete. The once-upon-a-time of unities surges forth with a power so great we feel we remember that time long ago. "*There did I live . . . ,*" my body alive with forest and river. Yet the national project instructs otherwise and will not easily allow this dichotomy between an alienating present and a prehistory of ramifying unities. For it is surely the aim of the national project, no matter what the tension with the past, to incorporate the one within the other, the ancient past with the here-and-now, so as to create a sense of home but on the national scale. The fullness of the land is nurtured as primordial within the abstraction that is the power of the map. Thus the enigmatic shapes of nations as set in borders drawn by cartographers are silhouettes that acquire the intensity of archetypal images.

---

3. Arboleda, *Tomás Cipriano de Mosquera*.
4. Sánchez, *Gobierno y geografía*, pp. 446–53; Jaime Ardila and Camilo Lleras, *Batalla contra el olvido* (Bogotá: OP Gráficas, 1985), p. 11.
5. Sánchez, *Gobierno y geografía*, pp. 443–58.
6. Soriano Lleras, *Itinerario de la Comisión Corográfica*, p. 43.

How could we suppose any piece of land detachable from human institutions? Nevertheless we persist: on one side, nature; on the other, artifice. An old story. First nature, then second nature. An old and well-rehearsed story, because even though the synthesis of nature with artifice is always the case, the old story separating nature out as an autonomous domain is easier on the ear, the land being conceived as a plane on which is then superimposed human history and law, especially the laws of states and of property from which springs the map as signature of the Fall. First the land. Then the law. But to contest this enduring tale, how might we evoke the true reality, which is the fusion of law and land, a fusion that conserves the autonomy of each, to some degree, yet in merging them creates something completely different? What is second nature? That is the question we need to ask if ever we are to glimpse the nature of nature. How might we evoke the way law and land mirror each other and enter into the fiber of each other's being, let alone the epiphanic moments when they appear to spring apart and catch us breathless?

"Miller owns this field," writes Emerson, "Locke that, and Manning the woodland beyond. But none of them owns the landscape. There is a property in the horizon which no man has but he whose eye can integrate all the parts, that is, the poet. This is the best part of these men's farms, yet to this their warranty-deeds give no title. . . . To speak truly, few adult persons can see nature. Most persons do not see the sun."[7]

Despite the static nature of its tables of statistics and of the map it eventually produced, Codazzi's Chorographic Commission was based on a body of men moving in a caravan across the landscape, sensing its peculiarities and wonders, absorbing and digesting it as lines between compass points and numbers in a table. There exists a disturbing figure in baroque tragedy, of history passing into landscape, the ultimate expression of which is a death's head. The maps and tables are the modern scientific equivalent of this chilling idea we now take as natural and commonplace, of what, in the gaze of Medusa, amounted to petrifaction. History becomes space, and space is held tightly in a clenched fist.

This sense of stillness in the landscape as you move across it can be

---

7. Ralph Waldo Emerson, "Nature," in *Essays and Lectures* (New York: Library of America, 1983), pp. 9–10.

abruptly reversed. For sometimes looking out the window of a train or of a car, you may think you are still and it is the landscape that is moving instead. This happens more frequently to people who are not used to trains or automobiles. Such may have been the illusion of a suspended sense of stasis of the chorographic commissioners as they lurched over the cordilleras carried on the backs of their peons knee-deep in mud. Having reified nature into numbers and tables, having gotten it figured as a map, the tables and the maps take on a life of their own and start to move. This must be why we love maps.

The important thing here is the scissors movement between one's body and what one's body—or rather, that of the peon carrying you—is moving across. Just as a skilled butcher finds the natural cleavage points, so the skilled chorographers of the commission butchered the carcass of the nation, finding the routes cut into nature by nature along which goods and humans flowed. For it is transport that underlies the map; transport in the sense of being carried across that which you objectify, and transport in the sense that this became pretty much the main preoccupation of the commission, concerned with roads, tracks, and rivers not only as the vital arteries of commerce but as the articulation of a nation.

For with independence of the country and hence the arousal of a new constellation of interests with Europe and North America, together with its new identity as a nation no longer a colony of Spain, the articulation of difference in the constitution of the whole found expression in an activity that bears a curious name, no less archaic than *miasma,* and that is *chorography*—as in Codazzi's Chorographic Commission—which, at first approximation, we may define as *the practice of evoking the genius of a part of the whole.*

Just as ethnography as practiced until the 1970s has been roundly criticized since then for concentrating exclusively on the tribe, the village, or the city block, so chorography is precisely this art of concentrating on a small unit detached from the whole. But what must never be forgotten here is that no matter how much an ethnographer is concentrating on a detached part, the ethnographer is perforce a translator, converting the genius of locale into terms that people living outside of that locale can understand and appreciate such that something of that genius lives on as vital force in the translation itself. Implicitly or explicitly, the ethnography of locale is simultaneously loyal to the imaginative life of readers living far beyond that locale. Similarly for chorography, because there can be no ethnography just as there can be no chorography that does not betray that which it seeks to translate and transmit. Jean Genet says as much in his memoir, *Prisoner of Love*. Traven gets around it by allowing the death ship to speak. The truest thing is the interzone that the translation creates between the two domains of us and them, fiction and nonfiction. Thus is genius of locale forever at risk, its true genius, we could say.

There is room for ambiguity here. There has to be. In insisting that chorography takes a small part of the whole and treats it exclusively as a detached unit, the authority of the ancient geographer Ptolemy is often invoked, insisting that what is required is not mathematics but art—including, I might add, the art of the ethnographer.[8] This tight connection with ethnography and art is clear in Joachim Vadian's book published in Vienna in 1518 in which he says chorography restricts itself to individual regions and describes them in the manner of a painting; it is limited to the local and the particular, which it depicts in precise detail, including human customs.[9] The *OED* cites a 1617 source: "Let a traueller observe . . . the fruitfullness of each Countrey . . . the healthfulness of the Aire, the Chorography etc."; and the following citation from 1683 similarly emphasizes the climate, while the third citation from 1850 reads, "a pictorial chorography and ethnography." Taken together these citations give a good idea of Codazzi's mid-nineteenth-century Chorographic Commission in which both Aire and pictorial representation as ethnography were important—as compared with today's maps and with what little remains of chorography in which climate and Aire have mysteriously disappeared, along with cosmic awareness and those chubby angels with puffed-out cheeks blowing wind in the corners.

But these citations also indicate to what extent Codazzi's Chorographic Commission was a misnomer or rather a misappropriation of chorography aimed at satisfying what were understood as the administrative needs of the modern state no less than the totemic need for a map of a newly formed nation in search of identity. Codazzi's translation is not from the genius of one locale to the genius of another, but is instead a translation from the particular to the general in which everything particular to the particular is erased for the sake of its enumeration and tabular presentation. Humans become so many functional

8. Lloyd A. Brown, *The Story of Maps* (New York: Bonanza Books, 1949), p. 61.

9. Cited in Gerald Strauss, "Topographical-Historical Method in Sixteenth-Century German Scholarship," *Studies in the Renaissance* 5 (1958): 99. Daniela Gandolfo pointed out this article to me.

male bodies (*hombres útiles*) capable of bearing arms. Cattle, hogs, horses, donkeys, and mules become so many head of this and that. Heat becomes so many degrees, and patterns of settlement become crossroads of degrees longitude and latitude, benchmarks demarcating leagues of military marching trisected into

level
ascent
descent.

It is so silly. It must have a reason. It is also scary.

Just how scary is indicated by Codazzi advising the governors of the Pacific Coast provinces to invoke vagabond laws to force ex-slaves to work two years after abolition.[10] As he saw it, the problem was the freed slaves had few needs. When they wanted cash, all they had to do was go down to the river, wash some gold, buy whatever trinket they wanted, then fall back into what he saw as their accustomed sloth and nakedness. And in that climate, whites died like flies. In comparison to his first visit to the coast in 1820, he found in 1853 far more blacks living along the riverbanks, the freed slaves were deserting the gold fields, towns were deteriorating, and there were no businessmen to be found buying gold. In the mines of Barbacoas, he said, "perverted or ill-intentioned agitators had infused in that ignorant and uncouth people the idea that they should not work for whites, and the lands of the latter ought to be divided amongst them."[11]

This is the advice he gave the governors:

In order that the province may progress at the same rate as other industrialized countries, it is mandatory that the working class be obliged to work by means of a well-organized police force. Without this the country will slip back day by day for lack of labor, or at best simply stagnate, with enormously grievous effects on the development of the nation's wealth. The land is useless for agriculture on ac-

10. Agustín Codazzi, *Jeografía física i política de las provincias de la Nueva Granada.* Vol. 4, *Provincias de Córdoba, Cauca, Popayán, Pasto y Túquerres. Segunda parte: Informes* (Bogotá: Banco de la República, 1959), pp. 323–24, 333, 336.
11. Codazzi, *Jeografía física,* p. 336.

count of the climate. Plantains, a little maize and a few plantings of cacao and sugarcane do nothing more than satisfy daily consumption, while fish and wild pigs abound. That is all the descendent of the African worries about. His necessities are almost nil. The man lives naked and the woman wears but a loin-cloth. From nearby palms they build a miserable hut. From the bark of the *damagua* trees they make a bed. A blanket of grass keeps them warm at night. If they want clothes they go to the gold-rich rivers or streams and dive down with their *bateas* to bring up gravel or get it from the banks and wash it until they've got the gold they think necessary for their purchases. They then go home to enjoy sweetmeats, smoke, talk, and sleep. Sometimes for pure pleasure a man goes into the forest hunting *zainos* and *tatabros* while the women get into a canoe to visit their *comadres*. A race of people which almost in its entirety spends its time in such indolence is not the race called upon for national progress. Out of ignorance, laziness, and misunderstood pride at being free, these people are slaves to their lack of need and hence live like Indians and barbarians.[12]

This pretty well sums up the role of science in mapping new nations and endorsing what in our time came to be called "development," as in the science of development, the economics of development, the sociology of development, and so forth. What a shock it was that day in Cali long ago when I came across a little book by a writer said to be Karl Marx's son-in-law, one Paul Lafargue, born and raised in Cuba (of course!). On the cover was an ever-so-relaxing picture of a person lying in a hammock. Its title? *The Right to Be Lazy.* Whoa! This outrageous idea of a "right" to be lazy gives me insight as to why our fevered mapper and measurer, Agustín Codazzi, is so very, very angry, with these no-good bums he wants forced into labor. Could it be that the hammock people represent for him a reversion from culture to nature that spits in the face of Enlightenment reason as much as its preferred forms of discipline? Could it be that it is their cu-

---

12. Codazzi, *Jeografía física*, pp. 323–24, for the Chocó. For Barbacoas, the same ideas are stated on pp. 333, 336.

rious form of life, "slaves to their lack of need," living in nature and not dependent on the market, that makes them so infuriating, especially when you take into
account that they are supposed to be sitting on mountains of gold?

Chorography relishes detail. "The more details, the better," says Lloyd
Brown in *The Story of Maps*. "Its concern is to paint a true likeness," writes
Ptolemy, "and not merely to give exact positions and size." It does not require a
mathematician. But it does require an artist "and no one presents it rightly unless
he is an artist."[13]

What sort of artist? Is not chorography part of everyday life itself, and do
we not practice it continuously? There is a sense of being-in-place evoked here
that is not in the mind so much as in the body as when one's body goes onto automatic pilot and finds its habitual way through the rooms of our childhood
along well-trod paths. There is intimacy here of landscape and body, the one in
the other dissolving time and space in an unconcealment of the being of beings.
Chorography, then, would be the attempt to express this intimacy as it is brought
to consciousness via the arts of representation. But is this really possible? Isn't the
very attempt flawed from the outset?

Where I go in upstate New York I know chorographically a tiny region
some three miles in diameter. I know it by walking through it in the changing
seasons, a bend in the path, a leaning tree, the glint of the sun in the rapids. To
travel the land and the river is to have it travel through you. Strangest of all is
how self-absorbed one becomes. You notice your surroundings less and your inner world more. But it's the surroundings that stimulate this. To travel the land is
to have it travel through you.

This is further knitted together through the people I know there and the
stories we tell each other, which inevitably make reference to the placeness of the
place. Truth to tell, however, such reference is inclined to be indirect and is cir-
cuited through accounts of conflicts over property, money, and the state, as each
or all of these impact the placeness of place. The placeness is displaced by vi-
ciously complicated conflicts over ownership, which a reader of Faulkner or

---

13. Cited in Brown, *The Story of Maps*, p. 61.

Thomas Hardy would quickly recognize. Even that, however, tends to recede into the background of daily life as so much white noise. The record has gotten stuck. You've heard it so many times before. What a mad world! First nature as in the realness of place becomes second nature as with real estate, and then second nature reverts to first nature as white noise like the river running over the rocks!

Is this why Emerson says there is a property on the horizon that belongs to nobody and for which warranty deeds give no title? You would like to think what he means is that once upon a time there was real nature, first nature, and then Manning and Locke and all that brood bought it up, swallowed it whole, and spat it out as commoditized nature, and all that was left was the stuff that couldn't be bought for one reason or another. The horizon therefore would be residue, what's left over or couldn't fit in. But I suspect this is quite the wrong way to understand what is special to us and what is thrilling in Emerson's invocation of the horizon. I suspect that it is precisely because Manning and Locke and all them have bought up nature that the horizon glows like a halo over a corpse. The horizon is not residue. It is not the last pitiful remnant of purity holding out before the Fall has completed itself. To the contrary, it is the miasmic glow of the commodity itself.

In the attempt to hold nature still, as representation, uncanny effects are created and the alienation effect of the map becomes congenial. It is the stuff misshapen and crunched that allows real reality, the road between here and there, to appear as a thin red line that car drivers, military gunners, and tiny children in the nursery cruise along tracing destiny on a map. Robert Louis Stevenson wrote *Treasure Island* after painting a map of an imaginary island together with his young stepson, Lloyd. A story unfolded in which a boy's perception adopted by an adult took center stage, resurrecting pirates from two centuries before. Didn't Emerson say few *adult* persons see nature?

In his reflections on *Treasure Island,* Stevenson writes, "I have said the map was the most of the plot. I might almost say it was the whole."[14]

He found its colors beautiful and he described how its shape "took my fancy beyond expression; it contained harbours that pleased me like sonnets . . . the names, the shapes of the woodlands, the courses of the roads and the rivers, the prehistoric footsteps of man still distinctly traceable up hill and down dale, the mills and the ruins, the ponds and the ferries." Staring down "on these few square inches of a flat projection," he formulated in an instant a list of chapters and in fifteen days had written fifteen of them.[15] The map opened the door to the child no less than to prehistory. Stevenson likened it to the perception of a child remembering how he laid his head in the grass, "staring into the infinitesimal forest and seeing it grow populous with fairy armies." As outcome of the adult's imagination of the child's imagination, this map traces Emerson's transcendental horizon as an island, Treasure Island, that in no way can be reduced to nature as alienated property, yet is the direct result of it.

Chorography relishes detail and treats small regions as if they are isolated units. How could we possibly equate chorography, therefore, with the mission of

---

14. Robert Louis Stevenson, "My First Book," in *Treasure Island* (1883), ed. Emma Letley (Oxford: Oxford University Press, 1985), p. 199.
15. Stevenson, "My First Book," p. 194.

mapping the new nation in which it is no longer a question of small and autonomous parts but of the whole, whose parts are surveyed as if they can be pasted together to make a whole? Is this why the parts come to seem precious and timeless as a reaction against their integration into a political mega-scheme, more full of a sense of place, as they are being absorbed into the larger scheme?

Horizon asserts itself because the whole can be achieved only when there is a common denominator into which the different parts can, as it were, be translated. Hence resorting to mathematical verities, to the surveyor as zealous map-maker bound to degrees of longitude and latitude no less than resorting to the survey in the form of statistical tables of men and cattle, bridges and hogs. Particulars become unified into a whole and in the process become hybrids, as they are now something apart from themselves because of the translation they are forced to undergo. They become universals but with their ghostly particularity barely concealed. In the German language, there is a word with a notable pedigree for this type of relationship, and this is the word *Aufhebung,* meaning not merely to cancel and transform, but also to incorporate and hence preserve the previous state in the succeeding one such that the former persists, annulled yet continuously formative. The fact that I feel forced to use a *foreign word* here suggests how active and complicated is this lingering of the extinct in the body of the new. You can't go home again, and as for the horizon, like the rainbow, the closest you'll get are the overlooked haunts of the homeless, vacant lots and subway tunnels, or the limitless space of the ocean beyond the three-mile limit where the state stops poised on a swell. This is where the pirates and the lost boys like Peter Pan gathered, at home in their chorography halfway across the Oedipal divide, drifting on stolen boats and hiding out on deserted islands such as the one Robert Louis Stevenson and young Lloyd painted, together, while on vacation.

But the Codazzi Commission in Colombia strove to recapture the placeness of place that it was destroying through an evocation of the new republic as panorama in watercolor paintings. There are thought to have been well over two thousand of these paintings, but most have been lost. I call them *chorographic cameos:* dramatic landscapes; towns seen from afar like mirages in the desert; markets; village churches; country people making canoes, weaving cloth, cooking, and dancing; and Indians on the verge of the forest drawing their bows, looking most serious as if posing for a snapshot by the chorographers. Indeed, the whole country was seen as if posing, drawing its bow. The paintings are stiller than any photograph. Everything is holding its breath.

Thus does the rationalization of nature split its representations into either art or science, into watercolors or tables of statistics. You see this with astonishing clarity in the new edition of Codazzi's reports edited by Guido Barona Becerra and his colleagues in 2002.[16] These large-format, handsome volumes combine the watercolors, the text, and the tables, region by region, such that the reader can now grasp the whole visual complex in its three interlocking dimensions. It is staggering to turn the pages and see the soft tints of the dramatic landscapes or the people like puppets or dolls, manifestly cute, side by side with entire pages given over to elaborate tables with their varying sized boxes and stepwise progressions of numbers measuring everything imaginable, reminiscent of a child's game with building blocks.

For just as a survey objectifies and hence can be thought to legitimate a new nation-state as a well-surveyed piece of sovereign real estate with a place for everything and everything in its place like a thoroughly inventoried store, doesn't each new nation-state require a self-portrait, like having your photograph taken for a passport? But here I think the map is a more powerful representation of the nation than the watercolors. The map we might say is all two thousand of the watercolors including the lost ones all boiled down into one. For the map gathers the imageric nature of painting together with the scientific pretension of statistics. Visual image and enumeration blend as map. Yet how strange this shape lifted off the surface of the earth, this shape we call the map, footprint of the nation-state.

The state is to its map as its citizens are to their passports. No map = no existence; that is the harsh verdict modernity hands down to upstart states no less than to travelers. Borrowing from the place-specific focus of chorography with its aim of rendering the genius of locale, the passport photo has come to characterize the official realm of the state, identifying each particular face as a unique place, stripped of context. Place as in a place in the land has given way to a lonely face glued to regulation paper to be scrutinized under ultraviolet light. And how

---

16. Guido Barona Becerra, Camilo Domínguez Ossa, Augusto J. Gómez López, and Apolinar Figueroa Casas, *Viaje de la Comisión Corográfica por el estado del Cauca 1853–1855*, tomos II y III (Cali: Imp. Feriva, 2002).

speedily we come to relate to this strange face that is ourself, the shape of the nation, whose profile remains embedded in our memory like a cave painting.

Photography forced painting into alternative modes of expression to realism such as impressionism and cubism. Light and color became the subject of painting, as did self-reflection as to the act of seeing with one's own eyes. But older maps had some of that too, with the fingerprints of the artist made prominent. There were angels blowing wind in the corners together with emblems of discovery such as naked goddesses reclining on seashells gazing fondly at warped perspectives as in a distorting mirror—or as in the reading of this book for that matter. For what is a book but a curved mirror with angels in the corners blowing hard?

When Codazzi began his survey, the Daguerreotype, the first form of photography, was beginning to displace painted portraits in Colombia no less than in France.[17] This is a critical moment in the history of perception and representation when painting and photography merge, mix, and contest each other's claim to represent reality. Codazzi's survey employed painters, not photographers, but the impulse in their portraits of places and persons is photographic, creating images that are meant to be of use to science and political administration no less than to folklore. The paintings are ethnographic and are aimed at capturing human types and regional culture. As *types,* the persons depicted are like the map, blending statistics with the visual image. And the nostalgia evoked by the paintings suggests strongly that of a disappearing world that the very same survey and the process it is part of are treading underfoot. This is modern magic; in "photographing" you with my folkloric watercolor as part of the scientific activity of the state's Chorographic Commission, you will disappear yet be preserved as in a time capsule. Thus are the modern and the archaic yoked together. This demonstrates how the "old" may gain renewed existence as an effect of the new, flaring into being in the field of representation at its moment of eclipse.

Emerging into the full flower of nationhood after more than a decade of bloody war for independence from Spain, Venezuela got a map in 1841 in the

---

17. See, for instance, the photographic portraits taken in Bogotá in 1850 by Luís García Hevia and other photographers, in Eduardo Serrano, *Historia de la fotografía en Colombia* (Bogotá: Museo de Arte Moderna, 1983), pp. 6, 35–58.

form of Codazzi's *Atlas* published in Paris, grand capital of Europe. From the recognition it received from the French crown and state, it would seem the map was indeed a passport to the club of the big boys, opening the door to the blessed state of sovereignty. Another eagle was soaring. Ten years later Colombia got its chorographic survey under way, but many years had to elapse before its map was printed in 1865 by Thierry Freres in Paris. The map! The map! How passionate the call, the hopes, starting with the savant Francisco José de Caldas at the beginning of the nineteenth century with the independence struggle from Spain demanding for Colombia a BIG MAP at least two inches to the league! This was no map, one is tempted to say. But then what would you call it? On Caldas's scale of two inches to the league, this would be a map measuring approximately 55 feet long and 39 feet wide.[18] As an elephantine miniaturization of the country, this would be a map laboring under nostalgia for the real, reluctant to let go of the actual country and wanting instead to copy it in its entirety, claiming it in its massivity as ours to dominate, now, as against the colonial usurper.

This is, I think, parallel to what came fifty years later with Codazzi's chorography; the desire for the genius of place, but on the grandeur and scale of the nation-state itself. Equally magical as this funhouse realism was the desire to have the map as an image that would open the door to divine knowledge and hence mastery of the earth and of the future. Beacon of Enlightenment in these dark corners of downtrodden empire, Caldas had himself proclaimed that the map he had in mind would be magical.[19] And how are we to understand this magic? Caldas said it lay in the fact that *each component of the state would now find its place.*

This bizarre combination of magic and grotesque miniaturization, mapping the earth as natural expression of the state striving for mastery over nature, brings to mind Doctor Faustus and his deal with the devil. This is especially so with his modern incarnation as Doctor Strangelove presiding over maps of the world in the war room as a U.S. nuclear bomber with full payload cruises silently over the Soviet Union locked on target. All is still in black-and-white, the bomber

---

18. Assuming a league equals three miles, and a width to the country east to west of some seven hundred miles, and a length north to south of some one thousand miles, not counting the three-dimensional realities of the extensive chains of mountains.

19. Sánchez, *Gobierno y geografía*, pp. 66–67.

serene and noiseless against the majesty of the mountains extending to infinity. The spell of sublime nature is but counterpoint to the caged hysteria of the war room, to sit in which is to sit inside the brain that determines the destiny of our planet. There is a glow along the circular desk around which the president sits with his advisers. Otherwise all is dark except for the huge map fitted into the curved ceiling of the dome, flickering with lights keeping track of the bombers. It seems like the leaders of the state have merged with the map hanging over them.

In an obscure corner sits Strangelove with his dark glasses and his mechanical arm, which threatens to rise up with a will of its own and choke him. Like the arm, the map is now useless, or worse. For it is the lonely bomber as destiny that charts its own way across snowy wastes. As part of the plan of war, radio contact has been cut off and the bomber flies too low to be detected by radar. Nature reasserts itself over technology. Despite its frantic efforts to call the attack off, the state is powerless to do so. Only when the pilot dons his cowboy hat and sits astride the plunging missile as it is released from the bomb bay do we abruptly break from the spell of abstraction to laugh as the world is blown to smithereens and the horizon rises as a mushroom-shaped cloud. Then did heaven and earth meet.

With satellite visualization by the United States of other countries, as of the coca fields in Colombia, Peru, and Bolivia, Francisco José de Caldas's dream of the big map as a truly mimetic replica of reality has been finally achieved. The abstraction of the map has been transcended by the photograph that can be blown up and read stereoscopically. Poor Caldas! Poor Codazzi and Mosquera! Their vision had been one in which mapping and surveying would redeem the new nation, but the vision has only been realized by a reassertion of the nation's subaltern status as supplier of cocaine within the American empire. One problem, however: Nature still has the last word. The satellite photographs of the coca fields are no good where there are clouds, like those that enshroud the Pacific Coast where the new coca fields are springing up.

There is something of an island about maps too; miniaturizing reality to the point where the immensity that is the territory becomes but a piece of paper we can hold in our hands, our "desert island" upon which as on a tabula rasa we can write our story. And just as an island sits secure in its containment by the ocean and takes its periphery for granted, so Codazzi's survey concentrates interiority. The nation is to be defined not by its external borders but by its internal constituents and by the ease or unease of communication between these constituents. The interior itself was made mysterious and ripe for mapping by virtue of the fact that the outsides had been mapped to some extent by emissaries of empire or by foreigners bent on pillage and contraband, men like William Dampier studying winds and currents along the coasts. Other pirates like Basil Ringrose had drawn their waggoners showing profiles of the land as seen from the deck of a heaving ship anxious for refuge and plunder. But even these views of the outside of nations belonged more to the domain of chorography than to mapping. Instead of the bird's-eye view, these maps offer fragmented views from the surface of the sea and are no less practical for so being.

Coasts were the natural maps of empire and piracy. With independence, the essential task is to survey what's inside, to measure and thence organize it in tables and numbers, just as when we look at a face, we take the outlines for granted and want to know what lies behind it. Statistical truth is Enlightenment's physiognomy. The external border of the nation's frontier, which is what legally distinguishes it from its neighbors, involutes into a myriad of mini-frontiers constituting the inner being of the nation-state as discriminations between way stations on the road, suggesting that the inside is dark and infinite were it not for these often fragile lines of interconnectedness like a nervous system connecting and coordinating the whole, blending nature with politics. This would parallel the long-standing military anxiety in Latin America and the United States to control the enemy within the miasmatic mass that can never, ever be mapped.

Did the surveyors mapping the new Republic of Colombia run around the periphery of the new nation with theodolites and put white pegs in the ground together with little orange flags as they do for housing lots nowadays? But a nation is not just any old piece of real estate; it is the real estate that defines real estate, allowing everything interior to its holy outline to be cut into squares and rectangles, bought and sold. And this is why these maps, so vital to the fate of us all, mix natural signs as icons of divinity, such as rivers, coasts, and mountains, together with white pegs or orange flags planted according to trigonometric calculation and the peace of wars. With utmost fairness it could be said that Caldas died for this map, executed by a Spanish firing squad, just as half a century later Codazzi would die for the map too, executed by the miasma.

Miasma killed Codazzi and killed him before he finished either the survey or the map. He was desperate. Five peons had died from tropical fevers and more would have died, he thought, if he had not gone into the Caquetá and Putumayo alone, hiring local Indians instead. But after examining the swamp of Zapatosa, Chimichagua, in the northeast of the country in January 1858, Codazzi fell ill with intermittent fevers. With his servants and six soldiers, he was offered a place to rest, but he was impatient to finish his atlas as soon as possible. He still had to measure and draw the states of Magdalena and Bolívar. "From my hacienda *Las Cabezas*," records Oscar Trespalacios, "he got down the first line from south to north and then left to stay in the village. . . . Three days later Colombia lost her geometer."[20] Ultimately nature proved insurmountable to the man on the front line of its conversion to stately forms of being. Codazzi's ghost joins the ghostliness of place in the map that takes his place.

Poor Codazzi! After all his effort to map and survey the interior, I found it impossible in the 1980s to obtain maps of the interior from the government's Agustín Codazzi Institute in Bogotá. Once again the interior was an enigma, aching for its map. It was forbidden to obtain a map then, probably forbidden now, and although no official reason was given, that being the nature of Authority, the word was that such maps were sought by the guerrilla and therefore not to be sold to the public. Indeed, in the front of the 1967 *Atlas de Colombia,* a splendid oversize volume of maps, tables, and photographs edited by Eduardo Acevedo Latorre and issued for sale to the public like any other commodity, there is nevertheless the following statement on a large white opening page:

PROPERTY OF THE STATE
Total or Partial Reproduction Is Prohibited
Without Authorization of the Instituto Geográfico del Estado

But of this you can be sure: Only the army of the state would need the map. Born and bred in the mountains and jungles where they have fought for decades, the guerrilla need no map. There is a story of a stranger lost in a town asking

---

20. Oscar Trespalacios quoted by Luis Striffler; cited in Sánchez, *Gobierno y geografía,* pp. 441–42.

children for directions to a particular address by street name and house number. But the children have no idea of where it is. "What's the matter with you?" demands the exasperated stranger. "After all, you live here!" "But you're the one who's lost," they reply. The savant Caldas had seen the map as a talisman that would dispel the enigma of the interior. But was it not the other way around? Was it not the very idea of the map that made the insides enigmatic?

beaches

To read Codazzi on the coast is to be overwhelmed at times by pestilence; by dark fetid overheated spaces where neither light nor fresh air can enter. If the Amazon is the green lung of the world absorbing carbon dioxide and pumping out oxygen, he sees this mangrove forest of the Pacific Coast on the opposite side of the Andes to the Amazon as the arsehole of the universe through which nature's rottenness is pumped into the clammy atmosphere. As a man of science, he discerns a landscape of cause-and-effect creating the chaos of the swamp. For him, the low coastal plain between the sea and the mountains amounts to a spongiform morass emerging and disappearing under different sorts of waters flowing at different speeds and in different directions geared to an all-consuming conflict. This is because the rivers that carry the Andean mass pell-mell downstream are blocked by the tidal movement of the Pacific Ocean with spring tides up to thirteen feet.[1] The consequence of this collision is a lunar-regulated stasis of mangrove swamps and small sandbanks, called beaches, on many of which a tiny proportion of the coastal population have built houses, sometimes on stilts, despite the threat of high tides and tidal waves. Perched between the mangroves and the open sea, these precarious beaches are the only healthy sites along the coast, whipped by the sea air, while the belt of mangroves immediately behind the beaches, says Codazzi, releases "an enormous quantity of noxious gases" that mix with other pestilential airs emanating from the huge mud mass exposed to the same heat. The roots of the mangroves are bathed twice daily by the sea and then left to the suffocating heat of the sun, and this miasmic efflorescence is made even worse by the rotting vegetation that is deposited in the mud by the force of the rivers and the tides.[2]

Sinkhole of abjection, the swamp is the source of a strikingly racialized geopoetics. Heavy and soulful when faced with the miasma, Codazzi lights up, however, when depicting the beaches. It is air, the open-spaced salty air that beckons here, pushing and pulling at the frenzy of whiplashed palms, open-spaced air circulating between neatly stacked slivers of mangrove wood drying for the kitchen fire that lights in an instant.

The newly freed slaves live along the edge of the dank estuaries by the swamps and inland up the rivers in the adjoining forest. But on the healthy beaches live "whites," says Codazzi, "descendants of Spaniards and Indians, or Spaniards and Mulattoes. They are strong, intelligent and active. They have cattle. And they make small sailing boats as well as canoes. They are always dressed and around their houses grow useful trees. One day the Republic will get its best sailors from these folk."[3] They are active, industrious, intelligent, and much given to travel.[4] The cultural ecology of the coast was not unlike a city in which the poor, generally of darker skin, live in the polluted slums while the rich have nice waterfront views, soft breezes, and an overall healthy living situation.

1. Codazzi, *Jeografía física*, p. 332. He writes thirty-seven "pies granadinos." Robert C. West in his article on "Mangrove Swamps of the Pacific Coast of Colombia," p. 100, written 103 years after Codazzi's text, states that the tides range from eight to ten feet on average, with a spring range of eleven to thirteen feet.

2. Codazzi, *Jeografía física*, p. 332.

3. Codazzi, *Jeografía física*, p. 333.

4. Felipe Pérez, *Jeografía física i política del estado del Cauca* (Bogotá: Imprenta de la nación, 1862), p. 127.

The number of such whites living on these beaches is tiny, maybe two hundred people all told, and there are but three contiguous beaches they inhabit, including that of Mulatos. This smallness of scale adds to their spectrality as "whites," like ghosts from an archaic past. Ricardo Grueso, my ex-miner friend from Santa María, long resident in Guapi, insists they are descendants of Vikings and of pirates such as Henry Morgan. With their blond hair, blue or green eyes, he says, they marry only among themselves, even brother with sister, in their anxiety to keep the race pure. Young Mario born and bred on the coast tells me: "Make no mistake. They will be tough on you, too, because you're not fair enough. They are Nazis!" Cecilia de Robledo recounts in a recent book the no doubt apocryphal story that when a black man arrived in an emergency some years back, he was well received, but the plates off which he ate were thrown into the sea.[5] Ricardo Grueso adds that they washed the floor where a black man had walked, with *hot* water! But even he has to admit things are changing and Mulatos now has more blacks than whites, even though there may be little by way of intermarriage.

Proud isolates on shifting sands, in my mind's eye I saw these whites as beaches themselves, defining the blurred morass of the coast by counterpoint. After hearing so much about them, never did I imagine that their beaches would be made of black sand! Yet if the whites stand out as windswept chips of purity providing the necessary contrast, it must be remembered that like the ex-prison island of Gorgona ten miles out to sea, these blue- and green-eyed folk have gained their sharp-edged capacity to define because of the mystery that has come to define them: their "whiteness" and their uncanny ability to build ships, not to mention the mysteries of their industriousness and their wearing clothes . . . intertwined in their incestuous aloneness with grand genealogies of piracy, Sir Henry Morgan who took Panamá in 1671, and, of course, Vikings.

It took years before I visited a beach on the Pacific Coast. My orientation had always been upriver. When I stepped off the launch at Mulatos, the first thing I noticed was the sound of the surf pounding. All night long I slept in the arms of that sound and as with Proust thought vividly of the same sound crashing

---

5. Cecilia de Robledo, *Gorgona, isla prisión; crónicas* (Bogatá: Pijao, 1997), p. 277.

through memory onto the glistening sand of Pittwater under the stars back in Australia when I was a child and my mother's good friend, who had rented a summer house, observed, as we stepped out of a rowboat into warm salt water, that there is no sound so sublime as the crashing of surf on a windless night. The sky is huge here at Mulatos, magnified by the dark shallow sea stretching over black sand. The wind never stops, soft wind, rustling the coconut palms so you never for a second forget that marvel of movement, the air cool and dry. You become aware of how much effort has gone into steeling your body upstream and in the estuaries so as to cope with the heat and humidity there. Here at Mulatos the high-water mark along the sand bristles with seeds taking root. It's not just the sweeping vista that the breeze manifests as touch on the cheek. It's the invisible life stirring, the animation that makes the beach a lookout on the cosmos.

At night it was pitch-black except for a solitary lightbulb on top of a set of cement steps some ten feet high forming an altar to the Virgin. I call them steps, but I guess the builder had thought of them as sacred architecture. I saw them as steps abruptly cut off, midair, leading to the void that must be heaven. At the base of this altar praying for over an hour was a skinny young white man with a group of black kids and, hanging back and facing the other way, into the dark, stood a gangly white teenager. The white man said he was a missionary, arrived only the day before from Bogotá with the teenager so as to cure him of drug addiction. It was an odd sight and as the days went by I was struck by the way nobody in Mulatos bothered them or thought them strange. They just let them be. Every night this little group crouched at the foot of their Virgin. There were no police, people said, with relief, it being the opinion of those with whom I spoke that police would bring crime and violence. The government has created a national park here, but unlike the park into which the ex-prison island of Gorgona was converted, ten miles out to sea, Mulatos seems untouched by state authority. But then it has strong internal cohesion and binding sentiments, a temporary autonomous zone if ever there was one. I heard a story that a few years back a U.S. citizen arrived but was told to leave straightaway because Colombians are not allowed to enter the United States. Imagine!

As in Codazzi's time, the inhabitants of these beaches and islets are famous for the excellence of their shipbuilding and knowledge of sailing and the sea. Early morning the majority of men cruise offshore for shrimp. But their identity lies with the few who refer to themselves as navigators and hire themselves out to captain coastal trading vessels or else stay home and build boats. So how did this begin? René Estupiñon, an unassuming blond man with brown eyes, is a master of shipbuilding. He told me that the whites here are descendant from Spaniards sailing north from Lima in a galleon with a cargo of gold and silver that was attacked by pirates in the vicinity of the island of Gorgona, directly opposite Mulatos. Fleeing the pirates, the Spaniards ran aground in the Río Tapaje and scuttled their ship so the pirates couldn't get at it. The site where the ship went down is still called *el estero del barco*. The survivors split into four groups, settling on Mulatos, Iscuandé, Playa Reyes, and Playa San Juan. Now and again when the tides shift the sand, you can still see the anchor.

Among the crew were ship's carpenters who started repairing and making ships, gaining a reputation for the excellence of their craft up and down this lonely coast from Ecuador to Panamá. Nowadays they build one new boat a year and reconstruct three. René Estupiñon employs a crew of twelve men, only four of whom are white. They place one tremendous hardwood tree down as the keel, then place the prow and the stern, and build up the ribs from the keel. These boats have to be strong because they are beached on mudflats up and down the Pacific Coast to take on cargo such as lumber. He says that a typical boat spends six hours out of twenty-four on land. While the majority of craftsmen build by eye alone, so-called *empíricos,* he is the only person in Mulatos who first constructs a model, some two to three feet long, and, when he's got it looking right, measures off the dimensions for the actual vessel from the model. Each boat he's built has its twin sister in diminutive form, ruddy brown and glistening in its smooth perfection back in his collection at home. Thus you can build any size you want by simply altering the scale. This is a mimetic approach. But he began as an *empírico* and is grateful because that teaches you skills you will need for working with models. But then how does an *empírico* figure things out? Does he

have a model in his head? Does he inch his way along, step by step feeling his way with the materials at hand? How might we compare and weigh the significance of these two methods?

Two changes are at hand. One is the sharply diminished supply of hardwoods such that René's next boat is to be built of steel. With the models it is easy to make the change, he says in his relaxed way. To me it would seem not easy at all to switch from wood to steel. René's calm manner seems to be telling me that my views of nature are hopelessly narrow, encased as they are by my idea that here at the end of the world on mudflats by immense rain forests the boats *have* to be made of trees and that no matter how adaptable local modes of construction are, steel has no place in the universe of the *empíricos* nor in that of the model makers. But to him it's all the same! No problem! It's me that's got the problem, trying to imagine René and his assistants managing sheets of hot steel and welding equipment in the blazing sun instead of sniffing aromatic sawdust and eyeing the friendly warm hues of Pacific hardwoods. But that's not all there is to this story of wood and steel. The diminished supply of wood also means less demand for boats because lumber was the principal cargo along the coast. And the reason there is less lumber, he says, is because of government restrictions on logging. I find that hard to believe and wonder how much his opinion is guided by ideology the same way mine is about the unnaturalness of steel. I think there is less lumber because of excessive logging. The mouth of this very river was chockablock with boats ten years ago taking off lumber. And then there's the guerrilla. If they forbid logging, then you can be sure there will be none.

The other change is drugs. Now René has to submit minutely detailed plans of every boat he is going to build to a state office in Bogotá and wait half a year for approval. The idea seems to be that if boarded by naval patrols searching for drugs, the navy can measure off every centimeter in search of false bulkheads.

René learned about models from Israel Estupiñon, who learned it from Gonzalo Estupiñon, who learned it from Jaime Martán, who had been sent by his father to Germany to study shipbuilding after the devastating earthquake of 1906 killed all the great shipbuilders living here except for the *empírico* Elías Estupiñon. Boat builders here also got tips from a U.S. engineer who came and lived on the beach for several years with his Colombian wife many decades back.

When I asked René for the date when the galleon was attacked by pirates, he said, after some hesitation, sometime at the end of the eighteenth century—exactly when Dampier, Ringrose, and all that pack of merry boys were cruising in these waters off Gorgona. When I asked him again, a year later, he said he couldn't remember but it must have been before 1906! Such is memory and such is the anxiety of the anthropologist to tell a good story. The year 1906 was when the tidal wave wiped out most people here. From the survivors came the models.

A few hundred yards from the open beach, René has his home on the edge of the swamp. He built his house there so as to reconstruct a boat. Years ago the boat had been floated up the estuary at high tide to its present berth on the mud, but the owner ran out of cash and the boat sits here still, prow pointed into the forest, staid and upright as if at any moment it will sail overland, a ghost ship of bleached white ribs in beautiful symmetry resting on the keel that was once a lofty tree. You will never forget this. I move to take a photograph but he will not come with me. It makes him sad to see this skeleton. One day soon he will move his house. It will take only a couple of days. How come? Oh! Each piece is fixed by bolts easy to undo. More like a ship than a house. And the ghostly ribs suspended so gracefully in the swamp, the real ship, it will stay and become part of the swamp into which it will slowly decay. Then it will sail once more, as pestilence and miasma rising from the fetid mangroves headed into the forest where the black folk live.

my co

ocaine mus

lightning

Barbacoas was the first town I knew on the coast. It was 1971. The bus zigzagged down the cliffs of the Andes along the border with Ecuador and arrived as night was falling. The main street ran in a curve down a slight hill to the fast-moving Río Telembí, green and wide. On either side of the street were tall houses of rough-cut planks, smoke from kitchen fires folding over them like mist. At ground level I could see a man in golden light making gold jewelry with hammer and pliers. The church had a Virgen, he told me, but the last batch of priests, from Italy, had little by little stripped her of her golden clothes until all she had left was a miniskirt.

Barbacoas is a word like *buccaneer*, meaning barbecue, derived from an Indian language, and it was once the name that the Spaniards gave to the entire southern half of the Pacific Coast. As the Indians disappeared, so the name shrunk, like the Virgen's skirt, and today it is no more than the name of this town famous in the nineteenth century for its gold and for serving as a port for small craft connecting the ocean to the road coming down the high Andes from the interior. In Codazzi's day, seventy Indian porters arrived there every day from the highlands carrying loads on their backs.

There is a small chain of hills separating the town from the mangroves by the sea, and it was these hills, according to Codazzi, that saved Barbacoas from the miasma. Being heavier than air, he writes, the particles emitted by the mangroves smashed against the peaks to become absorbed by the thick vegetation covering them.[1]

Everything comes down to particles. And what wonderful particles, Enlightenment's defense against miasma. But when you atomize reality like this, the uncanny may snake back stronger than ever. Take René Descartes, who said water was composed of long, smooth, eel-shaped particles, separated by different particles composing what he called the *subtle matter*. Vapor was caused by these two types of particles, the eel-shaped ones and the subtle-matter ones, reacting differently to heat. What's more, water's eel-shaped particles were unique. No other substance had particles so easily separable. Descartes expounded on these ideas in 1637 in a book entitled *Meteors*.[2] You may well check yourself at this point, reflecting on your own habits of mind, and ask, Why this urge of the intellect to dissolve matter's materiality into smaller and smaller parts? Why this urge to understand understanding as dividing and subdividing like this until one decides to call it quits when the parts become part/icles? And given the undoubted power of this style of thought in modern forms of reckoning, how come miasma still haunts us? But Descartes can help us here if we take to heart his subtle matter and eel-shaped particles, for they remind us of the crazy wild thought and subtle poetry swarming around the aggressive methodology of divide and rule. For this same poetry has the merit of estranging vapor, of making it a puzzle and a wonder, whereby the human intellect and the intelligence of nature can start talking to one another.

---

1. Codazzi, *Jeografía física*, pp. 334–35.
2. W. E. Knowles Middleton, *A History of the Theories of Rain and Other Forms of Precipitation* (New York: Franklin Watts, 1965), p. 20.

My liberty is this, lifting off with vapor's self-estrangement: Thinking of wind and spirit as one, allowing sheets and curtains of rain to intervene, the core being *vapor* as with eel shapes tumbling with subtle matter and daily life on the Pacific Coast. Vapor is a relation of *sun* to *water* as *movement* (= *wind*). I am told that in Baghdad in the tenth century, there was a secret society of Basra called the Brethren of Purity whose meteorology showed an advance over the Greeks. They thought that wind is air in motion, produced by vapor rising from the sea and by exhalations from the land warmed by the sun.[3] These same vapors and exhalations produced:

clouds
    rain
dew
    hoarfrost
                fog
    drizzle
thunder
    lightning
and hail.

Six hundred years after the secret society of Basra, Antoine Mizauld asked why raindrops are round. His book *Mirror of the Air* was published in Paris in 1548.[4]

In 1663 J. Jonston said raindrops fall in Mexico with such violence that they kill people.[5]

When I read today about raindrops and secret societies, I realize something has happened to wind and to weather. No doubt about it. What was before the source of conjecture as to the problem of Being and of the nature of

---

3. Middleton, *A History of the Theories of Rain*, p. 15.
4. Middleton, *A History of the Theories of Rain*, p. 177.
5. Middleton, *A History of the Theories of Rain*, p. 18.

the cosmos, namely, vapor and wind, seems now to have disappeared as a source of wonder. We no longer connect with the cosmos via weather or via earth, fire, air, and water—or, to put it differently, reading these ideas about the mundane play of rain and fog, we now see the roundness of the raindrop with new, estranged eyes.

In his *lèttera al dottóre G. B. Capponi* in Bologna in 1666, Father Urbano d'Aviso said vapor was little bubbles of water filled with fire.[6]

Bubbles filled with fire brings us back to electricity in this miasmic sky. Maybe we should think of this as a swamp sky, as if God had picked up the swamp and suspended it upside down in the air to make a sky of mud with red crabs running frightened, mangrove trees pointing downward from a canopy of cloud. The editor of Codazzi's papers, Felipe Pérez, reported that this coastal sky was "constantly raining and charged with electricity." There was barely an interval between thunderclaps, and the lightning struck five or six flashes at a time.[7] And from the first written records in the sixteenth century onward, one finds alarming comments concerning electrical storms. The pirate scribe Basil Ringrose described the lightning in 1679 in the Bay of Panamá as a power he had never experienced in his life. Forty years later, the British privateer Woodes Rogers records his first sighting of the island of Gorgona, June 10, 1709: "In the Night we have much Rain with Lightning and Squalls of Wind, by which the Havre de Grace lost her main Top-mast." So strong were these electrical storms that they impeded the careening of his vessels, despite the need to get the job done in double-quick time.[8]

Nature becomes a wizard's workshop of special effects. In 1809 Colombia's most famous scientist and a keen geographer, Francisco José de Caldas, portrayed the Chocó as the site of a continual apocalypse:

The wind blows in hard from the Pacific pushing clouds up against the *cordillera* which appears somber and threatening. Darkness

6. Middleton, *A History of the Theories of Rain,* 23.
7. Pérez, *Jeografía física,* pp. 123, 166–67.
8. Exquemelin, *The Buccaneers of America,* pp. 336–37; also see Rogers, *A Cruising Voyage,* pp. 158–59.

reigns and wherever you look there are clouds weighing down on every living thing. A suffocating calm prevails. This is the most terrible moment. Gusts of wind uproot enormous trees. There are electrical explosions and terrifying rolls of thunder. Rivers leap from their beds and the sea becomes a boiling mass with huge waves smashing along the coast. Sky fuses with earth as the end of the world is proclaimed.[9]

Felipe Pérez understood these awesome fireworks as due to the noxious vapors laden with maleficent particles rising from the swamps. The drumrolls of thunder and the lightning in the sky were divine counterpoint to the pestilence below. It seems truly fabulous, that is to say, of fable, this maleficence guarding the gold hoard that nature, in its prehistoric turmoil, bequeathed this lost region.

Of course they are related. Intimately. *Lightning & Miasma.* How low it hangs, this swamp sky charged with lightning! What troubled thoughts our geographers had concerning the noxiousness of its unseemly particles! Something has gone seriously wrong with the sliding movement between eels and subtle matter. Lightning signals the miasmic mix of invisibility and materiality that is so striking here, a secular equivalent, we could say, to spirits, which is to say breath, which is to say what lightning illumines at one stroke

> *pneuma =*
> *spirit =*
> *breath =*
> *song =*
> *God =*
> *wind =*
> *Discourse of Winds* (William Dampier, the pirate, cruising off the island of Gorgona)

---

9. Francisco José de Caldas, *Seminario de la Nueva Granada* (1809), cited in *Geografía económica de Colombia: Chocó* (Bogotá: Litografía Colombia, 1943), p. 46.

because, and for this we should be grateful, the *pneuma* of the *miasma* is heavy with particulate matter emanating from the swamp. All eel, we could say, with the *subtle matter* gone soggy on us.

If this sounds like metaphysics, it is also physics, the sort of metaphysics needed by people in the path of El Niño and sailors and weatherwomen the world over. For centuries in the Western world before the birth of Christ, the be-ing of Being was understood as composed of the interconvertibility of

Water—Earth—Air—Fire

In the sixth century B.C., philosophers living in Ionia on the Anatolian shore got to work on this formula. Thales of Miletus said all the elements came from one element, namely, water. This makes a lot of sense on the Pacific Coast of Colombia. Benjamin Farrington, to whom I am indebted for this understand-ing of early Greek philosophy, locates Thales in the context of the swamp world of ancient Egypt and Babylonia, whose economies and *hence* (!) cosmogonies were wrought through the labor of drainage as expressed by the Babylonian cre-ator, Marduk: "Let the dry land appear"!

Similar to accounts of the origin of the world among Native Americans in North America, in which the creator sends an animal down to the bottom of the sea to bring up mud or sand, the world was all ocean and what Marduk did was make dirt and pile it on a rush mat on the surface of the sea, and in this way be-gan land as we know it. Thales disagreed. In the inimitable words of the Enlight-enment via Farrington, he *"let Marduk out"* (i.e., Thales drained the swamp, the religious swamp). The prime force was discerned as in matter itself and not in a god. Matter is alive and power lies within things themselves. Immanence, not transcendence. According to Farrington, Thales held that the earth was a flat disc floating on water. There is water above our heads as well as all around us, and the sun and the moon are water vapor in a state of incandescence. Sun and moon "sail over our heads on the watery firmament above and then sail round, on the sea, on which the earth itself is afloat, to their appointed stations for rising in the east."[10]

---

10. Benjamin Farrington, *Greek Science: Its Meaning for Us*, 2 vols. (Harmondsworth, Middlesex: Pen-guin, 1947), vol. 1, p. 32.

I quote this as a form of encouragement—through estrangement, surrealism and dada in equal mix—the sun sailing on water above our heads. Can't stop. In a hurry. Tighten the sails. Got to get to the east by sunrise. Water, water, everywhere. True, we ascended from the sea and the slimy shore to become *men*, but it is still the same old thing: water, water, everywhere.

Then there was Anaximenes of Ionia for whom not water but mist was the first principle. He suggested that air might condense to cloud, then water, then earth, and finally stone, which makes us mindful of the prison island of Gorgona, it being the glance of the Gorgon Medusa that turned men to stone, which makes us mindful of those miners, men and women, cutting their way through stone in search of fossils and gold up the Timbiquí, where water and stone construe all being, all fire and all earth too. Stone, stone, everywhere . . . And pursuing these clever Ionians further, one sees how the four elements become elemental in a different way. They become poetic figures for a being that undoes itself: Being-as-indeterminacy, as with Heraclitus, "everything flows," for whom fire was the first principle.

"Take the thing we now call water," says Plato in terms that evoke the Pacific Coast and are breathtaking on account of the flow he perceives connecting water to stone, via fire. It's as if he is flowing himself, straight down that river into which Heraclitus told us you can't step twice. Not into the same place, that is, because by that time the water has become fire. When water is compacted, affirms Plato (and I want you to think back to cement, although he is thinking of *chora*), we see the water

> becoming earth and stones, and this same thing, when it is dissolved and dispersed, becoming wind and air; air becoming fire by being inflamed; and by a reverse process, fire, when condensed and extinguished, returning once more to the form of air, and air coming together again and condensing as mist and cloud; and from these, as they are yet more closely compacted, flowing water; and from water once more earth and stones: and thus, as it appears, they transmit in a cycle the process of passing into one another.[11]

---

11. Plato, *Timaeus*, trans. Francis M. Cornford (London: Macmillan, 1959), pp. 51–54 (sections 50c–51b).

His point is that it is the *chora,* meaning the womb or the nursemaid of becoming, that provides for this flow of one element into the other. Fair enough. But from this point on we may lose him, as this function of this womb to match and mix, to transform and dissolve, is in his opinion at the same time a *copying* process in certain respects like a photographic camera: "The things that pass in and out are to be called copies of the eternal things," he says, "impressions taken from them in a strange manner, that is hard to express."[12] What is fascinating about such a camera-as-*chora* is that it "translates" ideas, or should we say images, into material substances (just as the famous double helix of genetic imagery is translated into living creatures and materials, to invoke the womb once more).

This belief—or should we say conviction—concerning the conversion of form into substance resurfaces with the enthusiasm for Plato's ideas in the Renaissance magic elaborated by Marsilio Ficino, according to whom it was the magician's task to locate images that would mediate divine forms with the material world.[13] Ficino drew on the earlier work of Plotinus, who says:

> I think . . . that those ancient sages, who sought to secure the presence of divine beings by the erection of shrines and statues, showed insight into the nature of the All; they perceived that, though this Soul (of the world) is everywhere tractable, its presence will be secured all the more readily when an appropriate receptacle is elaborated, a place especially capable of receiving some portion or phase of it, something reproducing and serving like a mirror to catch an image of it.[14]

We trap the soul of the world through laying cunning images. All such images resemble *chora,* translating form into substance and vice versa. Poetry and matter become one.

---

12. Plato, *Timaeus,* p. 50 (sections 50a–c).
13. Frances A. Yates, *Giordano Bruno and the Hermetic Tradition* (New York: Vintage, 1969), pp. 62–83.
14. Quoted in Yates, *Giordano Bruno,* p. 64.

This gives us insight into how it is that one of my favorites, Walter Benjamin, such an object-riveted writer, could nevertheless give central place to the image—as when, for example, he says in a well-known thesis written in 1940 that historical materialism "wishes to retain that image of the past which unexpectedly appears to a man singled out by history at a moment of danger."[15] Where Benjamin's "magic" fusing of poetry and matter differs from that of Ficino and his friends is in its using a heady mix of Marxism, Jewish mysticism, 1920s film theory, and a serious interest in hashish and opium derivatives so as to dive back and forth through time to redeem the past and thus alter the future, not all that dissimilar in this respect from those Kogi Indian priests of the Sierra Nevada whom I mention at the beginning of *My Cocaine Museum*. William Burroughs took this further still, this same medley of dreams and drugs, bound in his case to image warfare in the very heart of the U.S. imperium. Nowadays we call it "spin," as in referring to the George W. Bush White House with its desperation for photo ops and the theatrical manipulations of reality including "weapons of mass deception." What is "spin" if not the intoxicating and unstable mix of power and fear bound to effervescent imagery plowed into collective memory so as to change the future? Burroughs wanted to democratize this mix by promoting what he called the Magical Universe as opposed to the One God Universe, while Benjamin put his money on what he came to call the "dialectical image."

Fundamental to the operation of the dialectical image, as I see it, is that it stands at the crossroads of a piled-up contradiction like a smash on the freeway of time such that several dimensions come into play, simultaneously. There is a juxtaposition of images; this is the montage dimension, and its task is to conjure forth all the tricks in the surrealist tool kit; surprise, wonder, and even shock. Then there is the tense stasis of shock itself, a phase of compressed nothingness in which memory, space, and time all coagulate and then reconfigure past and present, leading to the third dimension, which is the alchemical one wherein image and material being fuse and transform one another. Voilà! The dialectical image!

Benjamin must have been himself puzzled by this, his beloved brainchild, outcome of his fascination with Marcel Proust's concept of "involuntary mem-

---

15. Walter Benjamin, "Theses on the Philosophy of History" (1950), in *Illuminations: Essays and Reflections*, ed. Hannah Arendt, trans. Harry Zohn (New York: Schocken, 1968), p. 255.

ory" as joined to Karl Marx's theory of revolution and history. For he felt moved to quote his philosopher friend the redoubtable T. W. Adorno, quoting Benjamin with respect to the dialectical image, adding a strong image of his own, namely, that dialectical images are like "antediluvian fossils."[16]

Why fossils? I don't know exactly what Adorno had in mind with this bewildering attempt to understand human history and natural history as one, but the Pacific Coast certainly has a response. Fossils sleep the sleep of millennia consequent to untold planetary trauma. They are frozen images of the crash whose petrified being signals the enormity of that convulsion. Adorno couldn't for a minute forget the image Benjamin seized upon in his study of the baroque, namely, the death's head, the smiling absence of life, that winks from the horrors of the past frozen through time in a petrified, primordial landscape. Yet we know from the miners who cruise underground in search of primordial rivers of liquid gold that the fossils they find there at the doorway to the gold crumble to the touch. Petrifaction transmutes into the ash of time, gold itself. Voilà! The dialectical image!

This image that is also fact and trauma, the trauma that courses through facts, is the image of subterranean riverbeds of gold and fossil objects. The fossils are petrified memories like prehistoric cave drawings memorializing the event of a convulsed nature driven underground, what our chorographers called the upheaval that in prehistoric times shaped the land, throwing up the three mountain chains we know today as the Andes running north and south along the western rim of South America.[17] And if we look further, we discern something no less mysterious: a fourth chain of the Andes hidden under the warm waters of the Pacific itself. The founding violence that tore nature apart in its prehistoric turmoil laid out a mountain range parallel to the Andes, ten to twenty miles beyond the coast but *under* the surface of the ocean. Wonder of wonders, the *island* of Gorgona is the *peak* of that oceanic underwater range. The island upthrust from the ocean floor thus represents an inversion of the same founding violence that on the mainland drove rivers down into the earth, filling them with gold.

16. Benjamin, *The Arcades Project*, p. 461.
17. Pérez, *Jeografía física*, p. 123.

my co

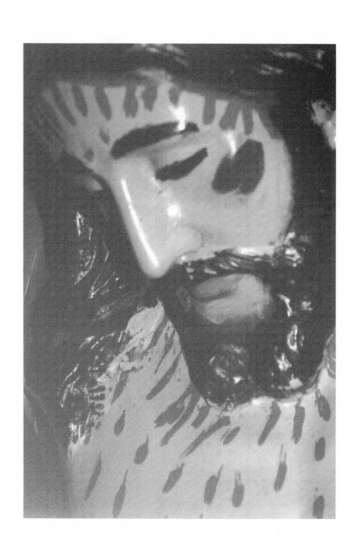

Only twice have I met a person who served time in Gorgona Island when it was a prison. The first was Blackmouth, Bocanegra in Spanish, Misael Bocanegra. "Eighteen years a prisoner" was the first thing he told me, "three years, three months, and twenty-one days in Gorgona." It was his sentence, his life sentence. For in reality it had never ended. He returned to live in the same town in the interior where he was born and where he had, so I was told, raped a woman who had jilted him, then killed both her and her baby with a knife. Some say he hacked off her breast and filled the baby's bottle with blood and stuck it in the baby's mouth. People wanted to lynch him.

Never once during the forty-five-minute interview in that small town in the interior did he look me in the eye. Not that I am one for baring of the soul either. But it was unnerving. Not even to try, I mean. To make such a thing of it. To give up like that. Hadn't he paid his debt to society? "A killer never looks you *en frente*," Rejina told me when I commented on it. Being a prisoner from Gorgona made him a freak. We had a curious power over him. It was like he never left Gorgona. But he had a power over us too. He lived alone as a watchman in his sister's warehouse on a quiet street leading to the river nobody used anymore, not for bathing, not even for washing clothes, ever since the paper mill had been installed upstream and dead fish floated by belly-up.

The warehouse extended the length of the block, tall enough to take the largest trucks. In its endless brick wall, there was but one window at which we stood out on the street conversing with him on the inside, for he made no effort to invite us in. Separating us were bars on the window, for all the world like a prison cell. It was hard to know what to make of our halting conversation. But then, what did I expect?

He must have felt our need for a suitable image, for his first statement was about the *botellón*, the box a prisoner was forced to stand in as punishment, two to three days at a time, unable to lie down or sit. Behind him in the dark, one could make out his tools. In prison he had learned to make shoes. Yet the more we talked about Gorgona, the more Gorgona slipped away. A handful of facts that could refer to most anything and nothing. What could he say? What would bring it into sharp focus? This was more than trying to resurrect the past. It was a question about justice for which the prison stood as a symbol stark yet enigmatic, the measure of which lay in the situation we presently found ourselves, inadvertently repeating the prison scene on a cul-de-sac in an impoverished and ecologically blighted Colombian town.

"Did you see the scar on his forearm?" Raúl asked as we walked away. It was like a tourniquet with puckered edges compressing the flesh into a balloon-like bulge. I had without thinking associated the scar with the violence of prison life and sharp-looking tools gleaming behind him in the darkness. But I was wrong.

It was New Year's Eve with skyrockets exploding, Raúl recounted. The watchdog quivered with fear under Blackmouth's bed. He tried to yank it out, but the dog lunged, biting deep into his forearm, and wouldn't let go. Eventually he was able to throw the dog's chain up over a beam in the ceiling and hoist it into the air so he could thrust one of his shoemaker's knives into its belly again, and again, until it went limp and its jaws opened. Time stands still at midnight, and fate—which is when time congeals—seeks out this opening in the passage of time.[1] Such was Gorgona, permanent midnight.

The prisoner has become a guard, or at least a watchman. Fair enough. "The deplorable thing," writes B. Traven in *The Death Ship*, "is that the people who were tortured yesterday, torture today."[2] But he is still a prisoner in his room alone in the solitary confinement of what now seemed like his own choosing, just as he had chosen to return to live in the town, scene of his crime. There was the community, gathered in its exuberance on New Year's Eve 'neath showers of stars. While there sits he, enclosed with but a dog for company, two watchmen, man and beast turning on each other, knife flashing. Was his room like his soul, a continuation of Gorgona, surrounded by the wild sea with sharks and moray eels? The name Gorgona in Greek, according to my copy of Bullfinch's *Mythology*, means strong billows. His own name was another name to contend with: Bocanegra. His was the black mouth surrounded by the billowing ocean, this murderer become prisoner become watchman on the wrong side of his bars. But what about me? Or you, for that matter? Am I not too much a prisoner of Gorgona's afterimage, fear and pictures shooting out of my black mouth? And that dog, under our bed?

There was a girl living next door to Bocanegra in the 1950s when he committed his murder. Years later she told me how he came home after his murder like any other day, *tranquilo*. His wife had no idea of what had happened. He ate his meal and went to sleep like any other day. And not too long after Bocanegra was put away, the neighbor on the other side of her home received a visit from her brother living in Medellin who wanted to leave his little daughter with her. He said he was going to kill his wife because she had a lover. "There are plenty other women in the world," his sister responded. "If it's not working out, leave her!" A few months later the sister received a cutting from a newspaper concerning the murder of the wife in Medellin. Forty stab wounds with a machete, assailant unknown. Years later the man's family came with a court order to take away the little girl he'd left with his sister. She didn't want to go.

---

1. Benjamin, *The Origin of German Tragic Drama*, p. 135.
2. Traven, *Death Ship*, p. 80.

Raúl told me Bocanegra died suddenly a couple of weeks after our interview and wondered about the coincidence. I promised henceforth to never interview anyone he liked. He laughed. He of all people had an ear for irony, his whole face cracked into a winning smile, skin taut across the cheekbones laid bare by years of coke addiction. I doubt he ever ate. It was our conceit, our mysterious power of death sociology in a country of killers. It was early evening, getting on for eight o'clock. All the shutters had been rung down except at the lottery. The plaza was empty but for the man selling candies and loose cigarettes from a stall on wheels. In the bar and soda fountain opposite, the town's businessmen brought in their children for ice creams. The trees in the park stood as sentinels across from the church as fear squirted like black ink down emptying streets while Raúl and I and Weimar told the same tired stories to each other seated on the corner, the last of the Mohicans sucking in hard on the vacuum.

In Guapi I heard of another ex-prisoner and I tracked him down playing billiards. Not here, he said, when I asked for an interview, a strange fellow with a bulging forehead, glasses that seemed to reflect passing light all the time, a tobacco-stained white mustache, and a skinny, tired-looking frame, so very different to the robust river men chalking their cues or the fat traders languishing in the heat. He was born and raised on the Río Timbiquí, had emigrated to the interior to cut sugarcane in the north of the Valle, and I was told he had killed his wife *por celos*, from jealousy, stabbing her twenty-seven times. These figures are like those proffered for bribes and corruption. Just as everyone can tell you to the last cent how much an official has been paid under the table, so they can tell you how many knife thrusts or bullets have gone into the corpse. Two sides of the same coin. He tried to kill himself with poison, permanently twisting one side of his face like a stroke victim. He remarried a woman with a solid government job. "What woman would want to live with a man like that?" my friend exclaimed, more than once.

When I got to his house the next day around nine o'clock, the wife already gone to work, he offered me a cigarette and, fixing me with a stare from those luminous glasses, informed me that people "outside of Colombia" were calling him by phone (at that time a feat of technical wizardry) so as to make a film about Gorgona, and they needed to speak with him about his "costs." I took the hint, thanked him for his trouble, and left, disappointed to miss out on the chance of hearing what it was like as a prisoner, but somewhat relieved not to hear about it, as well. Maybe, like him, I was too much a prisoner of Gorgona's afterimage. Maybe I endowed the prison with too much meaning until it became almost spectral, and this imposed an unbearable burden on ex-prisoners with whom I wanted to talk so as to both confirm and dispel that specter. I needed their prison experience as a gift and not as something to be paid for.

According to convention, Bocanegra and the man from Timbiquí who had killed his wife had paid off their "debt" to society by being imprisoned on the island of Gorgona. But in what had they paid and how does one estimate how much one has to pay for killing someone? This is the same sort of absurd but necessary question as asking in what and how much I should pay an ex-prisoner for telling me about his doing time. The prisoners' crimes had imbued them with an ineradicable contagion that no amount of prison could erase. It was this I felt at the barred window trying to converse with Bocanegra obscured in the dark, the same as what surrounded the strange fellow with the twisted face of a stroke victim whose eyeglasses reflected passing light. Fate decreed I enter the picture. I provided them with the opportunity whereby they could come forward with a gift and perhaps release the miasma, as the ancient Greeks had done through libations and sacrifice. But it didn't happen. Just as with cocaine and gold, it doesn't happen.

stone

stone

As you ascend the Timbiquí, the stones in the river get gradually bigger. Rounded and oval at the junction of salt with fresh water, they start off more or less the size of your fist. When you get out of the canoe at the first rapids, it is still comfortable to walk over beaches in the river's bend made of stones, thousands and thousands, who knows, millions of stones. A few miles farther upstream, however, and the stones are the size of your head, and you find yourself hopping like a mountain goat when forced to walk by the rapids. Your feet trip. The world spins. In all likelihood, a scientist measuring the stones would be able to find a mathematical equation demonstrating the infinitesimal gradation in size, the work of centuries, perhaps millennia, as the stones rub against each other, getting smaller and smoother as the river makes its way to the sea.

Way upriver in Santa María, there is beautiful stonework everywhere. There are deep drainage channels to divert the ceaseless rain. There are elaborate stone walls supporting the path by the river. There are loose stones serving as paving on the street, and there is the stonework reinforcing the walls of many of the shallow mines that go straight down into the earth for ten to twenty feet. The more recent the stonework of these walls, the lighter the stones are in color, like creamy white and yellow-streaked eggs, the size of footballs, or larger. In Europe such stonework is the sign of antiquity and stability, whereas here, although there is a dazzling beauty, such stones seem continuously temporary, part of the diffuse and never-ending work of mining shaking the ever-unstable earth.

Immobile in the surging sea, the island of Gorgona reminds us that stone presses hard against its opposite, as manifested by the movement of water. Stone and water coupled together is what everyday work means to the miners at Santa María, the men underground no less than the women washing gold by the edge of streams. Panning gold actually means adding water to dirt full of stones and working these elements together with centrifugal force such that the water comes to dominate the stone. Brecht makes the point in a poem following the Chinese Tao that Benjamin quotes approvingly: drop by drop, water wears away the hardest granite. Our recent language acknowledges this dialectic of stone in being stoned on drugs and music, which is the same as "being high." Being stoned suggests the dead face of the zombie, a person in a trance, passing as an inert object back into history and still further beyond to that mythical island, home of the Gorgons, near the night at the end of the known world where time is space.

Being stoned is what Benjamin was in Marseilles in 1932, contemplating suicide no less than the stones of the sidewalk, which, on account of a magical ointment with which he had covered them, could just as well have been the sidewalk stones he knew back home in Paris. "One often speaks of stones instead of bread," he said. "These stones were the bread of my imagination."[1] Being stoned is to enter into a conversation with the nature of second nature wherein history will return as prehistory, a message in a bottle or maybe in a body, but at any

---

1. Walter Benjamin, "Hashish in Marseilles" (1932), in *Reflections: Essays, Aphorisms, Autobiographical Writings*, ed. Peter Demetz, trans. Edmund Jephcott (New York: Schocken, 1986), p. 143.

event as an image that flashes forth from nowhere. It is "the primal phenomenon of history," writes Benjamin with reference to the *dialectical image*. "It is like lightning."[2] Lightning there is aplenty in this, the most isolated part of Colombia, if not the entire hemisphere, lightning and mountains soaring from four hundred miles of malarial swamps and prehistoric underground rivers running gold. Lightning is the aerial form of gold flashing through water, which brings us back to lightning-prone Gorgona and to the fantastic power the Gorgons had in Greek mythology of turning anyone who looked at them into stone.

Primal phenomenon of history it may well be, this famous dialectical image, yet is it not one of Benjamin's insistent insights that it is "precisely the modern which always conjures up prehistory," that "capitalism was a natural phenomenon with which a new dream-filled sleep came over Europe, and, through it, a reactivation of mythic forces"?[3] Is it this gathering of extremes, then, this excessive conjuring, that gives to the dialectical image its fixed-explosive nature whose logo is lightning and stone its petrified suspension out of time? The dialectical image bears the trademark of surrealism, the outcome of which for Benjamin is the *profane illumination* that resulted from an almost impossible stillness, which, at one point in his famous "Theses on the Philosophy of History," he calls a messianic cessation of happening, which is when thinking not only flows but is arrested, he says, into a monad, crystallized by shock. But what is a *monad*, and what relationship does it have to stone and to petrifaction? It is a strange word, indeed, like *miasma*, lying just there on the horizon of our knowing. What's more, it sounds like a stone, a heavy stone at that.

My dictionary tells me a monad is a most mysterious thing, neither matter nor spirit, but both and something else as well. It is mysterious because of its oneness, its being the "unit one," more than an atom, "an elementary unextended individual spiritual substance from which material properties are derived."

---

2. Walter Benjamin, "On the Theory of Knowledge, Theory of Progress," in *The Arcades Project*, ed. Rolf Tiedemann, trans. Howard Eiland and Kevin McLauglin (Cambridge: Harvard University Press, 1999), pp. 456–88.

3. Walter Benjamin, "Paris—the Capital of the Nineteenth Century" (1955), in *Charles Baudelaire: A Lyric Poet in the Era of High Capitalism*, trans. Harry Zohn (London: New Left Books, 1973), p. 171; Walter Benjamin, "Dream City and Dream House, Dreams of the Future, Anthropological Nihilism, Jung," in *The Arcades Project*, p. 391.

Like the gold and fossils in the subterranean rivers, or the curiously textured stones found on the island of Gorgona, this monad of Benjamin's crystallized by shock is an object violently expelled from the continuum of the historical process. But as crystallized shock, and true to its monad-being as a "spiritual substance from which material properties are derived," it dives through shock waves of time and space following the ghost train of the incongruous.

This crystallized shock resembles Roger Caillois's fascination with stones because they possess "a kind of gravitas, something ultimate and unchanging." A highly original writer, Caillois was associated with surrealism and wrote extensively about stones, so overcome was he by their beauty and philosophical significance, which led him into unusual and indeed uncharted waters of speculation and reverie. Stones evoke a mystery that is slower, vaster, and graver than the fate of that transitory species, humankind. Stones stand outside of history. They represent the primordial, the principle of the ages in whose presence a person becomes contemporary of the immemorial.[4] Yet this apparent flight into the sacred by means of stones is abruptly checked by what Caillois perceives as the base materiality of stone, containing "nothing divine that is not matter, lava, fusion, cosmic tumult." Such "negative divinity" is a stunning instance of the surreal "profane illumination" that stones provide. To say the least, Caillois's enthusiasm is composed of a lively mélange. He looks and talks like a scientist, a poet, and a philosopher starting from scratch. Stones allow him to bring a formidable intelligence and sensitivity to such white heat of intensity that the whole intellectual edifice melts and he is like a newborn child once more, seeing the world for the first time.

Lying "outside history," stones perturb more than their gravitas might at first suggest, a point seized upon by Jimmie Durham's stones, with their gentle mockery of gravitas, a mockery that says as much about the stony nature of stone as do appeals to their depth and timelessness. There were stacks of tiny hard stones of different colors, different shapes, and different textures on the table in his studio in Berlin in 1997; shiny stones, porous stones, bits of slate and marble,

4. Quoted by E. M. Cioran, "Caillois: Fascination of the Mineral," in *Anathemas and Admirations*, trans. Richard Howard (New York: Little, Brown, 1991), p. 207. For Roger Caillois on stones, see *Pierres réfléchies* (Paris: Gallimard, 1975); *Pierres* (Paris: Gallimard, 1966); and *The Writing of Stones* (1973), trans. Barbara Bray (Charlottesville: University of Virginia Press, 1985). I am grateful to Richard Kernaghan for these references.

tiny arrowheads, chips, plates, round, fistlike, rectangular blocks, green, white, light gray, dark gray, rust-colored stones—nine to each sheet of white cardboard onto which they were glued in rows and columns, entitled "Some Stones and Their Names." Each stone bore the name of a person written underneath in Jimmie's spidery handwriting.

SOME STONES
AND THEIR NAMES

C.H. LITTLEBELL

SANTIAGO CAMPANELLA

STELLA

ESTRELLA

ESMERALDA

MERCEDES GOMEZ

GUNNAR

GUNTHER

GRUNHILDA

When you sound out the names, you have a poem. You hear the music emerging from these chips of contingency fallen from the larger, cosmological scheme of things and found God knows where. Personified geological fragments at quite the opposite end of the spectrum to fossils, the stones thus narrow their separation and distance from us humans and the meaning of life, both human and planetary, which they render both sensible and silly. He gave me one of these stoned cardboard sheets as a present and signed it with a flourish for which I was pleased because it seemed to me to beautifully capture Benjamin's idea of the monad as something beyond belief unified, the dialectic at a standstill, petrified to the core, yet by virtue of that capable of being suddenly expelled by laughter from history as . . . Grunhilda.

Of course Jimmie has a long-standing love-hate affair with stone as with his amazement at how in the middle of the American continent, in a place sacred to all Plains Indians called the Paha Sapa, the heads of four Indian-killers have been carved into a mountain of stone now called Mount Rushmore.[5] Jimmie wants to free stone from the burden of history, as with the massive white marble slabs prepared by Hitler and his architect Speer for the future Berlin, most of it now lying in quarries in Sweden and Norway. His plan is to take the remaining slabs by barge across the Baltic toward Germany and tip them into the sea. Like those stone chips stuck on cardboard, this project manifests the urge to de-monumentalize stone and thereby monuments too.

The Gorgons lived on an island among the rain-worn shapes of men and wild beasts whom the Gorgon Medusa had petrified. Likewise, the rain-swept island of Gorgona ten miles off the Pacific Coast of Colombia is noteworthy for its petroglyphs and strange boulders. Reporting on the expedition of the *St. George* to the South Seas in 1924, James Hornell described such stones in the *Journal of the Royal Anthropological Institute of Great Britain and Ireland*. They were found at the water's edge at the low-tide mark, much worn by water and rain. There was a small alligator or iguana, a bird with out-curved mandibles on one stone. There were two squatting monkeys on another stone, together with a human face and what looked like an octopus as well. They were chiseled into massive boulders re-

---

5. See also Jimmie Durham, *Between the Furniture and the Building (Between a Rock and a Hard Place)* / *Zwischen Mobiliar und Haus (Im Gestein der Zwickmühle)*, trans. Stefan Barmann and Karen Laver (Köln: Walther König, 1998), pp. 85–87.

sistant to weathering, a hard and fine-grained type of stone called picrite. Two such boulders with designs were heaved aboard the *St. George* and taken to the British Museum. Archaeologist James Hornell tells us an immense amount of time must have been spent on the execution of these designs and regards as quite wonderful the smoothness and great depth of the grooving. "There can be little doubt," he writes, that the site where the incised boulders were found "was the chief sacred place of the island and probably the place of sacrifice."[6] Certainly much sacrifice went into the stone art itself.

Twenty years later in 1944 the island of Gorgona received a visit from a geologist named A. Gansser working for the Shell Oil Company of Colombia. Struck by the lack of geological research concerning the Pacific Coast, he said that wide areas had never been visited by a geologist on account of what he saw as its "very unhealthy climate, the extraordinary rainfall, and the luxurious tropical vegetation."[7] But his discoveries more than made up for that. What excited him most were the strange designs occurring naturally in certain rocks, and so he set himself the task of describing what he called "the extraordinary textural habits" of these stones.

And what are these "textural habits"? They include color; a dense dark green, strong luster, brownish augite partly altered in a hornblende, dirty green to brownish pleochroism, and greenish masses . . . blended with a variety of forms:

> *aborescent textures*
> *skeleton crystals*
> *marked fracturing without any predominant direction*
> and (so damn relevant to Gorgona, island of snakes and the stone
> gaze)
> *serpentization*

Commenting on these texts inscribed by natural history in the island's stones, our geologist suggests a "peculiar stress condition must have been respon-

---

6. James Hornell, "The Archaeology of Gorgona Island, South America," *Journal of the Royal Anthropological Institute of Great Britain and Northern Island* LVI (1926): 428.

7. A. Gansser, "Geological and Petrographical Notes on Gorgona Island in Relation to North-Western S. America," *Schweizerische Mineralogische und Petrographische Mitteilungen* 30 (1950): 219.

sible" and notes that Gorgona itself is the outcrop of a submarine chain of mountains torn off the mainland in prehistorical times. Here the natural sculpture, if we may call it that, has been executed not by man but by nature—a tortured nature, at that. Yet in both forms of sculpture, that created by nature no less than that created by man, we read the past frozen in the face of stone brought to a sudden standstill.

Then there are the faces of ancient figurines found close by, technically and aesthetically considered among the finest ceramics of aboriginal America and known as "Tumaco culture" on account of the site where they were first found by archaeologists. There are "snarling dragon-like monsters with long fangs and protruding tongues. Sometimes the head of an animal or monster is combined with a human body, or a human face peers through the wide-opened mouth of a monstrous owl-like bird or a jaguar. One headless figurine has its head placed inside the body from whence it looks out through a triangular 'window.'" Often the face is split vertically into two, each side with a different expression. In some figures, one-half of the face is a living person while the other is a skull.[8] Shades of the dialectical image!

Speaking of which, here comes another; for these old Indians would surely have gotten on well with T. W. Adorno, who was taken mightily by a figure that Benjamin used to describe the absorption of time by landscape, a landscape frozen and fixed like a painter's still life—"dead-nature," as the French say. This was the *facies hippocratica,* a fanciful image of the human face contorted and fixed at the moment of death, which seems to me pretty close to this Indian face, dead and alive at the same time. Why dialectical image? Because what the *facies hippocratica* does is speed everything up. Life dies but in dying lives on in this etched agony, recalling Nietzsche's chilling observation: "Let us beware of saying that death is opposed to life. The living is merely a type of what is dead, and a very rare type."[9] Such is gold, flowing underground as petrified lightning. Such is cocaine, crystallized shock.

What gives gold and cocaine their peculiar and privileged status—half-stone, half-water, half-fixed, half-mutating contingency—is the way they slide by

8. Gerardo Reichel-Dolmatoff, *Colombia* (London: Thames and Hudson, 1965), p. 112.

9. Nietzsche, *The Gay Science,* sec. 109, p. 168.

means of seduction through the life and death owed to transgression. Death stalks these substances in measure equal to the way they enliven life, enchant and compel, and if Benjamin's monad as crystallized shock amounts to a messianic cessation of happening, this is due to the fact that transgression expands and contracts time such that strange spillways of time flow into stationary ponds, like those Gustavo Díaz Guzbén talks about, enchanted ponds where gold lies and from which eerie music erupts like the sound of machines. As congealed miasma or the dialectic at a standstill, gold and cocaine are the contagion emitted by the breaking of a taboo—a contagion that is material, spiritual, and deadly. But then you have to ask yourself, Why is the taboo broken, and repeatedly so?

This is the same question we level at the eyes of the Gorgon. How could they turn men to stone, those eyes of the Gorgon so soft and liquid? Is it because this archaic creature living at the edge of the known world is the supreme representation of the rule, of the wrath that shall befall those of us who cannot withstand the temptation to transgress? And this is truth. For what makes a rule a rule is that built into it is the desire to transgress it.

Oh, Dairo! Let me be! In this swamp world, I dream with naked thighs of windswept beaches remote from the sludge that dissolves boundaries ever thicker into mud and rotting vegetation. I yearn for a world of hard-edged meaning, for the ripping salt wind and hard prehistoric stone with forms encrusted smooth and deep as petrified by the Gorgons, whose name was given by the conquerors of Peru in the sixteenth century to a tiny island ten miles out to sea from the swamp they dreaded. Was it on account of its fearsome serpents that the island acquired this name? Or was it with a premonition of its future as a prison island, such that whoever came there would be turned to stone? How far, after all, is stone from swamp?

I sit with some kids in Santa María watching a TV show for children, thanks to the Russians providing electricity to the village at certain hours of the day. We are being shown what the program calls "castles in the air," meaning skyscrapers in Bogotá. The children are quiet. Their attention fixed. The TV takes them all over Colombia, including the deserts of the Guajira Peninsula poking into the Caribbean and the Sierra Nevada of the Kogi Indians rising from the peninsula. The Guajira is displayed as home to wild dark women leaning sideways against the wind in flowing dresses that touch the sand. The Kogi men, with leathery faces, white pillbox hats, and long hippie hair, have deep dark eyes full of faraway dreams as they solemnly chew their cuds of coca leaves. How long before these kids watching become folkloric too?

A program on physical fitness follows from a university in California. There are interviews with a burly physical education instructor two to three times the weight of the biggest person in this village, and probably not even half as strong. There are pictures of machines people use to make their muscles bigger, as opposed to here where people use their muscles as machines and women may be as muscle-bound as men, a new ideal in North America. Later in the early evening, a movie star in Cali is being interviewed by another woman, asking how she feels when her parents see her with so few clothes on in the movies. Yet here it is not unusual for women to work topless the day long, panning gold.

But then there's fourteen-year-old Dairo, "a little touched," says a friend. He stops me from walking home from the High Canal dressed in swimming trunks and singlet. I should put on long pants because otherwise the sight of my thighs will impassion someone who will *ojear* and kill me. By *ojear* Dairo means the Evil Eye, an unconscious power—like electricity, people sometimes say, radiating out from the eye to kill beauty and life in the form of a blessed infant, but also, so now I learn from the "touched Dairo," adults too. Could this be the same eye as the Gorgon?

"They slay by a malign influence," says Jane Harrison with respect to the eyes of the Gorgon. They turn men to stone by virtue of a destructive exhalation from their eyes.[1] Can we call this destructive exhalation *miasmic*? Surely we can and surely this was why young Dairo warned me against this Evil Eye that seems

---

1. Jane Harrison, *Prolegomena to the Study of Greek Religion,* 2nd ed. (Cambridge: Cambridge University Press, 1908), pp. 195–96.

to combine with such brilliance of invention the emanations of the swamp with the hardness of encrusted form. Is this not the same transposing form of swamp and stone that Adorno has in mind when he says with reference to Benjamin that "the glance of his philosophy is Medusan"?[2]

There are many things that could be meant here. Undoubtedly, the most important is petrifaction, Medusa being one of the three Gorgons. But we might also want to take into account that Medusa was she whom the mythographer Robert Graves suggests stood for the older, matriarchal, and godless ancient Greece. In cutting off her petrifying head, Perseus was enacting not merely the triumph of patriarchy, but the creation of gods in place of personalized forces of nature. For the world without gods is the truly fascinating world—the world of heat and rain, swamp and stone, gold and cocaine—the world where myth and reality merge in the shapes of creatures and forces that are barely distinguishable from the muck and rush of nature, monstrous earth and sea creatures like the Cyclops, like Poseidon, and like the Gorgons, or else strange magical beings rooted on rocks in the open sea like the Sirens with their sweet song making sailors lose their minds, or hidden on islands like the witch Circe—all of whom had to be subdued and even more importantly had to have their powers appropriated by the new regime of reality shapers gathered around Olympus. To assert that the glance of Benjamin's philosophy is Medusan is to take all of that on board, no less than the contradictory relation of shamanism to Enlightenment, something Adorno, of all people, was well aware of and probed in his study of Homer and the movement of Western history as domination of nature.[3] What is at stake here is that "shamanism" stands largely for sympathetic magic in which like affects like, and that the domination of nature ineluctably turns in on itself such that nature "returns" in modernity as a curious sort of animated or potentially animated prehistory as worked with and theatricalized by shamans—at least the ones I worked with in the Putumayo region of Colombia, and that I read about in Siberia, on the northwest coast of the American continent, and in re-

2. T. W. Adorno, "A Portrait of Walter Benjamin" (1967), in *Prisms*, trans. Samuel and Shierry Weber (Cambridge: MIT Press, 1983), p. 233.

3. Max Horkheimer and Theodore W. Adorno, *Dialectic of Enlightenment* (1944), trans. John Cumming (New York: Continuum, 1989).

mote Australia. There is a real sense in which Benjamin is advocating above all a "shamanic take" on the artifactual modern world of capitalism. This is why Adorno gets it so right when he sums up Benjamin's method as "the need to become a thing in order to break the catastrophic spell of things."

To raise the question of such shamanism in relation to Benjamin's Medusan glance is to evoke another primary meaning of the Gorgons, and that is the way their image is used to prevent access by those who would pry into secrets and prohibited places. Greek bakers used to paint Gorgon masks on their ovens to ensure, says Robert Graves, that they would not be opened and the bread ruined by drafts. Neatly complementing this protection of the staff of life was the way the goddess Athene, according to Graves, placed the decapitated head of Medusa on her shield, "doubtless to warn people against examining the divine mysteries hidden behind it."[4] Of course, Enlightenment scoffs at this with its mandate to bring light to dark places, but then does not insight create blindness too? This is what Nietzsche asks in the opening pages of *The Gay Science,* where he wonders whether truth be a woman "who has reasons for not letting us see her reasons," and whether "perhaps her name is—to speak Greek—*Baubo.*" The *Oxford Classical Dictionary* cited in the relevant footnote tells us that Baubo, an obscene female demon, was originally a personification of the female genitals—precisely the equation Freud made with the face of the Gorgon.[5] As regards names, note the gaiety in *The Gay Science* with its implication that truth lies as much in that which cuts truth-seeking discourse off, namely, laughter. In lifting her skirts, Baubo not only shocked people but made them laugh. This is why she is remembered.[6] Laughter says what cannot be said about transgression and shock. Its virtues were highlighted by Benjamin in his essay on surrealism but a few years after he noted that truth was not a secret to be exposed, which would destroy it, but revealed in a way that does it justice. What sort of justice? you ask. The justice of the "Medusan glance," which petrifies like a fossil, yet liquefies and ferments like miasma from the swamp.

---

4. Robert Graves, *The Greek Myths,* combined edition (London: Penguin, 1992), p. 129.

5. Nietzsche, *The Gay Science,* p. 38.

6. Maurice Olender, "Baubo," *Encyclopedia of Religion,* 16 vols., ed. Mircea Eliade et al. (New York: Macmillan, 1987); cited in Winifred Milius Lubell, *The Metamorphosis of Baubo: Myths of Woman's Sexual Energy* (Nashville: Vanderbilt University Press, 1994), pp. 4–5.

Fossils bear the impress of time collapsed in an image. The image heaves and buckles. Time strains to be free even while it sleeps in petrified dreaming. Odd views and fragments like in a cubist painting or collage are preserved in stone. Parts of plants, shells, and animals, for instance, are preserved through the ages like three-dimensional X-ray prints in stone. I have one on my desk by my computer screen, the size and shape of an apple, which I picked off the ground in 1991 in the Andean highlands of Boyacá just north of Bogotá in Colombia. There are many volcanic-looking mountain peaks in the vicinity, and I have been told by archaeologists that the valley floor was important for shamans and their astronomy long before the conquest by Spain. The fossil is surprisingly heavy and of a light brown color flecked with black and white. Its sides are grooved in regularly spaced furrows, which give it a machine-made look except for odd excrescences and a fairly sharp point on one side as if the entire object had been drawn from a mold, leaving this "tail" of mud that subsequently hardened into the hardest stone. One side is flat and irregular, as if split off a larger whole. The bottom and top of this fossil sink inward like molds bearing in perfection the spiral form of a seahorse's tail descending into infinity.

Fossils not only bear the imprint of times long past, but are even more pertinent for a "Medusan philosophy" of dialectical imagery if we consider how they come into being. For the fossil is a snapshot, an abruptly stilled slice of time held fast by planetary hysteria, rupture and upheaval, world history in a fist. It is the self-destructing world taking a picture of itself as it destructs, a picture that will last forever in stone, an amazing phenomenon, only we don't quite see it that way because it is so quiet and still. Like the face of the dying, the fossil grants authority to the storyteller, in this case the world telling us the story of itself.

Baudelaire saw this same face of death in the ecstasy of lovemaking. "The human face," he writes in his *Intimate Journals,* "which Ovid believed fashioned to reflect the stars, speaks here only of an insane ferocity, relaxing into a kind of death."[7] But metamorphoses are what stand out in Ovid's rendition of the Gorgon Medusa, and rightly so, beginning with the salient flip-flop between

---

7. Charles Baudelaire, *Intimate Journals,* trans. Christopher Isherwood (San Francisco: City Lights, 1983), pp. 23–24.

images and things. Indeed, it is the image and the gaze that stand out here, thanks to their power to act on the material world. Let us not overlook how profoundly thinglike are the results of this imageric power; here you have her head dripping blood, this head now the epitome, if I may say so, of thinghood itself, insofar as we think things are dead and just killed things deader than dead. Severed from the living whole, the part assumes that stark objectness reserved for a corpse *fragment*.

But it is the traffic between image and body, image and thing, that stands out, no better expressed, I believe, than by the mirror and purse belonging to winged Perseus, the man who cut off the Gorgon's head. (Be it noted, by the way, that both these objects were gifts from the gods.) His mirror, by which he can see her face without being petrified, is actually a warrior's shield. Polished it becomes a mirror. In other words, what was originally a device to blunt a decidedly material blow from the enemy, namely, a shield, becomes a device to capture an image. Likewise, his purse becomes that which hides the material object, namely, her head, which has to remain hidden from sight because of its deadliness as image.

Added to which, how strange that despite all the talk of petrifaction, mutation is here such a striking theme. Annoyed with Atlas, Perseus flashes him the Gorgon's face, which converts him into a mountain. When drops of blood fall from the Gorgon's head onto the desert sand, there breeds a swarm of venomous serpents. As the Gorgon's head is severed, a winged horse and a warrior soar from the wound. And where Perseus lays Medusa's head to rest on some seaweed, the seaweed turns into coral like that which surrounds the island of Gorgona across from the swamp of the mainland.

Coral is like stone, not the stone of earth, but the stone of water. Yet just as the picrite boulders on Gorgona at the low-water mark lie incised with animal faces, coral too is petrified substance, carrying time in its intricate embrace as animated history—coral being the excretions of tiny animals acting in mighty concert on gigantic construction works, like children playing on sand between land and sea, as Pacific islands such as volcanic-peaked Gorgona rose like whales from the bed of prehistoric oceans. Coral is what comes to mind for Hannah Arendt, who sees a powerful magic in Benjamin's poetics of petrifaction as his way of coagulating the past into fossil-like things, a transformation no less organic than it is absolute. Just as the Gorgon's head is severed at one stroke from her body, so tradition has been severed from modernity, leaving bones and names scattered on the ocean floor to form forests of underwater coral: "Of his bones are coral made; / Those are pearls that were his eyes," meaning that the past can now speak only spasmodically in the form of *quotations lifted out of context.* These then are the pearls, these quotations out of context, and the critic sensitive to the play of past in present becomes like the pearl diver.[8]

Benjamin once likened his quotation-out-of-context method not so much to pearl divers as to highwaymen robbing travelers of their opinions. In his microscopic handwriting, he was forever copying down quotations for future use, microscopy, after all, being second cousin to petrifaction. It was a new art, finding and resetting these pearls; *the art of matter out of place*—exactly like that which provokes laughter and dissolves form into free-fall, perhaps into a color, or even a swamp. Then everything abruptly changes through being faithfully copied as quotation. Petrifaction, hand in hand with mutation. Coral is stone in the form of petrified forests and flowers. The colors are what get to you. The greens and blues of the water. Striped fish darting between yellow filaments clinging to cliffs like ancient ruins underwater. This is the world of the Gorgon from whose decapitated body sprang the winged horse, Pegasus, born from her sexual union with the sea god Poseidon; Pegasus, who gave Zeus his thunder and lightning while Athene, the daughter of Zeus, gave Ascelepius, the founder of medicine, two phials drawn from Medusa's blood. With the blood drawn from the Gorgon's left side, Ascelepius could raise the dead. With the blood from the right, he could cause instant death.[9]

---

8. Hannah Arendt, "Introduction: Walter Benjamin: 1892–1940," in *Illuminations: Essays and Reflections,* ed. Hannah Arendt, trans. Harry Zohn (New York: Schocken, 1968), p. 40.

9. I take my account from Graves, *The Greek Myths* vol. 1, p. 175. I thank Karina Rosenborg for pointing out this connection with the blood.

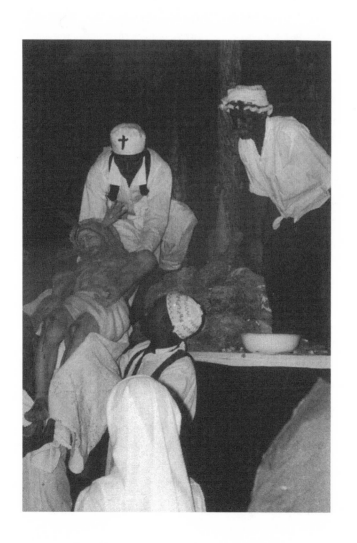

"I was petrified!" is how we sometimes refer to the impact of sudden fear, and there may be some biological truth to this figure of speech. Animals may mimic death and pass into the immediate environment when afraid, and shock, as privileged mark of modern times, has this petrifying component too. A human being in shock, as I understand current lore, often mimics the immediate environment in a posture of death, freezing time into the surrounding environment as a *tableau vivant,* reminding us that petrifaction is more than fear. It is a deep-seated configuring of time such that time becomes space reorganizing the qualities we ascribe to Being itself—which is precisely the nature of the island where the Gorgons hung out, where time is space at the edge of the known world. Contemplating volcanic craters and hardened beds of larva together with curious lizards and tortoises on the Galapagos Islands, southwest of the island of Gorgona, young Charles Darwin was moved to comment: "Hence, both in space and time, we seem to be brought somewhat near to that great fact—that mystery of mysteries—the first appearance of new beings on this earth."[1]

Grasping chronology in a spatial image—in this case that of an island—was thought to be prefigured by sadness, as with Plato's notion of the divine madness of sloth mixed with genius that the ancients attributed to the contemplative power of melancholia magnifying the fullness of objects. Such fullness has been attributed to an image Benjamin made much of, namely, Albrecht Dürer's angel *Melencolia I*, chin in hand, lost in thought gazing at the cold stone floor. Stone is what more than anything else emblematizes the magical spell of thinghood torn from history and sedimented into an image, chin in hand, wings inert.[2]

Such "profanation" as source of stoned illumination was what Benjamin seized upon in his interpretation of a watercolor entitled *Angelus Novus*, the *New Angel*, painted by Paul Klee, which he purchased for about fourteen dollars in 1921. His lifelong friend Gershom Scholem tells us that Benjamin considered this painting his most important possession; "it served as an image for meditation and as a memento of a spiritual vocation."[3] Benjamin informed Scholem that Klee was important because with him linear shapes dominate the picture, making painting a type of writing—not unlike the "writing" that Benjamin detected in nature as well, reminding us, surely, of those "extraordinary textural habits" of stones on the island of Gorgona, as well as of that fragment "The Lamp," which Benjamin wrote to himself in 1933 and which I now want to tell you about.

Inspired by his first stay on the island of Ibiza in 1932, this essay begins with the following quotation said to come from an eighteenth-century German satirist, Georg Christoph Lichtenberg:

In this way the marks on the bottom of a pewter plate tell the story of all the meals it has been used for. In the same way, the form of every piece of land—the shape of its sand dunes and rocks—contains in

---

1. Charles Darwin, *The Voyage of the Beagle* (1839) (London: Dent, 1959), p. 363.
2. Benjamin, *The Origin of German Tragic Drama*, p. 154.
3. Gershom Scholem, "Walter Benjamin and His Angel," in *On Walter Benjamin: Critical Essays and Recollections*, ed. Gary Smith, trans. Werner Dannhauser (Cambridge: MIT Press, 1988), pp. 62–63.

natural script the history of the earth; every rounded pebble that the ocean casts on the shore could tell that story to a soul chained to it, as our soul is chained to our brain.[4]

Lichtenberg was a feared satirist in his time (1742–1799) but is best remembered for his aphorisms, fifteen hundred pages of which were published along with his jokes, linguistic paradoxes, puns, metaphors, and quotations from other writers.[5] It seems blatantly contradictory that a person so delighted by wordplay could be also wedded to the notion of the natural script of the history of the earth. Yet this was manifestly not a contradiction for Benjamin, who, a few months earlier, in another Ibiza-inspired fragment on the topic of similarities, had evoked the notion of "the effects of an active mimetic force working expressly inside things," nowhere more so than with the newborn infant who, in the earliest years of life, "will evidence the utmost mimetic genius by learning a language."[6]

Nineteen years after he bought the *New Angel,* Benjamin found himself cutting it out of its frame to roll it up and enclose it in a suitcase of his most precious things to be hidden from the Nazis by Georges Bataille in the Bibliothèque Nationale. It looked as if the angel was on the point of fleeing from something it was staring at, said Benjamin. Like Dürer's angel, this one stares fixedly and, like the petrified victims of the Gorgons, the mouth gapes open, wings unmoving yet spread for flight. Benjamin transposed the name of Klee's *New Angel* into the *Angel of History,* facing not the Gorgon but the storm blowing from paradise, forcing it backward into the future. Yet for all its stark immobility and frozen form, this angel of history is nothing less than the *image of the dialectical image* and as such capable of swift reversals and sudden, life-enhancing flight.

This petrified angel hopes to reconfigure reality through strange laws of similarity. The sensitivity to similarities may have declined with the passing of centuries. No longer do laws of microcosm and macrocosm exert the force they

4. Walter Benjamin, "The Lamp," in *Selected Writings,* vol. 2, *1927–1934,* ed. Michael W. Jennings, Howard Eiland, and Gary Smith, trans. Rodney Livingston et al. (Cambridge: Harvard University Press, 1999), p. 691.

5. Editor's notes to Benjamin, "The Lamp," in *Selected Writings,* vol. 2, p. 693.

6. Walter Benjamin, "On Astrology," in *Selected Writings,* vol. 2, pp. 684, 685.

once did. Yet according to Benjamin, such laws, albeit in mediated form, lie hidden in our very language where memory and history intersect, nowhere more so than in times of revolution and states of emergency during which "the past can be seized only as an image which flashes up at an instant when it can be recognized and never seen again."[7] The recognition of the similarity is all of a sudden, a surfacing that can just as quickly disappear, equivalent to the messianic cessation of happening, which is, I think, where stone and swamp coincide.

Now you see it; now you don't! At first Benjamin called it the "doctrine of the similar," then changed it to the "mimetic faculty," which also surfaced on the island of Ibiza, along with many of his ideas about the storyteller. How can this be, something appearing and disappearing at virtually the same time? The other famous instance I know of is Sigmund Freud's notion of the fetish, which he suggests was a substitute for the phallus the mother was seen not to have.[8] In the same vein, Freud goes on to suggest that the Gorgon's face was the mythic equivalent to just such a fetish, her face being what he describes as "the terrifying genitals of the mother," an equivalence emphasized by the abundance of snakes as well as by the violent act of decapitation (read: castration).[9] But, he continues, to be petrified by seeing her face was not such a bad fate after all. In fact, it was a sort of victory, serendipitously preordained, we might say, in the very misfortune it at first seemed to be. Petrifaction was not only a sign of the fear of castration. It was also a countersign that one's body, like the well-functioning phallus, could become as hard as stone and was there in its thereness—just like the effect claimed for the magical medicine that the sorcerer Epifanio had wanted to sell me upriver at Santa María. This was magic, *apotropaic* magic, Freud calls it, meaning the use of a magical charm to thwart magic, of which the use of the genitals, in fact or in fantasy, is paramount, or at least on a par with the devil— as when, in Rabelais, the devil takes flight when a woman shows him her private parts.

Apotropaic magic sounds awfully foreign, like the *dialectical image.* But aren't they the same, using one image to counteract another, the battle rejoined again and again? When Adorno likens Benjamin's method to natural history and

7. Benjamin, "Theses on the Philosophy of History," in *Illluminations,* p. 255.
8. Sigmund Freud "Fetishism" (1927), in *The Standard Edition,* vol. 21, pp. 152–57.
9. Sigmund Freud, "Medusa's Head" (1922), in *The Standard Edition,* vol. 18, pp. 273–74.

says the glance of his philosophy is Medusan, he is at pains to remind us not only of the childhood world of magic, as with one of Benjamin's favorite toys, the snow globe, but also of the shamanic *"need that everything must metamorphose into a thing in order to break the catastrophic spell of things."*[10] This hugely important idea, crafted by Adorno for what he, as a philosopher, understood to be most at issue with modernity, puts Freud's thesis about the Gorgon Medusa in an altogether wondrous light.

In thinking through this need to become a thing so as to break the catastrophic *spell* of things, let us reaffirm this accent on the spell as we ponder the back-and-forth flow between *thing* and *image* that has come to light in the story of the Gorgon. For a spell implies not only enchantment but a set of words, like a prayer—or "secret," as such is called on the Pacific Coast—that can have a magical effect. Let us be in no hurry to reveal this secret, whose exposure would destroy it, but instead ponder its place in our everyday affairs, picturing the world by means of such spells, especially the apotropaic ones, although of course we don't see it that way, quite, and certainly don't call it that, *apotropaic* like the *dialectical image* being, as I said, awfully foreign-sounding and best held in reserve, like the secret, as it is elsewhere called.

So here's a delicate state of affairs, not just magic but apotropaic magic—meaning magic recruited to stave off magic, a cycle of action and reaction that seems endless, with neither beginning nor end. And this, I believe, is the origin of magic, which is equally to say its lack of origin and to place emphasis on the reaction rather than the initiating action, a chain of deferment linking things to words by means of strange sympathies. Magic may be rebuked for its insistence on art's priority over the things of this world, yet where would we be without gold or cocaine? Are they art or thing or both or somewhere in between? Anyway, does it matter how these substances kick up dust and flick their tails at us as they move with dizzying speed just out of reach of such questions? Transgression thrives on subverting norms and these transgressive substances, like art and magic, belong to no one kingdom of being but gain their power from moving, like water, between them all, a characteristic some have called *mana*. But what of the implications of *catastrophe,* as in Adorno's rendition of Benjamin's magic—

---

10. Adorno, "A Portrait of Walter Benjamin," p. 233 (italics added).

i.e., Benjamin's apotropaic magic, the magic of the dialectical image—by which everything must metamorphose into a thing in order to break the *catastrophic spell of things*?

The catastrophic spell of things refers to force, "petrifactive force" as it is called in Mary McCarthy's translation of Simone Weil's 1940 essay, *The Iliad or The Poem of Force,* which begins with these shocking words: "The true hero, the true subject, the center of the *Iliad* is force." Why shocking? Because as Adorno implies, a thing—meaning force—has become a person, indeed a hero, "the true hero" at that, while persons become *things* (the emphasis on things here is Simone Weil's, not mine). Exercised to the limit, force turns man into a thing in the most literal sense: it makes a corpse out of him. But then there is a more subtle force that hangs poised over the head of the creature it *can* kill. This is the force "that turns a man into a stone," she says, that turns a human being into "a thing while still alive. He is alive; he has a soul; and yet—he is a thing. An extraordinary entity this—a thing that has a soul. And as for the soul, what an extraordinary house it finds itself in!"[11]

Welcome to the penal colony of Gorgona.

11. Simone Weil, *The Iliad or the Poem of Force,* trans. Mary McCarthy. Pendle Hill Pamphlet, no. 91 (Wallingford, Penn.: Pendle Hill, 1983), pp. 4–5. [First published in French in Marseille, 1940, in the December 1940 and January 1941 issues of *Cahiers du Sud,* trans. Mary McCarthy, 1945, in the New York City journal *Politics.*]

my

Isla. de la Gorgóna
or Capt: Sharpes Isle

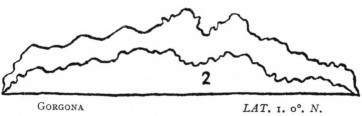

GORGONA   *LAT.* 1. 0°. *N.*

2

Our earth is a wounded island as we swing round the sun.

—H.D.

gorgona

Gorgona was Colombia's highest-security prison and is now a high-security museum of natural history with rare species of lizards and snakes. Before, it was wild men that were guarded. Now it is nature. There are many stories about the island, but they all boil down to the fact that just as death grants authority to the storyteller, so it is to natural history that the stories ultimately refer us. This brings the stories ever closer to myth, which I take to be not only stories relating to the time before time, but stories in which we delight in confusing humans with natural phenomena such as rain and heat, swamps and stone, gold and cocaine. Moreover, as the name of the island suggests, this is an island buffeted by mythology. So I leave it to you to decide which gets the better of it, story or myth, and whether it is worth our trying to decide. For even today—especially today—myth exacts its due in human suffering, calculated murder and cruelty, no less than in stupefaction and hopes of release. Such are prisons, such is gold, such is cocaine. For its part, the story brings the farawayness of myth closer to our senses and understanding and envelops us inside myth's fantastic self, such that, depending on the telling, the story not only embellishes the myth but may, at times, switch it onto a different track. To the uncertainties exploited by myth, the story adds others of a quite different sort, closer in appeal, less grandiloquent, certainly less Greek, less Gorgona, and we can perhaps then take the measure of our own collusion in myth making too.

The island's name can mean everything and nothing, just a name, you might say, a name that came with the Europeans on whose first maps Gorgona appears larger than life like a big jellyfish (medusae they're called), because it was from this island, where he was marooned for seven months, that in 1527 Francisco Pizarro launched the conquest of Peru. The island was thereby magnified in the imagination of conquest, being the only refuge from four hundred miles of mangrove swamps on the mainland with its terrible illnesses, fierce Indians, and rumors of gold, lots and lots of gold. Later on British pirates found the island a useful base for getting at the ships laden with the silver and gold that Pizarro's conquests farther south had uncovered, and still later, in our time, from 1960 to 1985, it became a notorious prison island fulfilling the petrifying destiny its name held in store until it was converted into a living museum of natural history, again fulfilling the destiny of its name, implicating serpents and stone.

Like names, myths have a logic that fans the fire within, nowhere more so than when they implicate prisons. To resurrect in memory a prison island like Gorgona is to uncork the dams of mythology generated by prisons as compacted state violence. In his novel *Government,* mystery man B. Traven lets us know that the sun-dried mud prison built by the Indians at the bequest of the state in the center of their village in a Mexican jungle around 1900 was of the utmost importance—"as everywhere on earth," he says, "the building of a prison is the first step in the organization of a civilized state."[1] Under the false name of Traven, this man wrote parables in the form of stories set in the Lacandon forests of Chiapas. His books are ethnographic and full of astute observations, offering practical wisdom on governance and rebellion. Yet although he depends on being there,

---

1. B. Traven, *Government* (1931), trans. Basil Creighton (London: Allison and Busby, 1980), p. 6.

and although the grit of place is what seeps into every particle of his writerly being, the Lacandon forest and surrounding mountains of Chiapas are also foreign
to him as a rank outsider and hence quite fabulous, like a stage set, allowing him
to work out even more precisely what he needs to say about human deception
and why we obey those who destroy us, including ourselves. In this sense, for me,
too, the island of Gorgona on the edge of the nation-state is my figure, my stage,
my fable—an offshore pirate base, then a penal colony, now a museum of natural history, always aware, then, that "the building of a prison is the first step in
the organization of a civilized state."

This is a story about a prison island. But are not all prisons islands? And
what could be more mythological than a modern prison? A calculated science of
incarceration and cruelty cannot but embrace myth, and that myth cannot but
embrace nature. Whether it be a concrete fortress on the mainland or an isolated
island, the idea is that society extrudes and isolates its evil across the storming sea
on some rocky fastness. Like seabirds and captive animals, the prisoners inhabit
bare caves called cells, stripped down to the bare necessities of survival. The bars
are their cages and they are fed like cattle. Their bodies are subject to periodic
review and belong to the state like so many wobbling kilos of the fatted calf. In
the United States, the most incarcerated society in the world, the prisoners are
black and their guards white. For all its brilliance of invention and dramatic display, not even Greek mythology could rival this brilliant color scheme of brutal-
ization at once so natural and so political, the bars and concrete, the fastness of
solitary, confining men as beasts held by stronger ones. All prisons are islands
and these islands are where nature and mythology become one.

Until that morning in 1993 when we slipped ashore through the mist to be
searched by some heavy-handed police waiting on the sand, Gorgona was little
more than a name to me, a chilling name, to be sure, where up till 1985 only the
worst of the worst had been put away by the Colombian justice system in which,
officially, capital punishment plays no part. For its prisoners had done unspeak-
able things, or so it was conveyed to me, the prison having been built to house the
worst offenders of La Violencia, that period of catastrophic killing and intimida-
tion to which dates may be tentatively applied (1948–1958), causing massive population displacements in rural areas in the center of the country and untold death.
People were killed not as people but as demonically possessed creatures owing

allegiance to either the Red or the Blue political parties.[2] Later the prison came to hold a mix of men, some accused of vile murders, others of political crimes.

Yet how much worse were these crimes than those of the justice system itself? This is not to say that many prisoners were innocent of the crimes of which they were found guilty, although that could well be the case. Nor is it to point out that the bulk of persons committing terrible crimes have gone unpunished because of lack of witnesses ready to testify or because of judges unable to act fairly. In the 1990s impunity for serious crime was running around an unbelievable 99 percent, which means only one bad deed out of a hundred was processed to reach the stage of sentencing, and I myself find little reason to doubt the situation was much different between 1960 and 1985 when the island of Gorgona was a prison.[3] Nor am I alluding to the fact that with but few exceptions, only the poor serve time. All this is true. But what I want to point to is the abyss that opens not when law is absent or weak but when law's lawlessness becomes law seeking out dramatic displays . . . as with nasty prison islands with exotic names off unspeakably lost coasts weighed down with miasmic overload. To my mind this is what situates Gorgona. Its prisoners were display pieces, sacrificial victims to the larger cause; the grim reality of a phantom justice system.

But I need to point out that it would be an error to assume such a phantom justice system exists only in Colombia or other corrupt Third World states. I am thinking of Nietzsche where he says prisons make men hard and cold. The mere sight of judicial procedures prevents the criminal from feeling bad about his act "because he sees the same kind of action practiced in the service of justice and given approval, practiced with good conscience: like spying, duping, bribing, setting traps, the whole wily skills of the policeman and prosecutor, as well as the most thorough robbery, violence, slander, imprisonment, torture and murder, carried out without even having emotion as an excuse."[4] He could be referring to

---

2. Germán Guzmán Campos, Orlando Fals-Borda, and Eduardo Umaña Luna, *La Violencia en Colombia: Estudio de un proceso social*, 2 vols. (Bogotá: Tercer Mundo, 1962 [vol. 1]; 1964 [vol. 2]).

3. Mauricio Rubio, *Crimen sin sumario: Análisis económico de la justicia penal Colombiana*, Documento CEDE 96-04 (Bogotá: Universidad de los Andes, 1996), p. 18. Also *La Paz: El desafío para el desarrollo* (Bogotá: Departamento Nacional de Planeación, 1998), pp. 103–12.

4. Friedrich Nietzsche, *On the Genealogy of Morality* (1887), ed. Keith Ansell-Pearson, trans. Carol Diethe (Cambridge: Cambridge University Press, 1994), p. 59.

New York City in the year 1999, where it had become common for police to go undercover, set up sting operations, and cruise the Bronx in unmarked cars prepared to murder as did the Street Crime Unit with their motto "We Own the Night"—not all that different from death squads in Colombia except the latter are illegal. Nietzsche's point could not be plainer. The justice system depends upon the methods it criminalizes, and from this inspired contradiction springs its mythic power.

We respect the law yet often feel sympathy and even admiration for the prisoner. Indeed, my first memories of the prison island of Gorgona go back to the late seventies by the bus terminals, early evening dark and cold in that most miserable of Colombian highland cities, Pasto, watching a Colombian-directed TV documentary about Gorgona in the roofed-over patio of what must have been the cheapest and to my mind the nicest hotel there, in the confusion of travelers, beggars, hungry dogs, and drizzle of rain and highland whisperings. It was the first time, incidentally, and you can take this as measure of my naïveté, that it was brought across to me that there is most definitely a "culture" of prison made as much by us on the outside as those on the inside. I also came to feel that those of us raised in a tradition of common law, and what I can only call "Anglo" prisons, are likely to be at a loss when confronted by what appears to be the quite different mix of freedom and coercion in Latin American prisons in which a strange degree of freedom is used to all the more coerce the prisoner. Of course, unless one has been a prisoner, one's understanding of prisons is likely to be a morbid and fantastic mishmash drawn as much from private nightmares as from film and literature. Yet . . . surely if we can ever speak of purpose and conscious design in the creation of social institutions, the prison is one place where such fearful ignorance fortified by fantasy is an intrinsic component of design and therefore enters, as living force, not only into the average citizen, but into the mind of the prisoner as well. What struck me there in the hotel in Pasto was the effusion of sympathy the TV documentary extended toward the prisoners. Barely deserving their cruel fate, they were martyrs to an unnamed cause. It was as if they were sinners bound to sainthood, redeemed by the enormity of their crimes as much as by their present suffering, both the illegal crime and the legal punishment bearing witness to a shared violence beyond the reach of law yet evoked by the plaintive songs of the prisoners accompanied by close-ups of fearsome iguanas said to abound on this reptile-rich, mountainous island, covered by lush jungle. We had transcended the justice system, or rather we had entered the transcendence of which it was capable and upon which, who knows, it rested?

It was there in the face of my friend, this same unfathomable mix of horror and sympathy. She had visited the prison in her youth. Without her saying as much, I got the feeling it was a site of pilgrimage like fingering Christ's wounds. The prisoners wore amulets of the saints, she said, encrusted into the skin and muscle of their chests. One had an insect on a cotton thread he took for walks. "And do you know what they most wanted?" she asked. "Women's panties. Unwashed. They begged for them when we left."

At the bus terminal in Cali in 1997, twelve years after the prison was closed, a man sold me a key chain made of a tiny fish petrified in plastic, its body arched, its little fins erect. Underneath on its flat belly in minute lettering was printed the name of the prisoner on Gorgona who, he said, had made it. Cabezas was the name, and it means "heads"; as with the Gorgon, the entire entity neatly petrified: not in stone but in plastic.

"*Impregnated with legend*" was how the Colombian journalist Heber Moreno C. saw the prison island of Gorgona in 1969. Its prisoners were not men, he said, but "wild beasts of the apocalypse." But what strange beasts he saw, quiet and subdued, surrounded by an electric fence against which one had fallen and been instantly carbonized. Other times he said he saw men like caged animals waiting to seize their prey, men who had gone crazy, walking up and down talking to themselves in ragged clothes. The tale he tells is of a country, an entire country, torn by a terrible violence. The famous Violencia. For its recuperation, the country needed a terrible prison. "The punishment had to serve as an example," he tells us, "so that such horrible acts, covering the republic in mourning, would never recur."[5]

Thus was born the idea of the prison isolated in the sea. Any prisoner with a sentence of more than twelve years, according to Extraordinary Decree No.

---

5. Heber Moreno C., "Isla prisión Gorgona," in *Crímenes que causaron sensación en Colombia* (Cali: Editorial América, 1969), p. 113 (italics added in first quote). I thank Juan Manuel Obarrio for pointing out this book to me.

0012 of 1959, was to be shipped there to serve his sentence. Many would never leave, and the handful of men who managed to escape were only too happy to be found and brought back from the even worse nightmare of the ocean straits and the mangrove swamps of the mainland coast.

An island is a bounded entity in a way that a country is not. It supplies the model of nature that a nation-state envies, for while the latter relies on flags, the former is framed by nature, not laws. Names are what bridge the realms of law and nature such that the name Gorgona and the name La Violencia sum up and fix a process of turmoil for eternity in the universe of petrified things: La Violencia, the Violence, an odd way of speaking, like saying, the Breathing, or the Dying, holding an ongoing action stock-still. Like an island, such naming provides what seem like natural borders comparable to the sea beating on the rocky shore and hence provides what is named with a special quality of being, a personality, we might say, and in that sense brings life to what it boxes in. When we name, we freeze reality, as with facing the Gorgon. In naming La Violencia, we make it protuberant in the vortex that is history. This naming not only petrifies but awakens life, no matter how spectral, in congealed things. This is the same mimetic magic of apotropaism that Freud postulates for the seizure of bodily process as erotic tumescence occurring when one looks at the Gorgon, but is also the work of God's naming the world into being. In its stuttering way, nicknames repeat this work of God.

Names abound in Heber Moreno's account of Gorgona, the nicknames of the famous bandits, killers, kidnappers, and other groups that by the early 1960s were being labeled as communist, such as the group of Manuel Marulanda or "Sure Shot" (Tirofijo) that became the formidably powerful guerrilla army of today known as the FARC. In the summer of 1999, the New York Times ran a photo of the chairman of the New York Stock Exchange in the jungles of Colombia engaged in discussion with leaders of the FARC, which, as far as I know, has no nickname. Like the state, which in so many ways the FARC emulates, a ponderous acronym does the job. It is said that something like three-quarters of the FARC's daily haul from extortion of around one million dollars a day is invested in Wall Street.[6] Money talks but names tell you more, especially those of famous

---

6. Alfredo Rangel Suárez, *Colombia: Guerra en el fin del siglo* (Bogotá: Tercer Mundo, 1998).

criminals whose activities elevate them into mythic figures precisely because they are lawless. The frequent use of tattoos by prisoners provides further testimony to this archaism. Perhaps the orgy of nicknames Heber Moreno provides us with is the verbal equivalent of tattooing? "For sure," he notes, "among the prisoners [on Gorgona] were members of the gangs led by 'Chispas,' 'Siete Colores,' 'Tarzán,' 'El Mosco,' 'Tijeras,' 'El Sultán,' 'Sangrenegra' . . ."[7] And here are some of those who ended up in Gorgona because they were allegedly responsible for kidnapping Harold Eder on March 20, 1965, and later killing him: "El Viejo o Nobleza," "Pielroja," "Tornillo," "Fulminante," "Pensamiento," and "Panela."[8] It appears that Harold Eder himself had no nickname, but he was surely one of the richest men in the Cauca Valley, owner of extensive sugarcane plantations and a pioneer in the agribusiness development—or should we say devastation?—of that once-beautiful valley.

The mystical paraphernalia of the nicknames, endearing and frightening at the same time, includes other neologisms such as the *corte de corbata* (the necktie cut), supposedly invented by the state's paramilitaries then known as *pájaros,* leaving the tongue protruding through a hole in the neck, and *bocachiquiar,* the mode of killing by cutting slits into the surface of the body so as to slowly desanguinate the victim, the slits reminiscent of the way the *bocachico* fish is prepared for frying.

How strange to read these terrible things, so long ago it seems, in old-fashioned books with cheap paper yellowing with age and brittle to the touch, yet present in every breath taken today in Colombia as I write these notes in 1999. Three days ago Paulina Palacios was telling me of a Colombian artist friend of hers, Juan Manuel Echavarría, who creates images inspired by the *corte de florero,* or flowerpot cut. This was the name of a mutilation in the early 1950s in Tolima, Colombia: cutting off a person's head and stuffing the thorax with their dismembered limbs so as to resemble a flower in a pot. In bleached black-and-white pho-

---

7. Moreno C., "Isla prisión Gorgona," p. 130. The names translated are "Sparks," "Seven Colors," "Tarzan," "the Fly," "Scissors," "the Sultan," and "Black Blood."

8. Moreno C., "Isla prisión Gorgona," p. 134. Translated: "the Old Man or Nobility," "Redskin" (also the name of a popular brand of cheap unfiltered cigarette), "Screw," "Detonator" or "Percussion Cap," "Thought," and "Brown Sugar."

tographs, Echavarría presents his "flowers" too. They are made of human ribs, femurs, the pelvis, and vertebrae. Art and terror emerge from similar roots apotropaically, we might say, quoting the terror so as to defend us from it.

Impregnated with legend, the same old legends we knew so well, the Count of Monte Cristo staring out year after year from his cruel prison on the rocky cliffs looking out on a desolate sea, the cruel sea of man-eating sharks, the waves breaking off the point, covering the sea like snow. And if the sharks don't get you, there are the venomous snakes for which, they say, the island was named in 1527 by Francisco Pizarro, "Conqueror of Peru," in honor of the Gorgons of ancient Greek mythology because they too were famous for the snakes that formed their hair. If that was the reason for naming this island, otherwise so generous to man with its healthy sea breezes, fresh water, and abundant fish and oysters, it was a mean-spirited judgment on the fact that the island stood out as a refuge from hostile nature. This is why of all the places on the coast, Pizarro had chosen to stay there, marooned for seven months, awaiting reinforcements and supplies from Panamá with the thirteen starving men who crossed the line he drew in the sand on nearby Gallo Island to stay with him, come what may. His crazed search for gold had bottomed out. The mud, the mangrove swamps, the ferocity of the Indians, the thunder, lightning, and pestilential rains were too much, even for these toughest of souls.

"It was singularly unfortunate," said Prescott in 1847 in his *History of the Conquest of Peru,* "that Pizarro instead of striking farther south, should have so long clung to what is today the Pacific coast of Colombia."[9] The golden countries seemed to fly before him. What had he and his men gotten in return? It was Gorgona that saved them, and months later when relief came and they sailed south to Peru, they were rewarded by unimaginable treasure. The Greek Pedro de Candia, one of the thirteen men who had chosen to stay the course and wait with Pizarro on Gorgona, described the bounty in a temple at Tumbes, their first port of call, once a small vessel had arrived from Panamá to take them south. Not only was the temple tapestried with plates of gold and silver, but artisans were at work making a garden from these same divine metals. It was as if the abundance of

---

9. Prescott, *History of the Conquest of Peru,* vol. 1, p. 257 n. 26.

mineral wealth provided by nature demanded that nature itself be recast in gold and silver as glowing plants. Pizarro himself later wrote that the Greek made it all up, but what he said was nevertheless true of what they later found in other Incan towns.[10]

Impregnated with legend, the island of Gorgona's heavily wooded mountain sustains a lake from which run thirteen streams of the purest water. In the mountain itself, so it is said, one finds tunnels that carry the name of Henry Morgan of Jamaica, the pirate who in 1668 sacked the fortress of Porto Bello on the Caribbean coast of Panamá. He then marched across the peninsula to sack the city of Panamá and is said to have used these tunnels in Gorgona to hide his treasure, although there is, as far as I know, no archival evidence that Morgan ever sailed anywhere near here.[11]

Impregnated with legend, we note that the crew of a pirate's ship, such as Morgan's, "was just about the most democratic institution in the world of the seventeenth century," yet "what is certain is that privateersmen were past masters in the art of torture" to make their captives reveal treasure, including, in Morgan's attack on Porto Bello, the burning of women "in parts that for decency will not be referred to," and *woolding,* which involves tying a band around the victim's forehead and tightening it until the eyes pop out.[12] The tunnels in Gorgona may be as fictitious as the stories of Morgan's presence on the island, but the connections at the level of the imagination are accurate as well as evocative.

Impregnated with legend, we add to the legend without realizing we are doing so, we who stand outside of this place yet are nevertheless enclosed by it. The simple fact of a prison is enough to drive the imagination. A prison island doubles that drive, and as a prison island off that terrible coast, the imagination is thrown into a frenzy of despair. As such, the island acts as a mirror image of the violence it was meant to contain, if not eliminate, and for which it had been constructed on the periphery of the nation where it falls away to the sea. Discussing reactions to the first sociological in-depth study of La Violencia, pub-

---

10. Prescott, *History of the Conquest of Peru,* vol. 1, p. 279.

11. See Earle, *The Sack of Panamá.*

12. Earle, *The Sack of Panamá,* pp. 66, 74–75.

lished in Bogotá in 1962, Orlando Fals-Borda, one of its authors, mentions the Gorgona theory proposed by Horacio Gómez Aristizábal: "Aggression is innate and the way of dealing with it is to employ it against itself. To eliminate *La Violencia* it is necessary to train prisoners chosen from the prison island of Gorgona to serve as a counter-guerrilla force deployed in the areas of the country affected."[13]

Impregnated with legend, the prison island absorbs the violence of La Violencia like a magical charm meant to cleanse the horror of the mainland. But where does the violence go after the prison has gone and the island assumes its new identity dedicated to the uplifting cause of protecting nature in a country brought to its knees by ever-more stupendous forms of violence? Looking across from the mangroves at Punto Reyes on the mainland, Gorgona lies blue on the horizon like a massive whale.

---

13. Orlando Fals-Borda, "Introducción," in *La Violencia en Colombia,* by Guzmán Campos, Fals-Borda, and Umaña Luna, vol. 2, p. 44.

ISLANDS

islands

For every prison island, there is a treasure island. The two are related in the same way as heaven is related to hell, the one turning into the other, to the extent that islands cease being inert pieces of land suspended jewel-like in the open sea.

Instead they take on a life of their own.

Here is a list of island prisons.

There are many more. Maybe you can think of some to add:

Devil's Island, some fifteen miles off French Guiana; actually one of three islands known collectively as the Islands of Salvation

Juan Fernández, a refuge for Robinson Crusoe. Later a prison island toward the end of the Spanish empire and thereafter used the same way by the enemies of that empire, known as the government of the Republic of Chile

The "still-vexed Bermoothes," or the Bermudas, where Prospero,
  rightful Duke of Milan, and his daughter, Miranda, were castaway
  as prisoners in *The Tempest* and where Prospero was able to exer-
  cise his vast knowledge of magic with the spirit Ariel and the sav-
  age Caliban

Elba, off Naples, and Saint Helena, deep in the southern Atlantic
  Ocean, almost fifteen hundred miles off the coast of Angola,
  where Napoléon was kept

Chateu d'If, island in the harbor of Marseilles where the future
  Count of Monte Cristo was imprisoned for delivering a letter to
  Napoléon on the island of Elba. Following his escape from the
  Chateu d'If, the future count made his way to the island of Monte
  Cristo to find the fabulous treasure hidden there.

Rikers, in New York City's East River

Alcatraz

Kafka's penal colony

Robbens Island, where Nelson Mandela was held

Pinchgut aka Fort Dennison in Sydney Harbor

Much of Australia, when you come to think of it, "world's largest
  island and smallest continent," was a prison island for Britain.

The Hulks in which prisoners were held in the Thames awaiting
  transportation to Australia

Galang, Indonesia

Numerous Greek islands in the Aegean

La Isla del Diablo, Orinoco River, Venezuela, under the dictator, José
  V. Gómez

The prison islands of Venezuela; Fernando Calzadilla, a Venezuelan studying Performance in New York, was kind enough to
  write me early in the year 2002 that "since I am Venezuelan, I
  thought it would be interesting to investigate prison islands
  there since there is a long tradition of them that goes back to the
  colony. I know right now there is one that is in use, El Dorado,
  on the piranha-infected Cuyuni River and others out of use like
  El Burro on Valencia lake. But also the Castillo San Carlos, on
  the mouth of the Maracaibo lake to the sea, was used as a

prison, as well as the one in Puerto Cabello during the Gómez dictatorship of the early 1900s, and Guasina, that was used by dictator Pérez Jimenez during the 1950s. I will be happy to help you. Sincerely . . ."

Green Island, high-security prison for Taiwan, especially for the White Terror period of martial law, 1949–1987. The minister of justice now says he wants to convert it from "an island of the devils" to an "island of paradise" by establishing a tourist industry there. But locals are worried. "To be honest," says one, quoted in the *Tapei Times,* June 17, 2002, "most visitors were first attracted to Green Island by the prisons."

El Frontón, Peru's high-security island prison just off Lima until the massacre there in 1986. My assistant and friend, Daniela Gandolfo, writes me: "If I'm not wrong (but I still need to confirm this), the prison was closed down after that incident and was reopened only to keep Abimael Guzmán [leader of the Sendero Luminoso guerrilla] in complete isolation, just like Ocalan [Kurdish rebel leader] in his Turkish prison island." It turns out that comrade Abimael was taken to the naval base on the mainland opposite the island, but the afterimage of the island prison is what sticks in her imagination. Later she sent me a news clipping from Scripps Howard News Service, February 20, 1999. It says that Ocalan's "new home" is a "small windswept island in the Sea of Marmara, 35 miles southwest of Istanbul. Naval vessels and helicopters patrol the exclusion zone which Turkey has now imposed around it." The island has been a prison since 1935. Ocalan will have scant opportunity to enjoy the views as he is in a small isolation cell. He and his guards have the place to themselves. A soap factory and a canning factory on the island have been temporarily deserted. Even the large selection of livestock that previous prisoners maintained is being evacuated; no one is left to look after the chickens and cows. Ocalan's interrogation continues and he still awaits a defense lawyer, although Turkey says his trial will be fair. It was the CIA that found him for the Turks, who have since 1992 conducted a genocidal campaign against the fifteen million Kurds living in

Turkey, the third-highest recipient in the world of American military assistance.[1]

Like a flag, an international telephone code, an airport, and a TV station, every state needs its island. As the pirates did.

The still-vexed Bermoothes: It all happened on an island where the mainlanders were shipwrecked. Making himself invisible, it was the spirit Ariel who sang to Ferdinand to wrap him in spells:

Full fathom five thy father lies;
　Of his bones are coral made;
Those are pearls that were his eyes:
　Nothing of him that doth fade
But doth suffer a sea-change
Into something rich and strange.

Mainlands are ordinary, the measure of reality for which islands in their eccentricity practice caprice. Islands are extraordinary and therefore likely to be enchanted, both utopias and prisons, sea-changed bodies into something rich and strange. None of Prospero's magic did him much good on the mainland.

Then there are the new treasure islands, now known as *tax havens,* where the money gets hidden and laundered. My list is incomplete:

Anguilla
Antigua and Barbados
Aruba
the Bahamas
Barbados
Bermuda

---

1. Chalmers Johnson, *Blowback: The Costs and Consequences of American Empire* (New York: Henry Holt, 2000), pp. 15–16.

the British Virgin Islands

Cayman Islands (where the Enron corporation has 692 subsidiaries
    so as to avoid paying U.S. taxes)

the Cook Islands

Dominica

Gibraltar

Grenada

Guernsey

the Isle of Man

the Maldives

the Marshall Islands

Mauritius

Montserrat

Nauru (with a population of 12,000, has 450 offshore banks regis-
    tered to a single government PO box and as of December 2001 is
    said to be laundering around 70 billion dollars of Russian mafia
    money)

the Netherlands Antilles

Saint Kitts and Nevis

Saint Lucia

Saint Vincent and the Grenadines

Samoa

the Seychelles

Tonga

Turks and Caicos (where Enron has 119 subsidiaries)

the United States Virgin Islands

Vanuatu

Alphabetical order suits them in their new role as banks, although they are
not that different from their archaic role as treasure islands frequented by pirates.
Most of these islands suggest a tropical climate, fertile soil, and exotic history—
an important asset these days. Money, you could say, finally meets its appropriate
environment. It burns down there like night soil under compost making rich
mulch. But this merging of money with islands as natural history occurs not
despite but because of the existence of the modern state with its banking and tax

laws favoring the rich with those famous loopholes. Indeed, it is this mix-and-match of the archaic with the modern that propels the natural into the super-natural spheres of billions of dollars afloat on islands of virtual reality. Described as but a mosquito-ridden island till the 1960s, the Caymans are now the world's fifth largest financial center.

"These are real deals, not paper transactions designed to deceive," says a senior partner of a law firm on Grand Cayman.

The radio announcer in New York City catches my ear when she asks: "What have Enron and Al Qaeda got in common?"

Answer: "Offshore island accounts."

"The Caribbean is full of places where security is pretty relaxed," says a professor at the University of St. Andrews in Scotland who studies terrorism around the world. As quoted in a *New York Times* article in January 2003, officials of the Organization of American States "are concerned that chains of remote islands, which are notoriously difficult to police, could become stop-off points for terrorists."[2] Perhaps this is because when it comes to islands, it seems at times difficult to separate terrorism from the actions of high-ranking U.S. government personnel. According to U.S. congressman Henry Waxman, U.S. Vice President Dick Cheney's long-term meal ticket, the Halliburton Company, is able to do a lucrative business with "Axis of Evil" countries such as Iran by setting up subsidiaries in territories such as the Cayman Islands.[3] At the same time, the island of Diego Garcia in the Indian Ocean—rented from Britain by the United States—serves as a holding pen for Taliban and other suspects, where they are probably being tortured by U.S. government personnel as I write these lines.[4] Imagine, renting another nation-state's island! For torture! And where would the U.S. government be without its prison at Guantánamo on the island of Cuba, a location beyond the reach of (U.S.) law?

Islands certainly make a mockery of sovereignty. Could this be why we cherish them so? Like tin-pot dictators too big for their boots, they are at one and

2. Associated Press, "Threats and Responses: The Caribbean; Islands Fear Becoming a Route for Travelers with Terror Plans," *New York Times,* January 9, 2003, sec. A, p. 15.

3. Bob Herbert, "Dancing with the Devil," *New York Times,* May 22, 2003, sec. A, p. 33.

4. Duncan Campbell, "US Interrogators Turn to 'Torture Lite': The Second Half of Our Investigation Finds America Bending the Rules in the Wake of September 11," *Guardian,* January 25, 2003, p. 17; *Washington Post,* December 26, 2002. Available at www.Commondreams.org.

the same time superstates and nothing but a mound of dirt or rocks framed by the cruel sea. Go rent one!

My guess is pirates were attracted to islands like moths to a light and that they felt good there. They certainly made it a point to visit them, these little nations of theirs, homes away from home tucked away in the secrecy of the open sea. To read the journal of Basil Ringrose, a pirate, is to read a succession of arrivals and departures from islands like names in a gigolo's date book. Restricting ourselves to this one voyage in the South Sea along the Pacific coast of northern South America, beginning in 1679, we find Ringrose and his pack of merry boys stopping off at the following islands in chronological order:

Tavoga

Otaque

Cayoba (off present-day Panamá)

Gorgona

Gallo

Galapagos

La Plata also known as the Isle of Plate or Drake's Isle (off Colombia
  and Ecuador)

Más a Tierra, about fifteen hundred miles due south of Gorgona and
  one of three that constitute the islands of Juan Fernández off
  Chile, that mountainous island with many goats, famous for a
  Scotsman, Alexander Selkirk, later to be known as Robinson Crusoe, having been castaway there in 1704 from a privateering vessel,
  the *Cinque Ports,* one of two ships under the command of William
  Dampier. In fact, it was Woodes Rogers, with the same William
  Dampier, demoted to pilot, who four years later found Selkirk
  nimble of foot, dressed in goatskins, and barely able to speak owing to his solitary existence. On Dampier's recommendation as to
  his skill as a sailor, Rogers made him mate on his ship and thus
  brought the future Crusoe back to England, where he resumed
  service in the British navy.

My point is that it was no accident, the encounter on Crusoe's island, later described as "a wasp's nest of buccaneers," five hundred miles off the coast of

Chile in the middle of nowhere.[5] Woodes Rogers had just completed six thousand miles at sea around Cape Horn in a 320-ton vessel, the *Duke,* with a crew of 117. His first port of call in the New World had been an island off Brazil, the island he called Grande, where his crew careened the ships and replenished the water. Later he would visit Gorgona, careen his vessels there, and await passing treasure ships to attack. Eventually all this experience in the nefarious trade stood him in good stead. The king asked him to eradicate piracy in the Caribbean. And he did. The pirates who refused amnesty, he chased and killed. This despite the fact that during his time hovering in the shelter of Gorgona, half his face had been shot away in a fiery engagement with the famous galleons sailing from the Philippines stuffed with treasure. I think of him lying there weeks on end in the heat and flies with only half a jaw watching the clouds scud by. But I'm getting ahead of myself.

By the time Woodes Rogers reached the islands of Juan Fernández, many men were sick from scurvy and frostbite rounding the Horn and needed to be taken ashore where sails and rigging were mended while other sailors hunted goats and drew off fresh water. "We have a little Town of our own here, and every body is employ'd," wrote Rogers, surveying his tent city made from sails on the beach at Juan Fernández. The future Robinson Crusoe provided them with turnip tops and other greens useful for scurvy to be mixed into goat stew. "'Twas very pleasant ashore among the green Pimiento Trees, which cast a refreshing smell," noted Rogers in his journal.[6] You bet! After six thousand miles at sea in a tiny boat with 116 other men! Idyllic as it was, they made haste, for they had been informed at the Canary Islands in the Atlantic that five French ships were coming to these seas. In fact, when they first approached Juan Fernández and saw Robinson Crusoe's fires there, they assumed they had been lit by their French enemies. Crusoe himself was scared that Spanish ships were close, as he feared he would be made a slave and put to work by them in the mines on the mainland. Yes! Busy, busy, places, these little islands stuck way out on the great nothingness of sky and water.

---

5. Walter De la Mare, *Desert Islands and Robinson Crusoe* (London: Faber and Faber, 1930), p. 23.
6. Rogers, *A Cruising Voyage,* p. 96.

It is impossible to imagine the abundance. They boiled up eighty gallons of sea lion oil to fuel their lamps and for frying their meals when at sea for want of butter. There were so many of these animals; they could have boiled up a ton of oil. Working ashore repairing rigging, the men enjoyed the taste of young seals. It reminded them of English lamb. Crusoe told them that in November seals lined the shore "very thick" for half a mile deep. "Their fur is the finest that I ever saw of that kind," wrote Woodes Rogers, "and exceeds that of our Otters."[7] An ominous compliment for the future well-being of the world's seal population. It is impossible to imagine the abundance. Twenty years earlier, in April 1684, the ever-observant Mr. Dampier had recorded that "Seals swarm as thick about this island, as if they had no other place in the World to live in; for there is not a bay nor Rock that one can get ashore on, but is full of them. Sea lions are here in great Companies, and Fish, particularly Snappers and Rock-fish, are so plentiful that two men in an Hour's Time will take with Hook and Line as many as will serve 100 men." The seals were the size of calves, with a fine, short, thick fur. "Here, there are always Thousands, I might say possibly Millions," he wrote. They are "either sitting on the Bays or going and coming in the Sea round the Island; which is covered with them (as they lie at the Top of the Water playing and sunning themselves) for a Mile or two from the shore." Although nimble swimmers, they were sluggish on shore and a "blow on the Nose soon kills them." Even large ships "might here load themselves with Seal-skins, and Trayne-oyl; for they are extraordinary fat."[8]

I sit back and try to visualize Dampier in his ship soaring across an ocean of seals, all that beautiful fur and salty Pacific making a magic carpet of his journeying—and ours too, this several centuries later, wondering, wondering what it was like back then in contrast to the death that followed, starting to see why islands figured with such elemental force in the European imagination as the world fell before its sailors and soldiers, merchants, and, of course, its scribes, such as Defoe. And I think of what it might have meant to Dampier, this sharp-eyed Englishman born in 1652 to a poor farming family at East Coker, Yeovil,

7. Rogers, *A Cruising Voyage*, p. 100.
8. Dampier, *A New Voyage Around the World*, pp. 68, 69.

whose father died when he was ten, his mother when he was sixteen, leaving him orphaned, transferred from the Latin to the Modern school to learn arithmetic and writing, and then a year later apprenticed to the master of a Weymouth ship bound for France and then Newfoundland. By 1675 he was in Jamaica working on a plantation belonging to a neighbor in Somersetshire, England. Quickly tiring of that, he went back to sea, cruising in trading vessels around Jamaica, settling in with the riffraff of merry boys cutting logwood at Campeachy, Yucatán, prior to joining pirates under Coxon, Sharp, and others, crossing the Isthmus of Panamá to the fabled South Sea, hitherto known only to the Spanish. What intrigues me is the matter-of-factness of Dampier's meticulous descriptions, in this regard similar to those of the Spanish chroniclers over the preceding two centuries. Here they were, emerging like butterflies from their mean lives in Europe, running away to sea and flung into amazingly different situations. Yet the wonder comes later, much later, in our time.

"I have made an estimate of more than three millions that have been carried to Canton from thence, in the space of seven years," wrote Captain Amasa Delano of Boston in 1817 in reference to seals killed at the Juan Fernández Islands. This is the same Captain Delano who described the smelting of gold in Lima in such detail, the same Delano whose story provided Melville of *Moby Dick* with one of his best stories. Delano thought that when the Americans arrived at these islands in 1797, there were without a doubt two to three million seals. Men would stand in pairs on the beach between the seals and the sea and drive the seals between them. A very small blow on the nose would stun them, and the animals were skinned by slashing them open with a knife from under the jaw to the tail, giving a stab in the breast that would kill them. Delano saw men who could skin sixty seals in an hour. At times there were fourteen sealing vessels moored off the islands. In China the skins sold on average for around a dollar, but three-quarters of the payment was generally made in tea.[9]

It was here in these islands of Juan Fernández that a ship limped into port under the command of don Benito Cereno with a cargo of slaves. It had been badly battered rounding the Horn, and Captain Delano helped out as best he

---

9. Delano, *Narrative of Voyages and Travels*, p. 306.

could. He found the atmosphere on the ship strange. For instance, he saw a young slave strike a crew member with a knife. And it was peculiar the way don Benito would never allow his slave to leave his side. As Delano rowed away, don Benito hurled himself off his ship into the long boat. It turned out that the slaves had control of the ship and were forcing the crew to sail them to Senegal. Delano and his crew subdued the slaves, but don Benito told the viceroy in Lima that Delano was a pirate and he owed him nothing. Herman Melville read Delano's account and wrote a famous story, "Benito Cereno." These islands of Juan Fernández have sustained more than their share of world literature with Robinson Crusoe and Benito Cereno. But even Marx, who used Robinson to great effect, failed spectacularly to understand just how bloody and wild a story of capitalist development these tiny islands in the middle of the ocean came to sustain.

"Man has always felt an extraordinary attraction for islands," wrote a Colombian general, Julio Londoño, in 1956 in the *National Police Gazette* of Colombia at almost the same time concrete was being poured on the island of Gorgona to build the prison there. Islands, continued the general, have exercised a strange fascination over man's "dreams of adventure and domination."[10] The general hits the nail on the head, I believe, and takes us beyond the usual idea that islands are attractive because they serve as an escape from civilization. For in the general's eyes, and they are hardly his alone, being eyes hardened to struggle yet open to adventure and fantasy, an escape from civilization means an escape from being dominated so as to become in turn the dominator. Thus we might say the reason Gorgona is a specter is not only because of its haunting history of having been a prison, but also because as an island it combines, as he says, "dreams of adventure" with those of "domination."

But how can one account for such dreams when it comes to islands? Why should an island, so innocent in its tranquillity, aloneness, and smallness, encourage thoughts of domination? Could it have to do with the graspability and boundedness of the territory in question, the sense of the whole leading to having it whole, a miniature universe in the palm of one's hand, the ultimate power trip? And something else; being without much by way of human presence, with-

---

10. Julio Londoño, "Islas del Pacifico," *Revista Fuerzas de Policía de Colombia* (March–April 1956): 85.

out buildings or apparatus of production, desert(ed) islands encourage not merely dreams of adventure and domination but the domestication of nature, as expressed in the image of a solitary man against the elements, like the fable of Robinson Crusoe.

Lying outside human time and place, the desert island is the tabula rasa awaiting the reenactment of human—meaning European—history. We might venture ourselves across the lonely sea to just such emptiness, endangering our sense of place and self so as to claim as consequence of our travail some sense, some fact, that history runs to a different time on the island, not clock time, but a time charged with a sense of the recurrent, the endless return, and the equally powerful sense of origin, of being able to start afresh.

Like the puppet theater or the play within the play, miniaturization in the form of an island allows one to hold the world in one's hands, play with it, observe it from different angles, and provide it with different fates. What Benjamin says concerning the theater of the baroque applies to islands as well: "The new theater has artifice as its god."[11] And such artifice supplies an essential ingredient of the dialectical image. Time is framed in a spatial image. Surrounded by sea.

In his police gazette article, the general makes another observation concerning the attraction of islands, and that is that they pull you toward themselves with an almost mystical force. Crossing the emptiness of the ocean, the navigator is drawn to the island as a magnetic point on the horizon. The reference here is to the loneliness of the voyage of discovery, the anxiety as to bearings, the rupture of sameness, and then the safety of the haven that is the island in such a situation, surrounded by a hostile unknown. The general ingenuously adds that islands are afraid of being alone, often existing in clusters, such as Gorgona with its smaller neighbor, Gorgonilla, or Crusoe's Island, Juan Fernández, one of three islands huddling together. Yet how much more of an anthropomorphizing jump is it, really, to assume that islands, in the depths of their solitude, not only want other islands for company, but human beings as well?

---

11. Benjamin, *The Origin of German Tragic Drama*, p. 82.

For is not an island like human consciousness, its vast bulk submerged in subaqueous moodiness like the human soul? Is it this that explains the coming and going of certain islands, one day mysteriously disappearing into the sea from which they came? Walter De la Mare (felicitous name) is rightly fascinated by islands that appear on mariners' maps only to be never found again by later sailors. What has happened? Could it have been a mythical sea creature instead? And when they disappear, these mystery islands of ours, they go with a bang. According to De la Mare, Crusoe's island of Juan Fernández, which later became a wretched prison island, was disappeared at least twice by tidal waves. And in 1835 this was followed by an eruption of flames and smoke from deep water a mile off the beach.[12] These outbursts mirror the destiny of islands to appear and disappear as prisons one day, utopias the next.

12. De la Mare, *Desert Islands and Robinson Crusoe*, pp. 124–25.

underwater mountains

The story of sailors anchoring themselves to some massive sea creature like a whale in mistake for an island only to be taken for a ride is a story that reinforces the shock and unease I feel on having to contemplate islands not as plates floating on the sea, but as tips of underwater mountains. It seems virtually impossible to think of islands as mere tips of something submerged, yet no doubt it is this enigma that lies embedded in the fascination with islands. It is striking how effectively the submersion of history is effectively symbolized by this image of depths invisible to the naked eye, surmounted by a placid, sunlit, but potentially treacherous surface. There is a diffuse awareness as to omens of the past made mysterious by its aqueous concealment. Writing about the sea as a symbol of the crowd, Elias Canetti says the mystery of the sea, unlike the mysterious suddenness of fire, lies in what it contains and covers: "The life with which it teems is as much part of it as its enduring openness. Its sublimity is enhanced by the thought of what it contains."[1]

In the mountains running along the Isthmus of Tehuantepec, which joins the southern states of Mexico to the rest of the country, there is a dam one and half hour's journey from the Caribbean port of Veracruz. It was completed in 1957 and is named after one of the saviors of the nation, President Miguel Alemán. The purpose, if indeed we can speak of such, of this dam is to supply electrical power to the national petroleum corporation Pemex, whose pumps and lakes of contamination run alongside strips of commercial development mile after mile between Veracruz and Tabasco. Folklore has it that the dam was built to benefit the Alemáns' family smelter in the industrial park at Veracruz, but folklore as you know is unreliable, almost as unreliable as etymology, the word *park* originally meaning a preserve for beasts of the chase.

As you approach the dam, the size of a small ocean, as I did with my seven-year-old daughter in the fall of 1995, the landscape is one of power lines and electrical substations foregrounding the mountains standing far away. We walk down a concrete slipway with a restaurant selling cold beer and fried fish to one side and climb aboard a metal dinghy with an outboard motor and an old boatman in a straw hat. It feels like the seaside. It takes a long time to get to where we are going, and soon the land falls behind us. The boatman steers the boat on a zigzag course as if obeying some ancient pattern that Juan Pérez, who has been here many times before, studying Mazatec shamanism, fancifully suggests might be the trail that went over the mountains before the landscape was flooded when the Indians lived here.

Some twenty thousand Mazatec Indians were moved from here to San José by the state in 1954 so as to make way for the dam. Some snuck back, maybe two thousand or more, and now live illegally on the islands that poke out of the water's surface, islands that used to be the peaks of lofty mountains. The boatman drops us off, and we spend the night on an island with a group of Indians: an adult man, his three wives, and a small boy. The island is tiny, less than a third of a mile in diameter. On it, there are two huts built close together, one a kitchen, the other for sleeping. They are built of sticks. The floors are beaten earth, cool

1. Canetti, *Crowds and Power*, p. 81.

and clean. Resting in the shade of the few trees on the island lie some twenty head of cattle with sweeping horns. There are other islands close by.

Late in the afternoon the sky grows dark with the flight of migrant birds from North America. One could not even imagine the world had so many birds. NAFTA birds, ancient emissaries of trade neither free nor state-controlled when the world knew other sorts of boundaries. How William Dampier, our seventeenth-century buccaneering naturalist from East Coker, Yeovil, careening on Gorgona in the Pacific Ocean off Colombia and cruising in search of prey between that island and the mainland in 1681, would have loved to study these birds for his *Discourse of Winds*. What insights must birds like these have given him about sailing the trade winds by mimicking the birds mimicking the wind so he could outrun Spanish galleons and prepare maritime charts that would help England become the supreme naval power of modern history. They settle into a floating forest a mile or so away, and the sound they create is like the roar from a football stadium, like the crashing of surf on the seashore, nature's cocktail party at the end of a long day on the wing.

In *Living on the Wind*, published in 1999, Scott Weidensaul says that biologists recently discovered that "Veracruz represents far and away the largest concentration of migrant raptors in the world, and one of the most critical migratory bottlenecks in the world." In one day he and his team counted nearly a million hawks in the sky. A raptor is a bird of prey, and he singles out Swainson's hawks and broad-winged hawks, the former flying seven thousand miles from Alberta, Canada, to Argentina. The broad-winged hawk reminds me of myself, a "chunky, crow-sized bird of the eastern hardwood forests, where it drifts beneath the canopy of oaks and maples on wide wings or sits quietly along the edges of small meadows and streams, waiting for frogs, snakes, mice, or other small vertebrates."[2] In the fall, however, it leaves me to fly off to the tropical rain forests of Colombia and Venezuela, stopping at Veracruz, where more than 75 percent of the land has been converted to agribusiness—in the form of sugarcane plantations and cattle ranches, presumably fed by the monster dam—which must make it hard for the migrants to find a rest for the night. Could it be that the dam, cause of the ecological and human disaster, is also in a backhanded way a

---

2. Scott Weidensaul, *Living on the Wind: Across the Hemisphere with Migratory Birds* (New York: North Point Press, 1999), pp. 124, x, 112–18, 107.

salvation for these birds? A mighty blow against nature by the combined power of capital and the state, the dam is nevertheless a sanctuary.

I take this irony to be something else as well; a manifestation—indeed, a sign—of how modernity creates layers of prehistory within itself, such that what we like to think of as nature—the immense stillness of the waters, no less than the immense chorus of the birds—becomes both intensely natural and intensely artificial at one and the same time. History conceived of as a straight line or as progress thus concedes the existence of another sort of time held fast in surprise no less than in an image framing all our thinking and feeling too—as with the boatman zigzagging his way across a placid surface, following ancient paths.

Such images are dangerous, yet should be nourished and held close to that organ we call our thinking. For they play mischief with the line we would and must draw separating the man-made from nature, no less than the long ago from the here-and-now.

We could this past imagine as the underwater mountains whose peaks are now islands. As the outcome of catastrophe transposed into landscape in which history is frozen, in this case in the petrified reality of the dam, the tugging at the memory of oppression is fraught with another type of standstill as well, a *profane illumination,* as when memory is bound to the fixed-explosive quality of surreal images that André Breton thought of as "convulsive beauty" in his book on mad love, among the first examples of which were coral and crystals. Benjamin himself referred not so much to *surreal* as to *dialectical* images in which history swam below the surface, citing "myth as long gone, nature as prehistory," which is why such images "are really ante-diluvian fossils," like a freeze shot of movement suddenly stilled.[3] When this occurs, for Benjamin it is equivalent to a Messianic cessation of happening, the greatest still shot of all time, and here the image of the fossil as the image of the dialectical image—for it, too, deserves its image—turns over to give way to flight and continental drift, birds, millions of migratory birds settling in the trees floating on the dam, millions of migratory birds soaring in thermal uplift, the very winds that Scott Weidensaul cannot stop trying to picture for us, this sense of birds filling the sky, dissolving space in a motion span-

---

3. André Breton, *Mad Love* (1937), trans. Mary Ann Caws (Lincoln: University of Nebraska Press, 1987), pp. 10–19; Benjamin, "On the Theory of Knowledge, Theory of Progress," p. 461; and Benjamin, "Surrealism," p. 192.

ning the continent north to south since time immemorial: kites, hawks, and vultures "sliding from thermal to thermal, forming enormous kettles that swirl and seethe with wheeling birds."[4]

The cacophony of birds settling in for the night is silenced by the pounding of hooves. Wide-horned cattle race along the crest of the mountain that is now the island and dive into the water. They seem crazy. Herd hysteria. There they were, grazing as contentedly as cows could be on a mountaintop become an island, and now for no good reason they are running as if their life depended on it. Every day late in the afternoon, they must sense the radical dislocation of land and water and decide to run. They are like the boatman zigzagging his craft for no apparent reason across the water, as if determined to retrace the antediluvial landscape. They swim vigorously to the next island, clamber onto it, and race along its crest to dive once again into the water and so swim back to the original island in a neat line, one bobbing behind the other. All you see are the flared horns dripping water, the beauty of their dark brown eyes, and the desperately dilating moist black holes that are their nostrils, black nostrils barely above the surface of the ripples marking their slow advance. Like the islands, their vast bodies remain out of sight.

---

4. Weidensaul, *Living on the Wind*, p. 108.

The smaller the object, the more likely it seemed that it could contain in the most concentrated form everything else.[1]

sloth

Then it was that the island of Gorgona was changed from a top-security prison to a top-security paradise to which Japanese, German, and U.S. ambassadors are flown in by helicopter, given lunch, and then, before the iguanas have time to blink, are flown back to Bogotá in time to see the next paramilitary massacre on TV, complete with chain-sawn-off legs, as a general, bloated with power and ugly as sin, reminds us IT IS FORBIDDEN TO KILL IGUANAS or stray from prescribed paths. Or walk without a guide. Or touch the animals. Or go to any but the two beaches designated. Or play music. Or any radio. Or shower anywhere but outside. And you must rent rubber boots from us to walk in. *¿Todo entendido?* Now we are going to explain to you how things are here. Come with me.

---

1. Arendt, "Introduction," in Benjamin, *Illuminations,* p. 1.

We go into a small hot room with school chairs neat in rows and bottles of various shapes and sizes glowing with a sickly luminescence. Dead snakes and marsupials like fetuses in formalin gaze at us from a long sleep behind hooded lids as he demands respect for the environment, clumsily embracing a bottle with a snake in it. And before we begin, "What is your name?" he asks in a commanding tone on account of which my daughter, aged five, refuses to give it, at which point he says, the light ever more luminous, the eyes ever heavier, "Good! Then we shall wait until you decide to tell us!" His pencil-line mustache quivers, the only sign of life on a granite face.

The director, so the police insisted on our arrival, wanted to see us. After all, we had arrived without permission in a small boat skimming the waves from the coast opposite. The police searched our bags and helped themselves to the *biché* we had been given as a present and never saw again. They called the director on a phone set up there in a shack on the sand. "*¡Sin sello ninguno!*" they told him. No seal! Not only was liquor prohibited on the island, but this was white lightning made without state license up some forlorn river under someone's rickety house. Plutarco grinned at me when I said this was nothing but another prison. He spun the boat and headed back to the mainland in drizzling rain. It started to dawn on me why the locals never visited.

A tall thin German-Colombian in his mid-thirties, the director appeared like a ghost, gliding through the mist. His way of introducing himself was to point out how much ocean the Colombian government controlled by virtue of islands such as Gorgona. He lived on the island with his wife, daughter of a high-ranking army officer. She seemed lost, chain-smoking her Piel Rojas like the lonely Russian miners way up the Río Timbiquí. His prior job had been in the national park of the Sierra Nevada on the Caribbean coast until he tried to get the marijuana growers there to stop and they retaliated with death threats. He carefully picked up a piece of glass from the sand. "Roads are the problem," he said. "They let the consumer society penetrate everywhere. Why do people want electricity anyway?" I thought of the people upriver in Santa María. What they most wanted in the world was a road and electricity. It seemed like the only thing he could relate to was his mobile phone into which he talked all the time. I wondered if he was talking to anyone.

The director and his wife left early in the morning on a speedboat. It took them a long time to get the boat into water as it was stranded on the mudflats on account of the size of the tides there. It was strange how much trouble they had getting anyone to help them. After all, he was the director. Eventually they sped south in a burst of spray and freedom toward the coast opposite. I had a feeling they spent more time escaping than living on the island.

Iguanas scuttled across the terrace. A contingent of police played volleyball with the radio on loudly. A young girl attached to the police cuddled a monkey. Those responsible for the rule of law were exempt from it. Like the iguanas, they freely crossed the boundaries.

After the mainland it was beautiful to be on the island. "But we have to leave something good for the children," a man says when questioned about the prison-like atmosphere. He can stay only three days but does not know why his time is limited. And you have to have a clearance to leave.

We wanted to put through a call to friends in Guapi on the mainland to come and take us away. But in an explosion of petulance, the man in charge of the radio refused. It was impossible to make contact with the outside world.

As the day proceeded, a picture of what sociologists like to call the "power structure" of the island started to emerge. At first it seemed grimly orthodox, the two whites directing a mestizo middle class of guides, technicians, and administrators, and a black underclass, cooking and cleaning. Only the latter were from the coast. The sociologist could take bleak satisfaction in its mute perfection and wonder at what the ecologically restored future held in store for the black denizens of a coast whose best bet was to become but the human part of the growing concern with "biodiversity."

But there was more to it than that, more than a class and color hierarchy. It was as if the island concentrated all the venom that the larger society across the straits contained and was able to do so because of the morally uplifting cause of ecological protection. Now nature itself had become the prisoner, an object of natural history to be ogled in its Otherness from rented rubber boots just like the specimens floating in formalin under half-closed eyes. What fairy-tale prince would plant a kiss on these cold lips and awaken them from their long sleep?

Right on sunset the director and his wife returned from across the straits. "Slavery is genetic," she announced angrily. Her husband nodded. The same government agency that administers Gorgona is forcing coastal people to stop shrimp farming, claiming it destroys mangroves. The director and his wife had met with these people, who then threatened them with the guerrilla. The director seemed scared. There's nothing more the guerrilla would want, he thought, than to occupy Gorgona.

But more than scared, I thought, was the humiliation and erosion of his dignity, caused not so much by the threat of a guerrilla assault, as by the violence he was forced to manifest as a state official against these poor people in the name of ecology. For like a zoo or anthropological museum with wire cages, guards, and vitrines, the island displayed not so much biodiversity conservation as control thereof—as with a malicious adult guide cuddling a dead reptile in its yellow formalin glass casket, bullying a five-year-old girl in front of her parents. It was theater wherein the violence of nature is absorbed into violence confronting nature, in the name of its protection. Thomas Hobbes held to this very same theater with his famous notion of the social contract creating the state that he called Leviathan, a sea monster in prehistory.

The token in all of this was the director himself, a towering prison of a man unable to acknowledge that it was not he who called the shots, but the police and the men under him, mestizos from the interior, strangers to the coast, who served as guides and guards. He could not even get his speedboat off the sand without their grudging help. But of course he was necessary, as a token, for without that the theater would collapse.

Awake before daybreak, I lie wondering in the dark if Plutarco will come through. For some reason my thoughts turn to Pacho and the way we would sit by the town hall downriver on the Timbiquí and he would illustrate what he was saying with geometric drawings, as if there was a link between these lines, circles, and dots spreading across the page and the events he was telling me about. I was asking questions about the Russians, how they came here, why they left . . . and I see him now hunched over these doodlings with furrowed brow as I wait for an answer in the no-man's-land between sleep and waking, rain pounding, and I ask myself why it didn't seem significant at the time, the labor of telling it how it was, words disappearing into meandering diagrams that spiral off one another until I see something else in the absence that this memory highlights. When you write, you feel you're short-changing reality. It's not even half the truth. And the more you write, the more it slips away.

Another way of putting this is that the signs he makes on the paper are oblique references to political and economic forces that have to remain obscure even if they could ever be clarified through the smoke screen of small-town politics, where every story breeds its opposite and truth is necessarily both imaginative and corrupt. This small town could well be yours, and mine, too, this small town we call our life, except Colombia is taking human existence into realms never thought of as possible before. The enigmatic and tortured shapes that Pacho reproduces on the page alongside his speaking are the allegorical signs of politics that everybody thinks they understand but in truth just add to the wild confusion as paras and guerrilla fight it out over the dying corpse of the state that is at least nine-tenths a fiction. Straight lines are explosions of force and sudden connections, betrayals and collusions concocted by cocaine. Circles are swamps of intrigue and possibilities for plunder worthy of further examination. Wavy lines are smoke trails of cover-ups and the bubbly wakes of lawyers in fast canoes with big outboard motors hastily summoned from the interior when the manager of the bank has been accused of stealing the pitiful amount of cash from the one and only bank on the river and the helicopter with the nurses' pay inexplicably veers away into an overcast sky. Erasures and smudge marks register the calculated deception disguising fake paras as real paras, fake guerrilla as real guerrilla, but most of all fake reality as real reality. Deep shading registers the plummeting price of gold as the postmodern condition of capital finally abandons the "naturalistic fallacy" of a need for something real to base value upon and the banks and governments abandon the "gold standard." Will the muscle-wrenching back bending by women in the river upstream, and the labor of men in the gloom hammering at the rock face, will all of that now pass away to add to the layers of fossilization sedimented by the Flood in prehistory? Years later as I read the proofs of this book before it goes to press, I see that on account of the world recession and war under the aegis of George W. Bush, the price of gold has shot up. Despite what banks and governments do, the "naturalistic fallacy" seems very much alive, tying gold to ultimate and real and basic-as-you-can-ever-get value. It appears that thousands of years of mythology do not disappear overnight, not even when the Federal Reserve signs off. Benjamin thought a good deal about this naturalistic fallacy; as in the mimetic faculty, as in the flash of similarity like the flash of gold in the black pay dirt at the bottom of the *batea* spinning in some women's hands, edge dipping into running streams. Here we return to Pacho's doodling. "Script," writes Benjamin, "has thus become like language, an archive of nonsensuous similarities, of nonsensuous correspondences."[2] Elsewhere he observed

---

2. Walter Benjamin, "On the Mimetic Faculty" (1933), in *Reflections: Essays, Aphorisms, Autobiographical Writings,* ed. Peter Demetz, trans. Edmund Jephcott (New York: Schocken, 1986), p. 335.

of the fragmented language of baroque theater that such language ceases to merely serve the needs of communication. Instead, as a newborn object, it "acquires a dignity equal to that of gods, rivers, virtues and similar natural forms which fuse with the allegorical."[3]

The director insisted on accompanying us to the beach. The rain became a fine shower. As we embarked, he drew himself to his full height and, arm extended, pointed prophetically. Through the mist were heaps of black clouds lit up by a golden ribbon of sunlight running along the crests of the high cordillera. "There is the continent!" he said slowly, accentuating each syllable, mindful of the paradise on which we stood. "Where the people are killing themselves."

As our boat coasted an hour later into Guapi, alive with the chitchat of people arranging their canoes for market, the bow cut through layers of putrid waste and plastic bags. It only gets worse as you go up the steps. It felt good.

Twenty years earlier on those same steps on the continent where the people are killing themselves was where I had first seen a sloth. It lay in the bottom of a dugout canoe. I thought it was a wet bundle of fur, a strange thing to come across in a canoe, and then I saw it was a creature. Like the iguanas happily crossing boundaries on Gorgona, the sloth did the same but without moving a muscle or so much as twitching an eyelid, and the categories it crossed were more basic still. It was as close to death as you could get in life, outside of being a clam. It not only blurred life and death, but in doing so it had a remarkable capacity for dissimulation of the one in the other. A sloth is a creature that plays games with death and hence with thought itself, especially thought as thought through the stillness of natural history. In this respect, the sloth is paradigmatic of the famous *tableau vivant* or theater of still life in which history is not so much slowed down as cut up into images. "He mov'd," noted the privateer Woodes Rogers in 1709 about the first sloth he had ever come across, while refitting captured ships on the island of Gorgona, "as if he had walked by Art, keeping an equal and slow Pace, as if all his Movements had been directed by Clock-work, within him."[4] Breaking down the fluidity of time into component still shots as with the heartbeat of the sloth

3. Benjamin, *The Origin of German Tragic Drama*, p. 208.
4. Rogers, *A Cruising Voyage*, pp. 179–80.

is to not only write a history of the Pacific Coast since European conquest and enslavement of Africans, but a history for which the allegory of a prison island named after the Gorgon as the history of modern Colombia is to my mind strikingly appropriate.

Years later there was another sloth tied to a bench at the same market by the river, a shapeless bundle of wet fur that matched and meshed with everything and nothing. I came back to take its photo but it had been sold. A few hundred feet upriver, I found it on a boardwalk leading to a plank house. It had been cut into pieces with a machete for a household's lunch, but they proudly showed off the pieces and tried to reassemble them into a whole for postmortem portraiture there by the muddy river under leaden skies.

No photo, no "last snapshot," but still, does not the sloth make us see the world anew? Is it not way out there, along with gold and cocaine, the quintessence of miasma? As a creature that plays havoc with life and death, should it not be a prime exhibit of my Cocaine Museum along with the golden *poporos*? And in describing the sloth as best we can, words running over its stillness, do we not mimetically, as it were, rework the language of nature no less than the nature of language? This must have been what Blaise Cendrars thought of a similar creature years ago: "Having such an extravagant animal as a pal opens your eyes to the mysteries of creation and allows you to touch, just with your fingertips, the absurdity of all the long history of the evolution of living beings."[5]

As for my Cocaine Museum with its rivers and stone, its swamps and miasma, it is really a lot closer than you think. For it not only lies in the Gold Museum, which itself lies deep in the heart of the national bank so as to anchor the modern economy with Indian religion and Indian gold, but it lies in the way we use words like fish nets to pass through water to catch whatever glistens and moves. In the process, the language merges with the light that radiates through the water like the lightning in the rivers where the gold once lay and to where the coca is coming. As a newborn object, this language "acquires a dignity equal to that of gods, rivers, virtues and similar natural forms which fuse with the allegorical," which is to say with the gods and ghosts of slavery awakened in the

---

5. Blaise Cendrars, *Sky: Memoirs* (1949), trans. Nina Rootes (New York: Marlowe & Company, 1992), p. 14.

museum, readied for our uncertain future. This glittering residue is also the dignity of friendship with the people who helped me up and down the Timbiquí, what stays as real despite race and money. It is what bathes me in light as I finish these notes in upstate New York and reluctantly make my preparations to go home, aware there is no alternative for a traveler such as myself other than to disappear inside my collection.

afterword

Species diversity. Biodiversity. Summer vacation. Lake Michigan 1985 watching TV as Jet Skis thump across the lake. Bearded professor with backpack, sensible L.L. Bean clothes, and L.L. Bean smile, walking through redwood forest in the state of Washington. Rays of sunlight filtering through the "cathedral" of the forest. It's a program about the "wilderness" and why we should protect it. "Species diversity!" cries the professor. Who then enumerates how many species this wilderness contains. I forget the number.

In my book, phrases such as "species diversity" belong to a strain of rhetoric better suited to stock-market portfolios than the play of light and water across the rippling rapids of a coastal river. Meant to marshal science in the fight to redeem fallen nature, such phrases actually give a further twist to its destruction. As such, this language takes its place alongside the rhetoric of "human capital" and the division of the social analysis into quantitative and "qualitative."

"Species diversity" was not exactly what Mary Wordsworth and her brother William, for instance, had in mind with their love of nature. We can see them as a "romantic reaction" to industrial capitalism. The word "reaction" suggests a mere reflex, an action smaller than itself, but for all of that the language made by these poets serves, by contrast with the eco-science of today, as a timely reminder of the desperate need today for a cultural revolution, meaning a sweeping change in the very basis of our way of life including not only shopping malls and SUVs, but our science and our language as well. What, then, of Fredric Jameson's notion that it is easier to imagine the end of the planet than the end of capitalism?[1]

So these thoughts began with mud—and the rocks and the hands and the water and the gravel and the hands—of gold mining up the Timbiquí with the heat and the rain and the overcast skies. Language was king. But this mud was my imminence. I mean, it was all around you and then inside you, as when the gods formed us, they say, from mud itself. All mud. The task then was the old, old one of getting the soul and the body to work together, meaning language and things, language and mud, but this time around the stakes are truly frightening. The end of the planet?

This is why I am fascinated by Walter Benjamin's mimesis project—meaning the mystical idea that words and things are materially connected, and that such connections open out like an artist's palette into pictures that come and go, at times with fantastic speed, depending on the state of emergency and the degree to which we enter into those pictures or, vice versa, the degree to which pictures engulf and absorb us. A movie. What is so strange about Benjamin in this regard is his equally strong conviction that such connections are intensely playful and political, what he called "allegorical," by which he meant that the

---

1. Fredric Jameson, *The Seeds of Time* (New York: Columbia University Press, 1994), p. xii. The actual passage reads: "It seems to be easier for us today to imagine the thoroughgoing deterioration of the earth and of nature than the breakdown of capitalism; perhaps that is due to some weakness in our imagination."

space between a symbol and what it means is always subject to history and is therefore forever incomplete.

In 1933 when he wrote an essay, "Doctrine of the Similar," which with slight changes became "On the Mimetic Faculty," Benjamin experimented with a form of *Denkbild,* or "thought-figures," which combined autobiographical fragments with an image, implying a more or less conscious philosophical curiosity and surrealist affinity for contradiction. He had started something like this earlier, with "One-Way Street," written between 1923 and 1928, but it was with his two summers on the island of Ibiza in 1932 and 1933 that the thought-figures acquired an autobiographical and ethnographic character, displaying, among other things, a marked interest in nature as well.

Such thought-figures were often embedded by Benjamin in stories he was told. But he went beyond that to create a form that combined ethnography with his own storytelling, and it was at this time that he wrote what is probably his most famous essay, "The Storyteller." As the Ibizan poet Vicente Valero has recently described in detail, this foray into thought-figuration also involved Benjamin's experimentation with drugs—namely, hashish and opium—and the recording of his dreams as well.[2] Benjamin thus represents an alternative track for anthropology, one that I have to some extent followed and modified according to my times and context.

In this I have been attentive to the claims of reflexive anthropology as I think it obvious that all objective recording is nothing more than what has been first run through and experienced by the observer. Such experience comes before representation, yet it is the writer's responsibility to the reader to try all means and modes to make that experience as full and as obvious as possible. Just as in this era of globalization, there is no place so remote as to remain unaffected by the world at large, so there is no anthropologist who does not straddle two or more worlds simultaneously. Indeed, what is anthropology but a species of translation made all the more honest, all the more truthful, and all the more interest-

---

2. Valero, *Experiencia y pobreza.*

ing by showing showing—i.e., showing the means of its production? The task before us, then, is to see what anthropology has been, all along; namely, telling other people's stories and—in the process—generally ruining them by not being sensitive to the task of the storyteller. We do not have "informants." We live with storytellers, whom too often we have betrayed for the sake of an illusory science.

The task before us, then, is to cross the divide, scary as it may be, and become storytellers as well—albeit, at least in my case, storytelling with a "modernist" curve, the sort of stuttering delivery that Benjamin endorsed, receptacles, no doubt, for his beloved "dialectical images." The traveler comes home and has a lot to talk about. It took a long time. Virtually the whole of the twentieth century chasing European nineteenth-century realism dressed up as science.

If what I call the "transgressive dynamic" in gold and cocaine seems both overwhelming and universal at this point, as value is increasingly tied to evil, and if I have tried to ride that storm and understand some of it at the same time, I have become acutely aware as to the claims of what I timidly call "place" as well. What I mean is this: that if it was mud and hands in gravel and sweat, all the time sweat and rain and heat, that took over my being—this ever so decided and decisive m-a-t-e-r-i-a-l-i-t-y—then so that, too, came to be overlaid by another set of sensations having to do with the placeness of place, in this case the Pacific Coast; the river, the village at the end of the river, the mines, breadfruit trees, swimming the *largo* with the kids in the bend in the river, the mountains beyond where Juan Pablo plays his flute and traps animals—and the endless connections people make with all that through history and the forgetting of history. (Julio Arboleda's sin was not that he was a slave owner, but that he denied being from Santa María.)

Gold and cocaine have real histories, as with African slavery in colonial times and the spread of coca up the Timbiquí today. By "real histories" I mean chains of cause and effect over time. But gold and cocaine take you on another, quite different tack, as well. Through their enchantment, their danger and beauty, they usher in a world of force and substantiality felt from within, a world that escapes from the time-based cause-and-effect reality we most of the time like to think we observe. This other world is the world of physics and chemistry, sex and silence, dreams and nightmares, and I call it the world of "immanence."

When in *My Cocaine Museum* I dwell on heat, for instance, or rain, or color, it is to that withinness that I am drawn, especially as it connects with the placeness of place and the strangely familiar but mute zone of the bodily unconscious for which I wish to provide something like a language—fearful that it might be better *not* to tamper with the mute wisdom of the body and that we should restrict poetry to the heavenly spheres, even as the planet descends into a fiery hell.

I like to think I am in this merely following the path laid out by those Kogi Indian priests I invoke at the beginning of this book for whom site-specific ritual is the essential ingredient in paying back the earth. With exquisite attention to the placeness of place and the importance of gold, they turn their attention to situation, social and spiritual, chewing coca for as long as it takes, which can be very long, indeed.

That is another story of coca quite different from the one now unfolding along the banks of the Timbiquí. But just as Kogi gold work occupies much of the Gold Museum in the heart of the Banco de la República, so the Kogi sense of place in the redemption of history underlies whatever is of value in this, *My Cocaine Museum*. In this way, then, and for that reason, I can only hope that the gods asleep in the museum—all 38,500 of them—will awaken and come to life with the tinkling of glass as the vitrines give way. This is my magic and this is why we write and why we write strange apotropaic texts like *My Cocaine Museum* made of spells, hundreds and thousands of spells, intended to break the catastrophic spell of things, starting with the smashing of vitrines whose sole purpose is to uphold the view that you are you and over there is there and here you are—looking at captured objects, from the outside. But now, no more! Together with the previously invisible ghosts of slavery, the awakened gods will awaken remote pasts and remote places previously congealed as soft whispers in the bank's ledgers and money-counting machines. Ghosts and gods peel back the money, back into mud, then stone—hundreds and thousands and millions of white and orange stones like eggs flowing yolk by the riverbanks all over Colombia where kids tumbling home from school in the midday heat make the stones make their jigger-jigger music, grumbling yet happy like the mad wail of the bells crying out for the dead all day long and longer still ringing in your ears.

acknowledgments

For their generosity from the day I first stepped ashore at Santa Bárbara on the Timbiquí River on the sultry Pacific Coast of Colombia in 1971, I am grateful to Maria Zuñiga de Grueso and her late husband, Jorge Grueso. I met them thanks to a letter of introduction written for me by my friend the schoolteacher and land-reform surveyor Alejandro Peña. I am mindful of how many worlds that little letter has opened. I am also aware of how much my survival from that time on, spiritual no less than material, has come to depend on everyone in the remote mining village way upstream named Santa María—especially Eustaquia Ocoró, Gustavo Díaz Guzbén, William Amú Ocoró, Benedita Grueso Ocoró, and Saturnino Grueso Herrera.

The director of the hospital in Guapi on the adjoining river, Dr. Demetrio Góngora, helped me in many ways with his calm advice, the beauty of his name, and the blessings he bestowed on my friendship with the sailor Plutarco Grueso and Plutarco's equally legendary wife, Mabby B. Obregón de Grueso, also a sailor on the rivers and high seas of these unpredictable waters. Ricardo Grueso Obregón of Santa María taught me about mining and the old days.

Arturo Escobar included me in his research team on the Pacific Coast in 1993 along with Alvaro Pedrosa, Libia Grueso, and Jesús Alberto Grueso.

The director, Clara Isabel Botero, and the staff of the Gold Museum in the Banco de la República showered me with kindness and information regarding their collection of pre-Colombian gold work. I am especially thankful for their hosting two memorable mornings of discussions in the museum in July 2003 with two miners from Santa María, Timbiquí—Lilia Zuñiga and Ricardo Grueso—as a first attempt to reconsider the museum's neglect of the tormeted history of three centuries of slave labor in Colombia's extensive gold mines when a colony of Spain.

Time after time, Hedwig Hartmann and her staff in the historical archive of the Universidad del Cauca, in Popayán, came to my rescue. Without their help, I would have been unable to locate documents on the slave mines at San Vicente, Timbiquí, or interpret them.

I owe much to the delight students made of our seminar "Prehistory: Between Land and Sea" at Columbia University, as well as to the conveners of the Carpenter Lectures at the Department of English of the University of Chicago for their invitation to give my talks on "Prehistory and the Dialectical Image" in May 2000.

At various times, members of my immediate family accompanied me to Santa María, for which I am eternally grateful. It is strikingly beautiful there, yet full of hardship. There is little food, the heat and rain are intense, malaria is endemic, and it takes a long time to adjust. Anna Rubbo accompanied me in 1971, and in 1976 we returned with our son, Mateo, then four years of age. In the late 1980s, I was accompanied twice by Rachel Moore and our two young children, Santiago and Olivia. Santiago returned in 1994, aged ten, and helped me through some tough times.

Jimmie Durham provided the necessary stonework and museum gift wrapping.

Upriver in Santa María, I went over the manuscript with Lilia Esperanza Zuñiga Asprilla. Other than what is in this book, I owe her more than I can say.

bibliography

Adorno, T. W. "A Portrait of Walter Benjamin." 1967. In *Prisms,* pp. 227–41. Translated by Samuel and Shierry Weber. Cambridge: MIT Press, 1983.

Albertini, L. *Étude de la concession miniére de Timbiquí, Republique de Colombie.* 2nd ed. Paris: Chaix, 1899.

Anderson, John Lee. "233,000 Acres, Ocean Views." *New Yorker,* November 29, 1999.

Arboleda, Diego Castrillón. *Tomás Cipriano de Mosquera.* Bogotá: Banco de la República, 1979.

Arboleda, Gustavo. *Diccionario biográfico y genealógico del antiguo Departamento del Cauca.* Bogotá: Horizontes, 1962.

Arboleda, Sergio. "La Colonia: Su constitución social." In *Corona funebre en honor del Sr. Dr. Sergio Arboleda.* Ibagué: Impr. del Depto., 1890.

Ardila, Jaime, and Camilo Lleras. *Batalla contra el olvido.* Bogotá: OP Gráficas, 1985.

Arendt, Hannah. "Introduction: Walter Benjamin: 1892–1940." In Walter Benjamin, *Illu-*

minations: Essays and Reflections, pp. 1–58. Edited by Hannah Arendt. Translated by Harry Zohn. New York: Schocken, 1968.

Artaud, Antonin. *Le Theatre et son double.* Paris: Gallimard, 1964.

Barona Becerra, Guido, Camilo Domínguez Ossa, Augusto J. Gómez López, and Apolinar Figueroa Casas. *Viaje de la Comisión Corográfica por el estado del Cauca 1853–1855.* Tomos II y III. Cali: Imp. Feriva, 2002.

Bataille, Georges. *The Accursed Share: An Essay on General Economy.* 1976. Vol. 1, *Consumption.* Translated by Robert Hurley. New York: Zone Books, 1988.

———. *The Accursed Share: An Essay on General Economy.* 1976. Vol. 2, *The History of Eroticism.* Translated by Robert Hurley. New York: Zone Books, 1991.

———. "Informe," *Documents* 7 (December 1929): 384; translated by Alan Stoekl as "Formless," in Georges Bataille, *Visions of Excess: Selected Writings 1927–1939.* Minneapolis: University of Minnesota Press, 1985.

Baudelaire, Charles. *Intimate Journals.* Translated by Christopher Isherwood. San Francisco: City Lights, 1983.

Bell, A. Colquhoun. "An Explanatory Note on *The Discourse of Winds.*" In William Dampier, *Voyages and Discoveries.* Introduction and notes by Clennell Wilkinson. London: Argonaut Press, 1931.

Benjamin, Walter. *The Arcades Project.* 1982. Edited by Rolf Tiedemann. Translated by Howard Eiland and Kevin McLaughlin. Cambridge: Harvard University Press, 1999.

———. "A Berlin Chronicle." 1970. In *Reflections: Essays, Aphorisms, Autobiographical Writings,* pp. 3–60. Edited by Peter Demetz. Translated by Edmund Jephcott. New York: Schocken, 1986.

———. "The Collector." In *The Arcades Project,* 203–11. Edited by Rolf Tiedemann. Translated by Howard Eiland and Kevin McLaughlin. Cambridge: Harvard University Press, 1999.

———. "Dream City and Dream House, Dreams of the Future, Anthropological Nihilism, Jung." 1982. In *The Arcades Project,* pp. 388–404. Edited by Rolf Tiedemann. Translated by Howard Eiland and Kevin McLaughlin. Cambridge: Harvard University Press, 1999.

———. "A Glimpse into the World of Children's Books." In *Selected Writings.* Vol. 1, *1913–1926.* Edited by Marcus Bullock and Michael W. Jennings. Translated by Rodney Livingston et al. Cambridge: Harvard University Press, 1996

———. "Hashish, Beginning of March 1930." 1932. In *Selected Writings.* Vol. 2, *1927–1934,* pp. 327–30. Edited by Michael W. Jennings, Howard Eiland, and Gary Smith. Translated by Rodney Livingston et al. Cambridge: Harvard University Press, 1999.

———. "Hashish in Marseilles." 1932. In *Reflections: Essays, Aphorisms, Autobiographical Writings,* pp. 137–45. Edited by Peter Demetz. Translated by Edmund Jephcott. New York: Schocken, 1986.

———. "In the Sun." 1932. In *Selected Writings.* Vol. 2, *1927–1934,* pp. 662–65. Edited by Michael W. Jennings, Howard Eiland, and Gary Smith. Translated by Rodney Livingston et al. Cambridge: Harvard University Press, 1999.

———. "The Lamp." In *Selected Writings.* Vol. 2, *1927–1934,* pp. 691–93. Edited by Michael W. Jennings, Howard Eiland, and Gary Smith. Translated by Rodney Livingston et al. Cambridge: Harvard University Press, 1999.

———. "The Lisbon Earthquake." In *Selected Writings.* Vol. 2, *1927–1934,* pp. 536–40. Edited by Michael W. Jennings, Howard Eiland, and Gary Smith. Translated by Rodney Livingston et al. Cambridge: Harvard University Press, 1999.

———. "Main Features of My Second Impression of Hashish." In *Selected Writings.* Vol. 2, *1927–1934,* pp. 85–90. Edited by Michael W. Jennings, Howard Eiland, and Gary Smith. Translated by Rodney Livingston et al. Cambridge: Harvard University Press, 1999.

———. "On Astrology." In *Selected Writings.* Vol. 2, *1927–1934,* pp. 684–85. Edited by Michael W. Jennings, Howard Eiland, and Gary Smith. Translated by Rodney Livingston et al. Cambridge: Harvard University Press, 1999.

———. "On the Mimetic Faculty." 1933. In *Reflections: Essays, Aphorisms, Autobiographical Writings,* pp. 333–36. Edited by Peter Demetz. Translated by Edmund Jephcott. New York: Schocken, 1986.

———. "On the Theory of Knowledge, Theory of Progress." 1982. In *The Arcades Project,* pp. 456–88. Edited by Rolf Tiedemann. Translated by Howard Eiland and Kevin McLauglin. Cambridge: Harvard University Press, 1999.

———. "One-Way Street." 1928. In *One-Way Street, and Other Writings,* pp. 45–106. Translated by Edmund Jephcott and Kingsley Shorter. London: New Left Books, 1979.

———. *The Origin of German Tragic Drama.* 1963. Translated by John Osborne. London: New Left Books, 1977.

———. "Paris—the Capital of the Nineteenth Century." 1955. In *Charles Baudelaire: A Lyric Poet in the Era of High Capitalism.* Translated by Harry Zohn. London: New Left Books, 1973.

———. "The Storyteller: Reflections on the Work of Nikolai Leskov." 1936. In *Illuminations: Essays and Reflections,* pp. 83–100. Edited by Hannah Arendt. Translated by Harry Zohn. New York: Schocken, 1968.

———. "Surrealism: The Last Snapshot of the European Intelligentsia." 1929. In *Reflections: Essays, Aphorisms, Autobiographical Writings,* pp. 177–92. Edited by Peter Demetz. Translated by Edmund Jephcott. New York: Schocken, 1986.

———. "Theses on the Philosophy of History." 1950. In *Illuminations: Essays and Reflections,* pp. 253–64. Edited by Hannah Arendt. Translated by Harry Zohn. New York: Schocken, 1968.

———. "Unpacking My Library: A Talk about Book Collecting." 1931. In *Illuminations:*

Essays and Reflections, pp. 83–110. Edited by Hannah Arendt. Translated by Harry Zohn. New York: Schocken, 1968.

Bennett, Wendell. "The Archaeology of Colombia." In *Handbook of South American Indians.* 7 vols. Vol. 2, *The Andean Civilizations,* edited by Julian Steward, pp. 823–50. New York: Cooper Square, 1963.

Bey, Hakim. *T.A.Z.: The Temporary Autonomous Zone, Ontological Anarchy, Poetic Terrorism.* Brooklyn: Autonomedia, 1985.

Bocarejo Suescún, Diana. "Fragmentos etnográficos y objetos prehispánicos: Representando lo indígena en el museo del Oro." *Arqueolgía del Área Intermedia,* no. 3 (2001): 151–82.

Bogue, R. H. *The Chemistry of Portland Cement.* New York: Reinholt, 1955.

Bois, Yves-Alain, and Rosalind Krauss. *Formless: A User's Guide.* New York: Zone Books, 1997.

Breton, André. *Mad Love.* 1937. Translated by Mary Ann Caws. Lincoln: University of Nebraska Press, 1987.

Brown, Lloyd A. *The Story of Maps.* New York: Bonanza Books, 1949.

Burroughs, William. *Cities of the Red Night.* New York: Henry Holt, 1981.

———. *The Letters of William S. Burroughs: 1945 to 1959.* Edited by Oliver Harris. London: Picador, 1993.

———. *The Soft Machine, Nova Express, The Wild Boys: Three Novels by William S. Burroughs.* New York: Grove, 1980.

———. *The Western Lands.* New York: Viking, 1987.

Caillois, Roger. *Pierres.* Paris: Gallimard, 1966.

———. *Pierres réfléchies.* Paris: Gallimard, 1975.

———. *The Writing of Stones.* 1973. Translated by Barbara Bray. Charlottesville: University of Virginia Press, 1985.

Caldas, Francisco José de. *Seminario de la Nueva Granada.* 1809. Cited in *Geografía económica de Colombia: Chocó.* Bogotá: Litografía Colombia, 1943.

Canetti, Elias. *Crowds and Power.* 1962. Translated by Carol Stewart. New York: Farrar, Straus and Giroux, 1984.

Céline, Louis-Ferdinand. *Journey to the End of the Night.* 1934. Translated by John H. P. Marks. New York: New Directions, 1960.

Cendrars, Blaise. *Sky: Memoirs.* 1949. Translated by Nina Rootes. New York: Marlowe & Company, 1992.

Cioran, E. M. "Caillois: Fascination of the Mineral." In *Anathemas and Admirations,* pp. 205–10. Translated by Richard Howard. New York: Little, Brown, 1991.

Codazzi, Agustín. *Jeografía fisica i política de las provincias de la Nueva Granada.* 4 vols. Vol. 4, *Provincias de Córdoba, Cauca, Popayán, Pasto y Túquerres. Segunda parte: Informes.* Bogotá: Banco de la República, 1959.

Conrad, Joseph. *Heart of Darkness.* 1902. Harmondsworth: Penguin, 1983.

Dampier, William. *A New Voyage Around the World.* 1729. New York: Dover, 1968.

———. *A New Voyage Round the World.* London: James Knapton, 1699.

———. *Voyages and Discoveries.* Introduction and notes by Clennell Wilkinson. London: Argonaut Press, 1931.

Darwin, Charles. *The Voyage of the Beagle.* 1839. London: Dent, 1959.

De la Mare, Walter. *Desert Islands and Robinson Crusoe.* London: Faber and Faber, 1930.

Delano, Amasa. *Narrative of Voyages and Travels, in the Northern and Southern Hemispheres.* 1817. New York: Praeger, 1970.

Departmento Nacional de Planeación. *La Paz: El desafío para el desarrollo.* Bogotá: Departamento Nacional de Planeación, 1998.

Dickens, Charles. *Great Expectations.* 1861. New York: Dodd, Mead, 1985.

Durham, Jimmie. *Between the Furniture and the Building (Between a Rock and a Hard Place) / Zwischen Mobiliar und Haus (Im Gestein der Zwickmühle).* Translated by Stefan Barmann and Karen Lauer. Köln: Walther König, 1998.

Durkheim, Emile. *The Elementary Forms of Religious Life.* 1915. Glencoe, Ill.: Free Press, 1965.

Earle, Peter. *The Sack of Panamá.* Bury St. Edmunds, Suffolk: Norman & Hobhouse, 1981.

Emerson, Ralph Waldo. "Nature." 1849. In *Essays and Lectures,* pp. 5–49. New York: Library of America, 1983.

Exquemelin, A. O. *The Buccaneers of America.* 1684–85. Edited by William Swan Stallybrass. Williamstown, Mass.: Corner House Publishers, 1976.

Evans-Pritchard, E. E. *Nuer Religion.* New York: Oxford University Press, 1956.

Fals-Borda, Orlando. Introducción to *La Violencia en Colombia: Estudio de un proceso social.* 2 vols. Vol. 2, by Germán Guzmán Campos, Orlando Fals-Borda, and Eduardo Umaña Luna. Bogotá: Tercer Mundo, 1964.

Farrington, Benjamin. *Greek Science: Its Meaning for Us.* 2 vols. Vol. 1. Harmondsworth, Middlesex: Penguin, 1947.

Fernández de Oviedo y Valdés, Gonzalo. *Historia general y natural de las Indias.* 5 vols. Biblioteca de Autores Españoles. Madrid: Ediciones Atlas, 1959.

Freud, Sigmund. "Fetishism." 1927. In *The Standard Edition of the Complete Psychological Works of Sigmund Freud.* 24 vols. Vol. 21, pp. 152–57. Edited and translated by James Strachey. London: Hogarth, 1968.

———. "Medusa's Head." 1922. In *The Standard Edition of the Complete Psychological Works of Sigmund Freud.* 24 vols. Vol. 18, pp. 273–74. Edited and translated by James Strachey. London: Hogarth, 1968.

———. "Totem and Taboo" 1913–14. In *The Standard Edition of the Complete Psychological Works of Sigmund Freud.* 24 vols. Vol. 13. Edited and translated by James Strachey. London: Hogarth, 1953.

Gage, Thomas. *Thomas Gage's Travels in the New World.* 1648. Edited by J. Eric Thompson. Lincoln: University of Oklahoma Press, 1985.

Gansser, A. "Geological and Petrographical Notes on Gorgona Island in Relation to North-Western S. America." *Schweizerische Mineralogische und Petrographische Mitteilungen* 30 (1950): 219–36.

García Márquez, Gabriel. *One Hundred Years of Solitude.* 1967. Translated by Gregory Rabassa. New York: Harper, 1991.

Gatrell, V. A. C. *The Hanging Tree: Execution and the English People, 1770–1868.* Oxford: Oxford University Press, 1996.

Genet, Jean. *Prisoner of Love.* 1986. Translated by Barbara Bray. Hanover: Wesleyan University Press 1992.

Glob, P. V. *The Bog People: Iron Age Man Preserved.* 1965. Translated by Rupert Bruce-Mitford. Ithaca: Cornell University Press, 1969.

Goethe, Johann Wolfgang von. *Theory of Colours.* 1840. Translated by Charles Lock Eastlake. Cambridge: MIT, 1970.

Granger, Henry G., and Edward B. Treville. "Mining Districts of Colombia." *Transactions of the American Institute of Mining Engineers* 28 (February–October 1898): 33–87.

Graves, Robert. *The Greek Myths.* Combined edition. London: Penguin, 1992.

Guzmán Campos, Germán, Orlando Fals-Borda, and Eduardo Umaña Luna. *La Violencia en Colombia: Estudio de un proceso social.* 2 vols. Bogotá: Tercer Mundo, 1962 (vol. 1), 1964 (vol. 2).

Haring, C. H. *The Buccaneers in the West Indies in the XVII Century.* 1910. Hamden, Conn.: Archon Books, 1966.

Harrison, Jane. *Prolegomena to the Study of Greek Religion.* 2nd ed. Cambridge: Cambridge University Press, 1908.

Heaney, Seamus. *Opened Ground: Selected Poems, 1966–1996.* New York: Farrar, Straus and Giroux, 1998.

Heidegger, Martin. "What Is Metaphysics?" 1929. In *Basic Writings,* pp. 89–110. Edited by David Farrell Krell. San Francisco: Harper, 1993.

Hemming, John. *The Conquest of the Incas.* New York: Harcourt Brace Jovanovich, 1970.

Herr, Michael. *Dispatches.* 1968. New York: Vintage, 1991.

Horkheimer, Max, and Theodore W. Adorno. *Dialectic of Enlightenment.* 1944. Translated by John Cumming. New York: Continuum, 1989.

Hornell, James. "The Archaeology of Gorgona Island, South America." *Journal of the Royal Anthropological Institute of Great Britain and Northern Island* 56 (1926): 401–36.

Howe, Susan. *Pierce-Arrow.* New York: New Directions, 1997.

Jameson, Fredric. *The Seeds of Time.* New York: Columbia University Press, 1994.

Johnson, Chalmers. *Blowback: The Costs and Consequences of American Empire.* New York: Henry Holt, 2000.

Kristeva, Julia. *Powers of Horror: An Essay on Abjection.* Translated by Leon S. Roudiez. New York: Columbia University Press, 1982.

Lacan, Jacques. "The Function of Language in Psychoanalysis." 1956. In *Speech and Language in Psychoanalysis,* pp. 1–88. Translated with notes and commentary by Anthony Wilden. Baltimore: Johns Hopkins University Press, 1968.

Leal, Claudia. "Manglares y economía extractiva." In *Geografía humana de Colombia: Los Afrocolombianos,* by María Romero Moreno, Luz Castro Agudelo, and Esperanza Aguablanca, tomo VI, pp. 399–429. Bogotá: Instituto Colombiana de cultura hispánica, 1998.

Lévi-Strauss, Claude. *Introduction to the Work of Marcel Mauss.* Translated by Felicity Baker. London: Routedge and Kegan Paul, 1987.

Llano, María Clara, et al. *La Gente de los ríos: Juntapatía.* Bogatá: Litográfia Sánchez, 1998.

Londoño, Julio. "Islas del Pacifico." *Revista Fuerzas de Policía de Colombia* (March–April 1956): 85–90.

Lubell, Winifred Milius. *The Metamorphosis of Baubo: Myths of Woman's Sexual Energy.* Nashville: Vanderbilt University Press, 1994.

Malinowski, Bronislaw. *Argonauts of the Western Pacific: An Account of Native Enterprise and Adventure in the Archipelagoes of Melanesian New Guinea.* 1922. Prospect Heights, Ill.: Waveland Press, 1984.

———. *A Diary in the Strict Sense of the Term.* 1967. 2nd ed. London: Althone, 1989.

Mauss, Marcel. *A General Theory of Magic.* Translated by Robert Brain. New York: Norton, 1972.

Menéndez y Pelayo, Marcelino. "Don Julio Arboleda juzgado por Marcelino Menéndez y Pelayo." *Signatura* #80. Archivo Arboleda, Archivo Central del Cauca.

Middleton, W. E. Knowles. *A History of the Theories of Rain and Other Forms of Precipitation.* New York: Franklin Watts, 1965.

Moreno C., Heber. "Isla prisión Gorgona." In *Crímenes que causaron sensación en Colombia.* Cali: Editorial América, 1969.

Müller, Grégoire, and Gianfranco Gorgoni. *The New Avant-Garde: Issues for the Art of the Seventies.* New York: Praeger, 1972.

Nietzsche, Friedrich. *The Gay Science: With a Prelude in Rhymes and an Appendix of Songs.* 1887. Translated by Walter Kaufmann. New York: Vintage, 1974.

———. *On the Genealogy of Morality.* 1887. Edited by Keith Ansell-Pearson. Translated by Carol Diethe. Cambridge: Cambridge University Press, 1994.

Nisser, Pedro. *La Minería en Nueva Granada.* 1834. Translated by María Victória Mejía Duque. Bogotá: Banco de la República, 1990.

Olender, Maurice. "Baubo." *Encyclopedia of Religion.* 16 vols. Edited by Mircea Eliade et al. New York: Macmillan, 1987.

Olson, Charles. *Call Me Ishmael.* Baltimore: John Hopkins, 1997.

Parker, Robert. *Miasma: Pollution and Purification in Early Greek Religion.* Oxford: Clarendon Press, 1983.

Parry, J. H. *The Discovery of South America.* London: Paul Elek, 1979.

Pavy, David, III. "The Negro in Western Colombia." Ph.D. diss., New Orleans, Tulane University, 1967.

Plato. *Timaeus.* Translated by Francis M. Cornford. London: Macmillan, 1959.

Pérez, Felipe. *Jeografía fisica i politica del estado del Cauca.* Bogotá: Imprenta de la nación, 1862.

Prescott, William H. *History of the Conquest of Peru, with a Preliminary View of the Civilization of the Incas.* 2 vols. Vol. 1. Boston: Phillips, Sampson, 1858.

Price, Thomas. "Saints and Spirits: A Study of Differential Acculturation in Colombian Negro Communities." Ph.D. diss., Evanston, Northwestern University, 1955.

Rangel Suárez, Alfredo. *Colombia: Guerra en el fin del siglo.* Bogotá: Tercer Mundo, 1998.

Reichel-Dolmatoff, Gerardo. *Colombia.* London: Thames and Hudson, 1965.

———. *Goldwork and Shamanism: An Icongraphic Study of the Gold Museum.* Medellin: Compañia Litográfica Nacional, 1988.

———. *Los Kogi: Una tribu de la Sierra Nevada de Santa Marta, Colombia.* 1950. 2 vols. 2nd ed. Bogotá: Procultura, 1985.

Restrepo, Vicente. *A Study of the Gold and Silver Mines of Colombia.* 1884. Translated by C. W. Fisher. New York: Colombian Consulate, 1886.

Rhees, Rush. "Wittgenstein on Language and Ritual." In *Wittgenstein and His Times.* Edited by Brian McGuinness. Chicago: University of Chicago Press, 1982.

Richardson, Ruth. *Death, Dissection, and the Destitute.* London: Penguin, 1988.

Robledo, Cecilia de. *Gorgona, isla prisión; crónicas.* Bogatá: Pijao, 1997.

Rogers, Woodes. *A Cruising Voyage Round the World.* 1712. New York: Longmans, Green, 1928.

Romero Moreno, María. "Familia afro-colombiana y construcción territorial en el pacifico del sur, siglo XVIII." In *Geografía humana de Colombia: Los Afrocolombianos,* tomo VI, pp. 105–40. By María Romero Moreno, Luz Castro Agudelo, and Esperanza Aguablanca. Bogotá: Instituto colombiano de cultura hispánica, 1998.

Ross, Andrew. *Strange Weather: Culture, Science, and Technology in the Age of Limits.* London: Verso, 1991.

Rubio, Mauricio. *Crimen sin sumario: Análisis económico de la justicia penal Colombiania.* Documento CEDE 96-04. Bogotá: Universidad de los Andes, 1996.

Sánchez, Efraín. *Gobierno y geografía: Agustín Codazzi y la Comisión Corográfica de la Nueva Granada.* Bogotá: Banco de la República, 1999.

Sass, Stephen. *The Substance of Civilization: Materials and Human History from the Stone Age to the Age of Silicon.* New York: Arcade, 1988.

Scheer, Edward. "The Uses of Critical Surrealism, Part ii: Defacement." *Cultural Studies Review* 8, no. 2 (November 2002): 194–200.

Schmitt, Carl. *Political Theology: Four Chapters on the Concept of Sovereignty.* Translated by George Schwab. Cambridge: MIT Press, 1988.

Scholem, Gershom. "Walter Benjamin and His Angel." In *On Walter Benjamin: Critical Essays and Recollections,* pp. 51–89. Edited by Gary Smith. Translated by Werner Dannhauser. Cambridge: MIT Press, 1988.

Serrano, Eduardo. *Historia de la fotografía en Colombia.* Bogotá: Museo de Arte Moderna, 1983.

Sharp, William F. *Slavery on the Spanish Frontier: The Colombian Chocó, 1680–1810.* Norman: University of Oklahoma Press, 1976.

Shore, Bradd. *Sala'ilua: A Samoan Mystery.* New York: Columbia University Press, 1982.

Sobieszek, Robert A. *Ports of Entry: William S. Burroughs and the Arts.* Los Angeles: Los Angeles County Museum of Art and Thames and Hudson, 1996.

Soriano Lleras, Andrés. *Escritos sobre Codazzi.* Bogotá: Aedita Editores, 1962.

———. *Itinerario de la Comisión Corográfica y otros escritos.* Bogotá: Imprenta Nacional, 1968.

Stevenson, Robert Louis. "My First Book." In *Treasure Island.* 1883. Edited by Emma Letley. Oxford: Oxford University Press, 1985.

Strauss, Gerald. "Topographical-Historical Method in Sixteenth-Century German Scholarship." *Studies in the Renaissance* 5 (1958): 87–101.

Striffler, Luis. *El alto Sinú: Historia del primer establecimiento para extracción de oro en 1844.* Cartagena, 1886.

Tisdall, Carolyn. "Bog Action." In *The New Avant-Garde: Issues for the Art of the Seventies.* Text by Grégoire Müller, photographs by Gianfranco Gorgoni. New York: Praeger, 1972.

Traven, B. *The Death Ship: The Story of an American Sailor.* 1926. Translated by Erich Sutton. New York: Collier Books, 1962.

———. *Government.* 1931. Translated by Basil Creighton. London: Allison and Busby, 1980.

Uribe, Manuel, and Camilo Echeverri. *Estudios industriales sobre la minería antioqueña en 1856.* Cited without other bibliographic data in Vicente Restrepo, *A Study of the Gold and Silver Mines of Colombia.* 1884. Translated by C. W. Fisher. New York: Colombian Consulate, 1886.

Valero, Vicente. *Experiencia y pobreza: Walter Benjamin en Ibiza, 1932–1933.* Barcelona: Ediciones Península, 2001.

Vergara y Velasco, F. J. *Nueva geografía de Colombia. 1901–2.* 3 vols. Vol. 3. Bogotá: Banco de la República, 1974.

Weidensaul, Scott. *Living on the Wind: Across the Hemisphere with Migratory Birds.* New York: North Point Press, 1999.

Weil, Simone. *The Iliad or the Poem of Force.* Translated by Mary McCarthy. Pendle Hill Pamphlet, no. 91. Wallingford, Penn.: Pendle Hill, 1983. [First published in French in Marseille, 1940, in the December 1940 and January 1941 issues of *Cahiers du Sud;* translation by Mary McCarthy, 1945, in the New York City journal *Politics.*]

West, Robert C. *Colonial Placer Mining in Colombia.* Baton Rouge: Louisiana State Press, 1952.

———. "Mangrove Swamps of the Pacific Coast of Colombia." *Annals of the Association of American Geographers* 46 (1956): 98–121.

———. *The Pacific Lowlands of Colombia: A Negroid Area of the American Tropics.* Baton Rouge: Louisiana State University Press, 1960.

White, Robert Blake. "Notes on the Aboriginal Races of the North-Western Provinces of South America," *Journal of the Anthropological Institute of Great Britain and Ireland* 13 (1884): 240–56.

Whitten, Norman E. *Black Frontiersmen: A South American Case.* Cambridge: Schenkman, 1974.

Wilches-Chaux, Gustavo, H. Meyer, and A. Velásquez. "La Costa Brava." In *Colombia Pacífico,* 2 vols., vol. 2, pp. 489–95. Edited by Pablo Leyva Franco. Bogotá: FEN, 1993.

Wittgenstein, Ludwig. *Remarks on Colour.* Edited by G. E. M. Anscombe. Berkeley: University of California Press, 1978.

Yates, Frances A. *Giordano Bruno and the Hermetic Tradition.* New York: Vintage, 1969.

Young, Michael W. *Malinowski's Kiriwina: Fieldwork Photography, 1915–1918.* Chicago: University of Chicago Press, 1998.

index

Adorno, T. W.: Benjamin's snow globe as magic of dereification, 178–79; dialectical image as antediluvian fossil, 236; on Benjamin's philosophy as Medusan, 257, 267; and still life or "dead nature," 252; and weather, 45. *See also* death's head (*facies hippocratica*)
alchemy, 29
Al Qaeda, and Enron, 288
angel of history, 264, 265
ánimas, 73–75, 83
Apocalypse Now, 37
apotropaic magic: and art and terror, 279; and dialectical image, 266–67; and mimesis, 276
Arboleda, Julio, 88, 94–95
Arboleda, Sergio, 30
archive (Popayán), 89–94, 151
Arendt, Hannah, 260
Artículo 55, 95
Aufhebung, 208

Banco de la República, ix–x, 13

Barbacoas, 227

Bataille, Georges: and the *informe*, xiii; and mining as accursed share, 121–27; and the swamp, 174–75; and the sun gives without receiving, 170

batea, 2–3, 8, 79

Baubo, 10, 258

Baudelaire, Charles, 259

beaches, 218–24

bells (of the church), 72, 75, 101, 127

"Benito Cereno" (story by Herman Melville), 23, 293

Benjamin, Walter: and archival investigation, 89–90; and Chaldini's sound-figures, 190; and collecting, xii; and color, 28–29; and Dürer's *Melencolia I*, 182; and hashish, 34–35, 313; and heat, 34–35; and Ibiza, 34–35, 313; and image and object, 235; and the Lisbon earthquake, 130; and *mana*, 49; and messianic cessation of happening, 247; and monad, 247–48; "the need to become a thing in order to break the catastrophic spell of things," 258; quoting out of context, 261; and recording of his dreams, 313; and shamanic practice, 257–58; snow globe as philosophical toy, 178; and surrealism, 25; and thought-figures, 313; and weather, 48–49; and writing in nature, 190–91, 307, 309–10. *See also* dialectical image; mimetic play; petrifaction; prehistory

Bennett, Wendell (archaeologist), 83n15

Beuys, Joseph: and bog action, 180–81; and primordial animals, 181; words as verbal sculpture, 190

Bey, Hakim, *T.A.Z.*, 185n19

biché, 117–19, 122

birds, 299–301

Blake, William: and excess, 122

bodily conscious and unconscious, 31, 46–47

bog, 176–79

bog people, 178–79

boredom: and ethnography, 62; in Heidegger, 60–61; and village life, 59

botellón (torture device in prison at Gorgona), 240

Brecht, Bertolt, 246

Brown, Lloyd: *The Story of Maps*, 205. *See also* chorography

bureaucracy, 136, 145

Burroughs, William S., 16, 27, 152, 185, 235

buzos. See divers

cachaloa (French mining company money), 112–13

Caillois, Roger, 248

Caldas, Francisco José de: and the big map of Colombia, 211, 213; and lightning in the Chocó, 230–31

Calzadilla, Fernando, 284

Canetti, Elias, 74, 297

Céline, Louis-Ferdinand: and heat, 39–40

cement: and cocaine production, 160–61; compared with speed as signs of the modern, 165–66; contrast with wood for house construction, 162–64; "discovery" of, 159–60; and mimesis, 160; and Rosendale, New York, 159–60; and water, 161–62; and wharves, 164–65. *See also* wood

Chaldini's sound-figures, 190

children: and adult's imagination of the child's imagination, 207; and color, 207; and maps, 207; and prehistory, 178–79; and rain, 55–56

chora, 233–34

chorography: and cameos, 208–9; definitions, 201, 202; and displacement by abstraction, 203; and early ethnography, 201; and Genet and Traven, 202; as genius of locale, 201, 202; and Peter Pan, 208; and pirates, 208; and visual imagery, 202. *See also* Codazzi; Emerson; maps

church, 72, 124

Cieza de Léon, Pedro de, 84

cocaine: between life and death like gold, 252–53; compared with *biché* and gold, 118–19; as congealed miasma, 253; as crystallized shock, 252; and devil, 4; as magic, 127; smuggled through U.S. diplomatic pouch,

144; spread to Pacific Coast, xvi, 11, 132, 144, 150; and technology of production, 153; as transgression, 253; and wood and cement, 161, 169

cocaine museum, 13–20, 309–10

Codazzi, Agustín (Italian cartographer): death due to miasma, 213–14; and the guerrilla not needing a map, 214–15; and Instituto Agustín Codazzi, 214; and miasma, 217–18; and pestilence of Pacific Coast, 217–18; tasks, 197–98; vagabond laws against blacks, 203–4. *See also* chorography; maps

color: and Burroughs, 27; and Goethe, 26–29; makes mockery of language, 27; and money, 26; and transmutation, 26; and *Treasure Island,* 207; and Wittgenstein, 27. *See also* Benjamin

Conrad, Joseph. See *Heart of Darkness*

coral, 260–61

corruption: coastal government, 137; and gold and cocaine, 173

Crusoe, Robinson, 290–91, 295

Dampier, William (pirate and later officer in the British navy): and miasmatic mix of invisibility and materiality, 231; and Robinson Crusoe, 291; and seals; 291–92; and wind, 43–45

Darwin, Charles, 263–64

DEA (U.S. Drug Enforcement Agency), 15

death's head (*facies hippocratica),* 236, 252

Delano, Amasa, 23, 292

Descartes, René, 228

devil: and the accursed share, 122; and the Antichrist, 125; appears in form of animals, 125; and cocaine, 4; and gold, 4, 6–11, 80–81; mediates form with substance, 125; and women's distance from, 9

dialectical image, 90, 235–36, 246, 247, 253, 265, 300

Díaz Guzbén, Gustavo, 8, 74, 79, 89, 121

Dickens, Charles: *Great Expectations,* 182–85

diluvios (fossils in gold mines), 2

divers (*buzos),* 70–71, 77–80, 170

Doctor Faustus, 211

Doctor Strangelove, 211–12

documents, xiii

dogs: bomb sniffing, 130; and the guerrilla, 130–34; and U.S. customs; 15; use in Spanish conquest, 130–31; and Walter Benjamin's story for kids, 130: whine before person dies, 129

dredges (*draguetas),* 70–71

Dürer, Albrecht: *Melencolia I,* 181, 264

Durham, Jimmie, 248–50

earthquakes, 7

Easter week, 54, 73

Echavarría, Juan Manuel (artist), 278

Echeverri, Camilo: and treatise on nineteenth-century mining in Colombia, 77–78

ecological politics and the guerrilla, 142–43

El Dorado (the Golden King), 107

El Niño, 232

Emerson, Ralph Waldo, 200, 206–7

emigration (from Santa María), 101

Enron, and Al Qaeda, 288

esteros (swamp channels), 192–93

Estupiñon, René (shipbuilder), 221–24

Evans-Pritchard, E. E., 126n1

Evil Eye: according to Jane Harrison, 256–57; and eyes of the Gorgon, 256–57; and miasma, 256; in Santa María, 256

Fals-Borda, Orlando (sociologist), 281

FARC. *See* guerrilla

Farrington, Benjamin, 232

Faulkner, William, 204

Fernández de Oviedo y Valdés, Gonzalo (sixteenth-century Spanish chronicler), 82

Ferro, María del Rosario, xi

fetishes, xviii, 24–25, 266

Ficino, Marsilio (Renaissance magician), 234–35

figurines: on Gorgona, 251; Tumaco style, 252

Flood (biblical), 2, 25

formless. See *informe*

fossils, 2, 6, 91, 236, 258–59. *See also* Adorno; dialectical image; Medusa; petrifaction; shock

four elements (air, earth, fire, water), 80, 232

Fourier, Charles, 31–32

Freud, Sigmund: and apotropaic magic, 266–67; and fetish, 266; and gold as matter of place, 5; and holy dread, 176; on Medusa, 10; and pirates, 185

Galapagos Islands, 263–64

Gandolfo, Daniela, 285

Gansser, A. (geologist) 251–52

Genet, Jean, 62–63, 65–66, 83

Gil, Ramón, xi, xv

global warming, 31–32, 40. *See also* heat

Glob, P. V., 177–80

Goethe: and color of gold, 5; color theories, 27–29

God (Christian and Jewish): love of gold, 5

gold: and coca, xi, xv–xvi; and cocaine, xvii, 252–53; and enchanted music, 8, 89; and fairy tales, 24; as fetish, xvii, 25–26; and the four elements, 80; and God, 5; as a *grano,* 4; and Indian graves, 83; and the Lima mint, 23–24; as magic, 127; melting down by Spaniards, 26; as menstrual blood of the earth, xv; and Panama, 37; as petrified lightning, 252; as sacred, xvi; and speed, 170; and spiritual caretaker, 123; as transgression, 4, 5, 253; and water, 84, 106; and yield from panning, 3–4. *See also* devil; mining

Gold Museum, ix–xix, 13

Gorgon: and the Gold Museum, xviii–xix; and transgression, 253. *See also* Medusa

Gorgona (island): and dialectical image, 236; and guerrilla, 305–6; and naming, 255; as national park, 303–10; and prisoners, 239–43; and rainfall, 52–54

Granger, Henry G. (mining engineer in Colombia), 87–88, 94

grano (measure of weight of gold), 3. *See also* gold

Graves, Robert (mythographer), 257–58

Grueso, Mabby, 189, 191

Grueso, Plutarco (*motorista*), 132, 189, 192–93, 306

Grueso, Ricardo (gold miner): and *dragueta,* 70–71; and the Flood, 2; on paddles vs. motors, 191; and petrified leaves in mines, 6; and sluice mining, 81; as storyteller 192; and the whites of Mulatos, 219

guerrilla, xvii, 18, 132, 140, 144, 146–47, 154, 155; and fake guerrilla, 140–42; and threat to national park of Gorgona, 305

Gustavo. *See* Díaz Guzbén

Hardy, Thomas, 206

Harrison, Jane: and Evil Eye, 256–57

hashish, 34–35, 313

Heaney, Seamus, 177–78

Heart of Darkness (Conrad's novella), 37, 194

heat, 31–40; and the movies, 32. *See also* boredom; Céline; Fourier; global warming; rain; weather

Hegel's master and slave, 105

Heidegger, Martin, 60–62

Herr, Michael (author of *Dispatches*), 35–37, 40

Hobbes, Thomas, 131

horizon. *See* Emerson

Hornell, James (archaeologist), 251

Howe, Susan: *Pierce-Arrow,* 190

human rights speak, 157

ibaburas (native boats), 191

image: and doctrine of the similar, 266; and Ficino and Neoplatonic magic, 234–35; fossil as image-plate, 259–60; and petrifaction with Medusa, 260; and spells, 267; and sudden emergence in state of emergency, 266; and thing, 267. *See also* dialectical image

informe (Bataille's concept), xiii–xiv, 6, 173. *See also* Bataille; miasma; swamp

islands: analogous to layers of mind and prehistory, 297–98; analogous to maps, 212–13; and Benjamin on the baroque, 294; compared to the nation-state, 277, 288; list of prison islands, 283–86; list of tax-haven islands, 286–87; and pirates, 289–90; and puppet theater, 294; as tops of mountains in Mexican dam, 298–301; treasure island as prison island, 283, 295; and Walter de la Mare, 295

justice: and the guerrilla, 142–43; and magical medicines and poison, 125–26

Kalimán, 152–53
Kernaghan, Richard, 248n4
Klee, Paul, 264
Kogi Indians, xi, xiv–xvi, 235, 256, 315
Kristeva, Julia: and abjection, 39

Lacan, Jacques, 186–87
Lafargue, Paul (Karl Marx's son-in-law): *The Right to Be Lazy,* 204
landscape: moving through the body, 201, 205; and photography, 209; and watercolors, 208–9; and writing, 264–65. *See also* chorography
language: of the fetish, xviii; of matter and myth, xviii; of nature, xvii. *See also* second nature; writing
laughter, and transgression, 258
La Violencia, 273–74, 276
Leal, Claudia, 113n1
Lichtenberg, Georg Christoph, 264–65
lightning: and dialectical image, 247; and eighteenth-century reports, 53; as gold, 247; and miasma, 231–32; and stone, 246
logwood, 292
Lilia. *See* Zuñiga
Loñdono, Julio (Colombian police general): and prison islands, 293

Mabby. *See* Grueso
magic: 9, 74; apotropaic magic, 266–67; and dialectical image, 268; and spells, 267; and transgression of categories, 267. *See also* devil; mining

Malinowski, Bronislaw, 33–34
Mamo Luca (Kogi priest), xi, xiv–xvi
mana: and bodily unconscious, 47; and magic, 267–68; and weather, 46–48
mangroves. *See* miasma; swamp
maps: and *Aufhebung,* 208; Caldas's big map, 211; as the death's head, 200; displace sense of place, 199, 208, 211; and Doctor Strangelove, 211–12; and Emerson's sense of the horizon, 200; and independent Colombia, 197–98; insides vs. outsides of newly independent nation-states, 213; and islands 212–13; and lines of transport, 201; and Medusa, 200; and nature vs. culture, 200; and pirates, 213; rearticulation with Europe and United States with independence, 210; and shapes of nations, 199. *See also* chorography; Codazzi
marimba, 54, 73
Mauss, Marcel: on *mana* in relation to weather, 46–47
mazamorreo (panning for gold), 3
Mazatec Indians (Mexico), 298–301
Medusa: and Freud, 10, and the Gold Museum, xviii–xix; in Greek mythology, 256–57; and maps, 200. *See also* Gorgon
Melville, Herman, 23, 292
miasma: and Codazzi, 217–18, 228; and Descartes, 228; and Evil Eye, 256; and Greek idea of contagion, 175; and hosts of African slavery, xvi; and lightning, 230; and particles, 228. *See also* Bataille; Codazzi; Parker; petrifaction; prehistory; swamp
Middleton, W. E. Knowles: *A History of the Theories of Rain,* 228–30
mimetic play: between the guerrilla and the state, 134; and cement, 160; and the devil, 125–26; and diving for gold, 80; and doctrine of the similar, 266; and gold ingots, 26; and gold mining, 8, 80–82; and image suddenly emerging in state of emergency, 266; Indian gold and silver replicas of gardens, 280; and naming, 277; and prison of island of Gorgona and La Violencia, 281

Made in the USA
Middletown, DE
23 January 2023

22854980R00215